HOW THE BOY NEXT DOOR TURNED OUT
AN AUTOBIOGRAPHY

DIARMUID
GAVIN

HOW THE BOY NEXT DOOR TURNED OUT
AN AUTOBIOGRAPHY

CASSELL
ILLUSTRATED

First published in 2010 by Cassell Illustrated
a part of Octopus Publishing Group
Endeavour House, 189 Shaftesbury Avenue, London WC2H 8JY
www.octopusbooks.co.uk

An Hachette UK Company
www.hachette.co.uk

Distributed in the United States and Canada by Hachette Book Group USA,
237 Park Avenue, New York, NY 10017

British Library Cataloguing-in-Publication Data.
A catalogue record for this book is available from the British Library.

Hardback ISBN: 978 1 84091 562 4
Paperback ISBN: 978 1 84091 575 4

Printed in UK

To Mum and Dad, with love and thanks

CONTENTS

PART THREE: MOVING ON AND MOVING BACK

PROLOGUE

We dropped our suitcases and stood facing the grassy slope. In front of it, a few trees, then the spiked railings that enclosed the Chelsea Flower Show, in the grounds of the Royal Hospital. Traffic whizzed down the Embankment and the great Thames flowed by. Our plot had been neatly marked out with white spray paint. There were twenty-four sites marked for gardens. Twenty-three of them were full of men with mobile phones, surrounded by contractors, teeming with machinery. Our plot was the first in a row of eight. At our feet, written on a railway sleeper, the same white paint spelt out the name 'Gavin'.

Vincent and I had £300 in our pockets. This small ten-by-ten square metres of London would be our home for the next month. To transform it and change my life, I was short by £60,000. We knew nobody in the city and the city didn't care. Right beside us a crane was unloading giant boulders, swinging them through the air, a wrecking ball. The Japanese were garden-building. This afternoon the Irish would start.

It was Wednesday 3 May 1995, and I had an impossible dream – to change the face of gardening. I was twenty-nine. I'd failed often. In Dublin I had twenty tonnes of stone lying in a pile; in County Kerry plants dug from the countryside rested in old fertilizer bags – all waiting to be transported and replanted. I had talked my way into the heart of the British gardening establishment. This was the last chance saloon. If I could make it here, I could make it anywhere. If I failed, it was curtains.

Overcome with a mixture of fear and terror, we paced the site. And then we laughed. Nervously. Dragging our bags behind us we retreated through the ornate gates and went back towards Victoria Station and a dingy, windowless basement room. From the luggage Vincent retrieved the Chelsea Flower Show contractors' manual, and we set about putting our plans into action.

13

The nearest builders' merchant to the flower show, Travis Perkins, occupied a curious position in the heart of upmarket antique land. An uncaring assistant behind the counter listened to my request for a wheelbarrow, two shovel and two spades to be delivered to my Chelsea plot. 'You'll be lucky, bank holiday on Monday. Delivery will take a week.' 'OK, we'll take them now.' The first of many humiliations.

I handed over my £55 and wheeled the tools down the street. Taking a wrong turn, we went the long way round. Crossing Sloane Square, I dodged the black cabs and pretty girls laden with shopping bags. Sophisticated European types perched at their café tables, cappuccino in hand, gazed as I trudged past. My face reddened. While thousands of other Irish were changing the nation's image in London as bankers and company directors, solicitors and business consultants, I was back on the barrow. And the barrow led me in the Bull Ring entrance, past the cranes and the walkie-talkies, the security men in their Day-Glo jackets, past the PR ladies with clipboards, and on to my first garden.

We started to dig. We had nothing else to do. And for three days we excavated our site. We shifted the soil from the front of the garden, where grass had met the kerb, up to the very back, and when no one was looking, we shifted it back again. Designers and contractors stopped for a chat. The Irish boys were everybody's friends. There was nothing to be jealous of, we weren't a threat.

As we dug, in County Kerry, a cow pushed her way through the rickety wire fence. Our plants tasted good…

The last fifteen years have been eventful, packed with ups and downs. I started life as the boy next door on a suburban street in a society that by and large wasn't sure of its relationship with gardens. I wanted to do things differently, to make gardens that would appeal to me as a young lad, ones that would have a stronger relationship with people and houses. I wanted to take influences from all I experienced, and I wasn't sure how to go about it. Creating a series of gardens in a park in central London changed my life. How could this be? And why did I attract so much trouble? I started off jotting down my memories of six Chelsea Flower Shows. Along the way this became the story of my life so far. A lot has changed for me and for gardening. It's been a roller coaster adventure, of dreams and a passion to achieve.

I've created my own road. It's not a route that I would advise others to follow. Much of my life has been a black comedy, a series of events that knock into each other. I haven't made things easy for myself or taken the obvious paths. The passion that drives me on is often the one that gets me into the greatest bother. I respond to events emotionally, and I have high standards that don't sit well in a world of compromise. I haven't learnt to play the political game. My mood can be read from my face instantly, and though I could wish for an easier life relaxing with the rewards of some turbulent years, this will never be. A sense of adventure fuels me. I'm an optimist, continually exploring possibilities in gardens and in life. I have a public profile that opens some doors. I'm in a position where I can meet people, pose questions, and sometimes achieve.

Relating this story has been a challenge. There are many things I'd rather forget. But by writing this book, I feel I'm closing one set of adventures and leaving room to open another. This is my story, the tale of how the boy next door turned out.

PART
ONE
ROOTS

MOVING HOME

Mum and Dad were both brought up in Dublin, on the south side of the Liffey. Mum came from the heart of the old city, James Street, the home of Guinness. In 1969 they moved their young family further south to the new suburb of Rathfarnham, the last village before the Dublin mountains, the last tram stop away from civilization.

I can remember visiting the place as they searched for a new home. I was four. Built on the site of an old golf course, the road is called Fairways. It stretches from what was then a newly built shopping centre through a series of turns and curves down towards the old village. The houses are almost all semi-detached, mirror images of each other, joined at the hip. Six miles as the crow flies into the heart of the city, through Terenure, Rathgar and Ranelagh, suburbs of red-brick terraces or Georgian town houses. The occasional villa. Thousands of people had moved out from the city centre for a better life, into sometimes sprawling estates. Some had been built by the council, others were private. Rathfarnham was very desirable. Buying a home here had been an achievement for Mum and Dad. We were to live on the edge of pastoral countryside, surrounded by shops, good schools, parks and rivers.

The village itself was pretty. On the main street there was an old post office, a tiny courthouse and a pub called the Captains. A small factory turned pieces of Connemara marble, a beautiful green speckled stone from the west coast, into rosary beads. A couple of tiny kiosks sold bottles of cola and gobstoppers. There was a newsagent, butcher, delicatessen and bookies' shop. The line-up was completed by a pharmacy, two or three other pubs and the odd clothes shop full of out-of-date, out-of-town fashions. It had character and characters. Both churches, Catholic and Protestant, are made from silver granite block. The Protestant one is sited at the far end of the village. The other, where we prayed, is opposite a landmark, another pub, the Yellow House. Religion dominated lives. Each morning a steady stream of pious heads would wander from village to church for eight o'clock mass. On Sundays, our family would leave the house at a quarter past nine for the short walk. We always sat at the front. When school was closed we were sent to ten o'clock mass every day. It was repetitive and boring. Soon I would skip the ritual.

It was a happy community. Young parents found contentment on the street. The River Owendore flowed behind one stretch of houses and into another river, the Dodder. The Dodder was faster, colder and deeper, and separated us from Bushy Park. The park had been carved from the grounds of what once was the ancestral home of the Shaw family, distant relatives of George Bernard Shaw. It was divided into two sections by a steep slope. Below lay a great expanse of deciduous woodland with large ponds and dramatic bamboos, winding shady walks and shell grottos. Clambering up the steep front incline led to the discovery of an old stone ice house, built to hold ice for the preservation of food. Or taking the hundred generously splayed wide steps, you emerged from this sylvan splendour to find playing fields, tennis courts and a putting green.

This was my locality – rows of houses carved from a golf course. Fields and fruit farms, bordered by rivers and with quick access to city, mountains or coast. Young people saving hard, visiting banks, building societies and credit unions weekly to deposit small sums of money.

In the first few years it was probably paradise. The open areas in front of our house hadn't yet been tamed. The weeds that first summer grew six foot tall. It made a perfect playground. Inside the garden, I watched Dad digging. Out back, garden soil sloped from the hawthorn down to a six-foot-wide concrete path, which ran across the back of the house. Dad and Uncle Brian excavated an area. They built a concrete-block retaining wall with two steps leading up to a triangular rotating washing line. They laid a patio, using two-foot-square grey paving slabs. Two front lawns were prepared. Dug and raked, over and over. Brown bags filled with seed were purchased and sprinkled like chicken feed. A few weeks later, a faint blotching of green emerged, then a carpet.

Trees were bought from a garden centre and planted in the centre of the lawns: ornamental cherries, two on one side of the driveway and one on the other. Borders were dug. In the front garden they were eighteen inches wide, bare soil. In the back, a narrow, shallow trench was created around the grass, five inches wide. Then some plants. It was blue and white, blue and white, blue and white, bedding plants purchased in polystyrene trays, lobelia and alyssum. That was our garden. In late spring the cherry buds would burst in time for the procession of cousins, the girls in their white bridal outfits and boys in pastel suits, proudly sporting religious medals, posing beneath the pink flowers, hands clasped together, draped with rosary beads and drawstring purses, and pockets bulging with coins. Freckled faces, beaming, special for a day.

Outside the gates of number 98, I felt free. The busy roads that would soon zip through the green areas between our road and the river were still only lines on a planner's map. Life was an adventure. One evening I gathered my friends. We had been driven to the park across the river in the family Hillman Hunter weeks before. The river was dangerous, we'd been told to keep away. I persuaded a group to follow. We clambered through rough grasses and thorny thistles. Down the river bank. Large self-seeded marginal planting created a jungle along its edge, willow leaves dripping down like green curtains. We took off our sandals and socks, abandoning them on rocks, and set out gingerly to conquer our Amazon. The hope was to return with them dry, so no one would be any wiser about our adventures.

But the uncommon silence on the road led to suspicion. Search parties set out. When pairs of shoes and socks were found by the river, the worst was feared. Having been unable to scale the big walls around Bushy Park we returned dejected. Caught red-handed, we were grounded.

I liked building dens, forts and houses. Abandoned concrete blocks and pieces of wood provided plenty of construction material. Even the long grass allowed me to disappear and create a hideaway. This continued through to my teenage years. I love being in charge of my own environment and creating enclosures, from tree houses right through, these days, to grand garden pavilions. Creating a space that I feel comfortable in makes me feel secure and confident. And also excited. From the time I left school, people have always examined my interest in Lego and the construction of enclosures. It's often suggested I should be an architect. That's a profession controlled by too many rules and laws for me. A den in an unexpected place, a temporary hideaway in the middle of a building site, a place to escape to up a tree, or a giant egg that opens – this is what I love.

A GOOD-LOOKING COUPLE

My parents, Joan and Jack, were two young people who had left school early through necessity. They cycled through the countryside, went hostelling, had fun boating on ponds and in parks. Dad had his music and Mum her unshakeable determination to achieve. They were a good-looking, clever couple. Dad worked at the General Post Office, at night studying for national exams. He achieved some of the best grades in the country. Mum was a prize – beautiful, elegant and strong-willed. Family albums of black-and-white photographs show a different world, with Joan and Jack dressed up to the nines for dinner dances, or going to the opera. I would have imagined that to be a rich man's entertainment, but not so. There were plenty of music halls and societies through which to further this passion. Among Jack's mates at work and also a follower of opera, was Bob Hewson, Bono's dad. Mum and Dad found each other, courted and married.

They made the decision to leave Ireland and set out for London – prospects weren't good in Dublin. Arriving in London with nothing, they were confronted regularly by signs in boarding house windows reading:' No blacks, no Irish, no dogs'. Dad held down three full-time jobs. Mum was a top shoe sales person at Lilly & Skinner on Piccadilly Circus, where she served Cliff Richard's mum, among others, and observed the preparation of footwear for the royal party at Princess Margaret's wedding.

They lived in Willesden, and soon, in 1961, their firstborn, Declan, arrived. Three years later, on 10 May, I arrived as a companion, and the family moved back to Dublin. In just a few years they had managed to save enough to buy a home. Dad was a manager in an established company. Through this he was transferred back to Dublin with relocation costs taken care of. They left Britain with an enduring fondness for the place, a love of both city and country.

A year to the day after me, Conor was born. And two years later, on 8 May, came the first girl, Niamh. The final member of the family, Emer, arrived on 11th November 1968. We were still living on the north side of the city, in Coolock, opposite the Cadbury's factory. Dad brought us to visit Mum in hospital. The baby had brought presents for us: a model fire engine and lots of different plastic zoo animals. Happy days.

Delving into family history can be illuminating. People are conditioned by their circumstances. What were our circumstances?

WHO DO I THINK I AM?

When the BBC first commissioned the genealogy series *Who Do You Think You Are?*, I was considered as a candidate for forensic examination of my family's past. At Sunday lunch on a visit home from London, I announced this to the family. I was greeted by silence. My achievements in London were celebrated, but not in front of me. A week later, Mum called, an unusual occurrence as generally she waits to be rung.

'Your Dad's very depressed', she said.

'Oh', I said, 'Why?'

'That programme you're thinking of making. He says you'll find nothing good there.'

I was intrigued, but the programme went no further. 'You'll find nothing good there.' No explanation, conversation over.

Ten years later, I was back living in Ireland and working for the state broadcasting company, RTE. They had bought the rights to the series. Again I was approached. Delicately I raised the idea at home, and after I'd given some assurances about how non-invasive the process would be, I was given the go-ahead.

A month later I was in Edinburgh, gazing at a stately end-of-crescent house – Georgian, four storeys over a basement. Dad's great-great-great granddad John Gavin had lived here with his young family. John Gavin. Dad's name. His antecedent, it was revealed, was a Scottish Presbyterian, a shipbuilder by trade. In Leith, a short distance away, an elderly maritime enthusiast spilt the family history. John was the father of Crichton. He built and owned ships that sailed from Scotland's west coast to the Baltic. An influential member of Edinburgh Presbyterian society, he was a land and property owner, controlling vast swathes. His sons continued in business and developed the Gavin Brewing Company. It was whispered to me that he had hated Catholics. How and why Crichton had ended up in Dublin, no one was quite sure. When John died, his estate was divided up by one of his other sons, with permission to do as he saw fit with Crichton's share. So Crichton had been cut out, in effect. What mischievous deeds or misfortune had caused this? And was he exiled to Dublin? Letters emerged showing he had begged for advances from the trust fund. He claimed his wife was ill. The replies from Scotland were heavy with the scent of disapproval. Crichton had ended up in a boarding house in Dublin. A Catholic family also renting space there had a young daughter, Mary. Soon she was expecting Crichton's baby. The news was not appreciated in Scotland. A son was born and given his father's name, Crichton Strachan. The Dublin branch of the Gavins fell further from grace and far from the table. Crichton Strachan junior would eventually adopt another name and end his life a blind beggar. Dad remembers visiting his granddad during lunch breaks from school, running down a laneway to meet this blind beggar. History for me had been brought alive: the fall from grace of a member of a prosperous Scottish dynasty, the deliberate abandonment of his cultural roots, and the emergence in the ghettos of Dublin of a new generation of Irish Gavins.

London also featured in the archive. There was a family of Tibberts in Oxford who had a daughter, Martha. She married Crichton Strachan senior. And her dad worked at Covent Garden, translating librettos of Rossini operas and Meyerbeer's *Le Prophète* from Italian and French into English. He was obviously well educated, with the gift of many languages, which must have been unusual in the 1830s. This news, revealed to me by a historian standing outside a theatre in Covent Garden, was fascinating. In his younger days, Dad had a wonderful voice, and he had charted the rise of many great tenors since that time, having seen Pavarotti perform at the Dublin Opera Society as an unknown. He idolized the Swedish tenor Jussi Björling. Just as my life is gardening, so opera is Dad's true love. He followed Björling in life and in death, only recently disappearing from home carrying but a passport and pyjamas in a Marks and Spencer plastic bag, boarding a flight and travelling to an obscure Swedish town to pay homage at the tenor's grave. Dad can have difficulty walking the few hundred yards to buy a daily newspaper, but his passion for opera allows for no such frailties.

The more I delved the more I found out, piecing together a family portrait. Mum and Dad both came from large families. In Mum's there had been seven or eight children, with her own mum a strong role model. She ran a sweet shop in one of the oldest parts of the city, a place where people had little but didn't realize it. Granddad worked for the railways. When Granny died young, Mum assumed a parental role, helping to look after her siblings, including a younger sister who suffered from spina bifida. Granddad remarried, taking one of Granny's friends as his new wife. It wasn't a popular move with his sons or his daughters, but Aunty Connie, as she was known, eventually attained the position of the family matriarch.

Mum's brother Noel emigrated young to Liverpool and became a radical socialist. He was soon consumed by that great city. Uncle Brian was a passionate republican who, in the small parlour at the front of the house, would play a recording of the national anthem at the start and at the end of any session listening to records. A single man, he was close to our growing family and for a while lived with us in the new house in Rathfarnham. A love of the outdoor life led to him joining the scouting movement.

Every year on Christmas Day his act of rebellion was to place a toilet roll on top of the television as the Queen's speech began. This would send the arch-royalist Connie into a state of fury.

Betty was the fun one, with flaming red hair, a larger-than-life personality, and a huge interest in all her nieces and nephews. Her home was full of fun, fizzy drinks and chocolate bars. She married Chris, a former RAF pilot. Peter, the youngest brother, was good-looking, solid and hard-working. Much younger than the rest was

Pat, a pretty girl who belonged to a different generation. Pat also lived with us in the early days in Rathfarnham. She worked in a pharmacy in town.

On Dad's side it was different. He doesn't talk about his background. But I have clear memories of his parents, and there are lots of brothers and two sisters. The Gavin side has always been a bit of a mystery. Like many men of his generation, Dad doesn't talk about family or feelings. I remember visiting Granny and Granddad in their red-brick terraced house, with Granny –grey hair, cigarette, blue housecoat and a worn face – busying herself and probably inundated by visits from grandchildren. Dad's desolation at her passing was crushing.

Granddad was another matter. A character. He was a true Dubliner, loved his pint of Guinness. He features on a classic Dublin postcard, a man sitting at a bar.

Dad's eldest sister, my godmother Betty, is a great lady who brought up a large family with her husband Mick. And then there's Aunt Marie, again wonderful. The boys, seven or eight of them, are a bit different. Fiercely loyal to each other, often they don't talk, for years: wives do the communicating. Between them they cover life's full range of social and economic achievement. Funerals are the main gathering times. And these are similar to mafia meetings. Gavin men aren't very tall, and often wear old-fashioned thick spectacles and dark overcoats. Jack, my Dad, is referred to as the Don by his sons-in-law. The Don will silently nod at the other dons. It's often the beginning and end of the conversation. The next generations are uninhibited and we will gladly sidle up to any of these bespectacled men and chat away. 'How's your dad?' they'll ask. Dad meanwhile will be ambling along right behind. If dads don't talk, cousins do.

George is the wealthy uncle. At the funeral of one of his brothers he told me and my brother how he coped with such occasions, dampening his emotions by humming the *Match of the Day* theme tune repeatedly and continuously throughout the hour-long service. Wives and cousins natter, and then the group disperses until the next sad occasion is dealt with in similar manner.

THE TROUBLES OF THE PAST

Mum had been convinced that her family held the key to rebellion, her dad having been a very young member of the old Irish Republican Army (the respectable forerunners of the Irish Army, not the terrorists of the 1970s and 80s). Recent history in Ireland is an emotional and sometimes complex web of rebellion against our colonists in Britain.

The Troubles ensuing from this complex situation continue. The year 1970 saw the beginning of decades of terrorism on both Republican and Unionist sides. Throughout my childhood, atrocities carried out by both sides would dominate the world headlines. We grew up through turbulent times. Belfast was only a hundred miles up the road from Dublin, but it might as well have been Timbuktu. Images of armoured cars, tanks and guns dominated the six o'clock and nine o'clock evening news. Stories of cold-blooded killings and reprisals, rivers of blood, butchery. Catholic communities oppressed, Protestant ones threatened. Relative peace, a seemingly unobtainable gift for thirty years, has seen the abandonment of violence for politics. Brave people, politicians and fighters, have made big decisions. Ireland is no longer scarred by murder and mayhem and is enjoying a chance to explore, develop and get to know itself as a contemporary European nation.

Mum felt that *Who Do You Think You Are?* would reveal her dad's part in the formation of our young republic. He worked on the railways, at a depot called Inchicore that was the receiving base for steel brought over from London to make armoured cars. As a young member of the IRA, his role was to help keeping this material away out of the hands of the British Army. They discovered it couldn't easily be broken up with sledgehammers, as was the original plan, so they would load it into trucks and drive it far from the city. Granddad's truck broke down just a few miles from base.

His heavy cargo was tipped out into the Grand Canal, where for some time it lay in a watery grave. When he went looking for a pension from the Irish Army that emerged from the old IRA, these details were on his file, along with the fact that his other role had been the protection of farmers.

I was with the television crew, filming in a church in the Liberties of Dublin with a jovial priest. We were examining the baptismal and wedding certificates of my grandparents. Suddenly there was a shocking revelation. There had indeed been a family death on Easter Monday 1916. One of my great-grandparents had lost his life during the Rising. Dad's other grandfather, not Mum's, had been shot dead. I rang Dad from the church. Did he know, I asked him, that his granddad had been killed during the Rising? No, came the simple answer. Then silence, followed by a worried, 'I hope it was the Brits'. I laughed: it would never do to have a collaborator in the family.

The mystery was solved the following day. I was brought to another part of Dublin, a gentrified area way down the canal near Mount Street. I learned that Dad's granddad on his mother's side, who worked in sales for Independent Newspapers, had been visiting his mother, probably concerned for her safety. Setting out to return to his own young family, he was caught in crossfire, mown down by a stray bullet on a small bridge. This unremarkable site had been the spot chosen by the British forces as an entry point to the city for reinforcements newly arrived off the ferry from Holyhead. The Republican fighters had taken up positions in surrounding Georgian buildings, and a bloodbath ensued.

CHILDHOOD HOLIDAYS

That's the basis of our family: slightly complex, lots of turbulence, and many grey areas. Out of this emerged a young couple, Joan and Jack, who wanted the best that life could offer. The life of the Gavin family, a mini Brady Bunch, was set up to unfold nicely in this new suburb. Dad had a good job working as a personnel manager. He was also making a name for himself within the business community as secretary to the Irish Management Institute. Their conference week was a big event in the family calendar. We'd troop off to some hotel, often in Galway. Mum and Dad would get dressed up and go off to a ball on the Saturday evening, while we ran rings around the babysitter. Mum had to buy a present for an attending dignitary, the President of Ireland. She chose a sterling silver rose bowl.

There was great excitement when Dad travelled to Geneva as part of a business delegation. The postcard from Lake Geneva arrived home before he did. All was glorious. Dad was impressed with the city. Leaves falling from the trees didn't have a moment to settle on the ground, he wrote, before they were soon swept up by an attendant.

I was playing at the top of our road when his taxi turned the corner. I raced to meet him at the garden gate, heart pumping. The presents flowed. A cuckoo clock whose brass weights in the form of conifer cones chimed from then on, on the hour every hour. Wonderful chocolates. And tales of this distant land where everything was run with precision. He promised to bring us there, and a few summers later he kept his word. We travelled by car from Rosslare to Le Havre, a never-ending journey initially made delightful by the all-you-can-eat lunch buffet – for which each and every one of us paid the price on that night's turbulent seas!

We camped by Lake Geneva, where our tents were invaded by swarms of frogs. We took cable cars up the Matterhorn and admired the quaint wooden cabins of the Swiss farmers. We drove through France and visited the Tomb of the Unknown Soldier under the Arc de Triomphe. By the Sacré Coeur we had our photos taken outside the guest house where Mum and Dad had spent their short honeymoon. We visited the Louvre and saw the *Mona Lisa*, and we travelled to Versailles to see the magnificent Hall of Mirrors and gazed at Le Nôtre's famous gardens. The parts I really remember, though, are the playgrounds in the campsites.

My parents' love of the countryside found expression in regular jaunts throughout Ireland – north, east, south, west – to Cork, Kerry, Wicklow, Antrim, Sligo. For annual holidays or long weekend escapes we'd be packed into the car – three, four, then five of us – and shown Ireland. All we wanted was to play on the beach, and there was always one to be found. If the sun came out we'd spend long Sundays at Brittas Bay, a sandy stretch on the coast of County Wicklow, just over an hour from Dublin. As we approached along winding roads and saw the first glimpses of blue sea meeting the horizon, the same chant would always ring out: 'I see the sea, the sea sees me, God bless the sea and God bless me!' The car would be unloaded: deck chairs, wind break, rugs, flasks and picnic basket. There'd have been a telephone call to cousins before we set out. We'd all meet up, swim in the sea and play in the dunes.

On summer Sunday evenings we'd go to Sandycove, a Dublin coastal bathing spot, where first we would watch and then join Mum and Dad as they swam strong lengths. When visitors came from England, friends from days in Willesden, we'd travel to Powerscourt in County Wicklow, a wonderful Palladian mansion whose grounds contain a dramatic and picturesque waterfall, Ireland's highest.

Soon after the birth of the youngest, Emer, Mum contracted yellow jaundice. We laughed with her in the secluded hospital room as she peered at her discoloured face in the mirror. Three little boys, wearing home-knitted Aran jumpers, laughing at their Mum.

Suburban pioneers exploring playing fields, new roads being built, new people moving in, Rathfarnham growing, pushing out right to the foot of the Dublin Mountains.

At home, life was all adventure. Conor and I went to school at the convent, where little people ran riot in the playground at break. Huge clear plastic bags of jam sandwiches arrived at lunchtime, strawberry jam squeezing out through half slices of white bread, with tiny glass bottles of milk. The Abbey in Rathfarnham was, I am sure, a nice posting for the nuns. Their quarters were impressive, consisting of big rooms with lots of marble and wood, filled with religious paraphernalia. A stone grotto in the garden sheltered a statue of the Virgin Mary, hands held in silent prayer, eyes lifted to heaven, wrapped in a blue shawl.

AN ORDERED LIFE

Suburban gardens in the 1970s consisted of grass. Lots of it. To some people from a rural background, they were places to grow fruit and vegetables to harvest for the table. For Mum and Dad the garden, like the house, had to be kept clean, tidy, immaculate at all times. Inside, carpets were hoovered daily. Windows were kept spotless. Painters and decorators arrived each spring. Nothing was allowed to fade. The same ethos applied outside. Mum and Dad made sure the lawn was kept tidy and hedges neatly trimmed.

They also collected stones. No trip to the country, whether Dublin, Wicklow, Cork or Kerry, was complete until Mum had weighed the car down with another stone for her rockery. This lay at the base of the hawthorn , and they bought small flowering plants – alpines, campanulas and aubrietias and saxifrage – to plant in the cracks and crevices of this haphazard rock face. Oxalis was divided repeatedly and planted as neat mounds with bursts of pink flowers, forming garlands at the base of the trees.

Every evening during the longer spring and summer days saw Mum on her hands and knees planting, with Dad somewhere in the distance, dressed casually in his pullover and gardening shoes and walking behind his lawnmower. He'd look up and wave at a neighbour. Cleaning, mowing and planting, keeping things correct. Mum's people a hundred years back had come from the Dublin Mountains, where they had lived in granite cottages. Her dream was a picture postcard one.

What was I like back then? I'm told I was angelic looking as a small child with a shock of blond hair, doted on by all. Gaining a brother or a sister, moving country, moving house, losing grandparents, getting chocolates off the man who waited by the garden gate to collect his son from the Cadbury's factory opposite – it's all a blur now. I'd love to be a fly on the wall, looking back at the blossoming family, understanding my parents then, seeing their dreams come alive. Were their hopes for the future evident in every move they made? They were strict. Chores had to be done and television was rationed. They encouraged a healthy outdoor life and expected us to pay attention at school. Christmas or birthday cash, secured from kindly uncles, soon found its way to the post office or building society.

Finances weren't a fun issue. On top of a chest of drawers in my parents' bedroom was a money box. It had five slots for coins and notes – electricity, mortgage, food, etc. – labelled in Dad's beautiful handwriting. Pennies were watched, hawkishly. The weekly shop was packed at the check-outs into brown paper bags, sewn together with white twine at their end. When they were unpacked on our kitchen table, every item – eggs, sugar, porridge, bags of peas, bread – was checked against the till receipt.

TRAGEDY

From the age of ten, I'd rifle through Dad's desk. This is in his office, at the top of the house. The attic had been converted into a large room for the children, a place to do homework. The smaller room next to it, overlooking the garden, was Dad's crow's nest, his escape. Mum liked to keep things tidy, so we were bundled away up a second flight of stairs. Here opera would blare from his hi-fi systems. Photographs from family holidays and other occasions were mounted in a few albums, while others were packed away in the paper sleeves that they'd arrived in. They ranged from tiny squares, black and white images bordered by white margins, to big, glossy graduation pictures or embarrassing images of debs balls. The desk was a mock period piece, a bureau. The drawers didn't slide out easily: they were heavy and had to be pulled firmly, when they emitted a protest groan. Beside a few newspapers that he kept, perhaps charting the Pope's visit to Ireland in 1979, there were our school reports, house deeds, bank statements and books full of lyrical handwriting – verses and chorus of songs he had collected. Dad would smoke in this room, at one time a pipe, occasionally a cigar but usually cigarettes. Mum never chanced the stairs to these rooms.

The bureau contains mass cards, small laminated paper memorials with pictures, prayers and religious insignia, sent out as acknowledgements by the families of the departed. A bundle of cards is wrapped in elastic bands in a brown envelope. Opening it has always been difficult. But every so often the need to remember leads me to it. A page from a newspaper. On that page is the report of a tragic accident. A little boy going to school with his brother, knocked down crossing the road.

The remnants of the attic space on one side, reaching under the eaves, are used for storage: Christmas decorations, suitcases, piles of junk and dolls that Mum used buy for herself. A new one always left under the Christmas tree, never emerging from its box. And somewhere there's a wooden cross. Conor Gavin. It marked his grave in the early years.

Mum wasn't long out of hospital. We were collected by the school bus every morning from the main road. All the proper safety procedures were in place, with people looking after us every morning. Conor did something unexpected.

It was 1 February. The accident took place a couple of hundred yards from the police station. I was brought to the house next door and later collected by Dad. I didn't understand. Conor had been brought to the doctor. Doctors fix people. He must be OK. Dad said he was gone. I was brought upstairs to Mum. She was being comforted by nuns. She grasped me. The blur of the next few days. Spending time in different people's houses, neighbours and friends. Being walked up the aisle of a packed church to the front pew. Aunty Betty waving and smiling through tear-filled eyes. Afterwards, standing outside in a row with little class mates as Conor's coffin emerged. The cars left the churchyard for the grave. We didn't go that day.

The family was crushed. Every week we would visit the cemetery. I remember the bill coming in for the funeral. Regular breakdowns, visits to the doctor. In one of the mass cards someone had written 'remember your four other children', and that's what Mum and Dad did.

It's hard writing about Conor. I do it with tear-stained cheeks. It's a private story but it's important to always acknowledge that he lived. Conor was number three son in our family of Mum, Dad, three boys and two girls.

His death was another beginning for me. Curiosity means people want to know who you are, where you come from, what your reasons are for doing things, what makes you as a person, what has formed your ideas, what motivates you. It can be a difficult road to navigate.

Tell people about Conor and they will want to know more. But Conor's story doesn't belong to me. It belongs to everyone who knew him. It belongs to those caring nuns who a few weeks later welcomed me back to school and read from a little book they had written about his life. It belongs to Mum and Dad and my brother and my sisters, my aunts and uncles, my neighbours. In interviews I have been asked about my happy childhood growing up in Dublin. And you try to say, yes I came from a lovely family, grew up in a lovely area, but then this thing happened. And I want to tell you it happened. Not to tell is to deny a life; but if I tell, you will probe, and it is not only me you are probing but all the other people who Conor belonged to.

We decide what to tell people about ourselves. We make choices every day, based on different situations and scenarios. If you achieve fame or notoriety you develop layers of defences, mechanisms for dealing with questions. You develop boundaries to suit yourself; sometimes you play a game. Being prominent means being probed, interviewed. I'm fairly articulate and appear to have a nice easy way about myself. Part of my work is being a hired spokesperson for products, services or causes. So for a portion of my life I leave myself open to questions. I have a label, as a 'gardener off the telly'. You go through waves of interest. Sometimes, at some times of the year, people want to know a lot about you. At other times they don't care. I'm closely associated with the Chelsea Flower Show, so for months leading up to the show every year, whether I am due to be there with a garden or television coverage or not, I become a story.

SURVIVAL

The years after Conor become a blur of heartache combined with a busy family life. We dealt with it differently. Mum and Dad acquired new strength. They had to carry on, to go out to work daily, to run a house, to take care of babies.

It was a while before there was laughter again. But it did return. Family holidays to England and within Ireland and the exotic jaunts abroad continued. Declan developed an interest in sport. I withdrew into a fairly solitary dream world. I liked arts and crafts, watching *Blue Peter* on television and reading my collection of Enid Blyton stories. Whatever the difficulties, however withdrawn into their own thoughts they were, Mum and Dad provided unconditional love. And there were happy occasions. Once Mum met me on my way home from school. I had just been through the ritual of my first confession and had been bemused by the ceremony, but her sheer joy at my advancing through another Catholic ritual, my first since baptism as a babe, was infectious. My Holy Communion, a pious event for little people, came soon after. Back at home after the church service, I sat at the kitchen table, just me, Mum and Dad. A cardboard box with a brand new shiny watch was produced. This was followed by howls of grief. I went out for a lonely cycle ride in the square at the end of the road.

On Christmas Eve, Dad dressed up as Santa and crept into my sisters' bedroom. The magic he created as the two little faces realized they had a very special visitor lived on for years. Opera took a back seat for a while. He went through a phase of singing rebel songs, whistling away contentedly as two or three of us had our baths. In the summer he was in charge of sports day at work, and he'd bring home all the medals and cups in the week before they were awarded. We would parade around the garden with them. Moments of light and darkness, hand in hand. Memories, troubles, and the need to carry on.

I enjoyed the cub scouts, an organization that I was encouraged to join because of Uncle Brian's involvement. It focused on morality and achievements. During the Easter holidays we bob-a-jobbed, going from house to house asking was there any work needing doing – polishing shoes, say, or bits of gardening. Wearing a uniform of short trousers, pullover, little cap and neckerchief tied with a woggle, I learned a lot about knocking on doors. There were badges to be earned, achievements to be garnered. To get one award, I had to germinate some seeds. Mrs Flynn lived down the road. She had a reputation for being green-fingered. I arrived with my packet of cress seed, and in her larder we shook these onto damp blue blotting paper. After a few days little white seedlings topped by two tiny leaves pushed up.

Every birthday and Christmas would see tonnes more of red and white Lego bricks arrive. I built houses, cars, hotels, offices, monsters, lighthouses. I liked comic books and action heroes. And while Mum and Dad were out I watched copious amounts of television.

Our playing fields had now been replaced by a new road running behind our houses, a bypass to feed traffic away from the little village. A new bridge over the river created easy access to the park, and the dark, shady deciduous woodland became my playground. I wasn't happy with how it looked. I wanted to change it. This vast park had probably been laid out as a private pleasure ground in Victorian times. Enslaving my sisters, I made them follow me with shovels, spades and garden fork over the road and across the bridge. Under some dense canopy on the slope, I began to make a garden.

The aftermath of tragedy would affect everything. I grew up without a notion of how I fitted in to life's grand plan. Outwardly fine, smiling, probably always smiling, dressed in woollen knit jumpers, short trousers, socks, sandals, I was a pleasant little boy. I always said my pleases and thank yous and was an exemplary guest in anybody else's house. Plates were always wiped clean and parents' orders obeyed.

Mum and Dad had never really been given a chance to develop as the people they could have been. Exploring talents or inherent skills, making a career out of what they loved – none of this was on the agenda. As soon as you were able you went out to work. Your wages were handed over to your parents to help the family budget. So that's why they pushed us so hard to achieve our potential. The fact that I didn't appreciate my schooling and didn't have any inclination towards an academic or safe career worried them enormously. I wasn't bothered by school. I wanted to pursue a life doing something creative, and although they had enjoyed theatre and opera, these pursuits didn't figure as career options. Hard work meant a steady wage. If Dad had been able to enjoy the opportunities he was to give to his children, and had worked in the arts doing something he loved – writing about opera, or researching – his life would have been more fulfilled. This wasn't even a consideration. Everything centred on him being the primary provider. It was the cause of angst in my early days of education that I showed no dedication towards learning. From a young age I possibly knew that my road to fulfilment would be different from that of my parents.

If Dad had had a second chance to be young, he'd have had the benefit of a great education. Whatever his background, he would have been able to go to university in Ireland because there are no tuition fees. He has a sharp intellect. Among the sharpest. This has passed cleanly to my brother, who works for one of those big international firms so cleverly profiled in a John Grisham novel and hops from continent to continent, spending some years in Manhattan, a posting in Mumbai and now a swanky pad off the King's Road in London.

This would have been open to my Dad if he'd been born later. Instead, everything was a fight. With both my parents the fight was always for their children. The fear was always of not doing a good job. They had seen many fall by the wayside, many opportunities not taken. They had gone to London, worked so hard, achieved so much, and within five years come back home with the beginnings of their family. And their role was to provide financial, educational and moral guidance to us, to give us chances – and if one son was a dreamer who lurched his way through life excelling at nothing, well then that person wasn't making the most of what was on offer.

Starting out today, Dad would probably have the opportunity to turn his passion for opera into a career. Setting out on life's journey when he did, this wouldn't have been allowed, it wouldn't have paid the bills. In the eighties he'd listen to pirate radio programmes which on Sunday afternoons would devote a few hours to classic operas. He started writing in to these programmes and was soon writing scripts, sending stories. He'd often hint that we should listen to the radio at a particular time, as he would have some contribution. But this fell on amused ears – why would we bother to listen to Jussi Björling just to hear Dad's name read out? But it was impressive enough that he did it. It was great. How much more fulfilled would his life have been if the circumstances of his birth had been different? Opportunities exist now, whatever your background, that didn't then.

Mum is a romantic, as may be seen in the pristine dolls in the attic, and the collection of Lladro figures, Spanish porcelain images of pretty peasants, goose girls, nuns and the like, invariably purchased with pesetas on holidays and still displayed in a large illuminated mahogany cabinet. And her desire for flowers, sweet little country flowers and not only those in the garden. But she was also a lioness. Her iron will was what pushed the rest of us. She managed the family budget very carefully, which meant that we had the foreign holidays, and she was the first woman on our road to have a car.

LOST AT SCHOOL

After the convent I went to a variety of schools, including Ballyroan, where the future golfer Padraig Harrington was also a student. And then St Joseph's in Terenure. I connected with little around me. Long walks to school and long walks home, satchel on my back, mind lost in dreams.

I was desperate for a pet, and used to walk to the city to buy white mice. They lived in hidden compartments in my room, complete with hinged doors under my wardrobe. One escaped into the attic. I'd lie awake night after night as it scampered loose across the plasterboard ceiling. Eventually I trapped the hungry beast with tempting cheese.

I'd keep gerbils in wasteland, creating homes for them. I wandered through my school years not feeling much at all. Exam results weren't good. I was regarded as a bit 'slow'. There was a visit to a child psychologist. After twenty minutes she and I had agreed I was OK. It had been recognized that I had changed since the tragedy, and my parents worried. They tried to understand what might be going on in my head, while dealing with their own loss. My way of coping was withdrawal and disobedience. When I'd disappear I'd be up to no good. It didn't help that as a creative person I was different from the rest of the family. My goals or achievements would never revolve around study, the jobs that were held up as examples of achieving in life didn't appeal at all. I'd no desire to work in a bank or the Civil Service. I wanted to make stuff and grow stuff. This is why I disappeared with shovels and spades. Mum and Dad couldn't see a living being made this way, so they steered me in the academic direction that was never going to suit. Nobody in our environment painted or made stuff. The examples of creativity that came into the house were bits of reproduction furniture and porcelain figures. These meant nothing to me. It wasn't that there was no taste or artistic flair, it was just that I had different tastes that served to push me further from the fold. I regard my parents' achievements in battling against their odds highly. It was what they provided that allowed me the place and the time to dream. I didn't have to go a nondescript job at the age of fourteen.

Behind a shy but smiling façade, I was lonely and withdrawn. A lack of interest in sports didn't help. In schools obsessed by Gaelic football, hurling or rugby, it was easy to go unnoticed. I enjoyed swimming, and joined an after-school club where dive-bombing and messing around were fun. I put my name down to join a fledgling cross-country running team, but was left behind by the coach. Daydreaming to the detriment of any homework became my skill. I'd wrap myself in a huge mess of worry rather than put any energy into allotted tasks. At home every evening, two hours' study was required. When homework was finished, Dad would check it. I'd either make up excuses and pretend, or present the same work in a different guise. Dad would just nod, sign a report card. The following morning I'd hastily try to copy somebody else's work into my book.

The art room was a refuge. At Templeogue College I had caught the eye of the art teacher. Mr Weafer liked my enthusiasm. Soon I had a key to the art room door. I'd bunk off classes and escape to marvel at the store room, packed with paint and paper, powder, oils, acrylics, palettes, easels, every type of brush imaginable, pastels, different coloured cardboard, scissors, blades, knives, clay for modelling – all that you needed to create.

My brother Declan was in the same college. Occasionally I'd see him run past with a rugby ball. He studied hard and achieved. I coasted, keeping as much as possible under the radar.

GARDENS, GARDENING AND SUBURBAN LIFE

Saturday was chore day. I would polish the family's shoes. I was also to weed the garden, front and back, and the rockery. I'd spend hours pottering, on my hunkers, trowel in hand. Plants at 98 Fairways were growing. A row of conifers had been planted behind the front garden wall. They grew to be thirteen, fifteen foot high, dark green, conical in shape, each of a slightly different height and girth. They stood beside each other like a parade of army reservists. There were also hydrangeas Uncle Chris had grown, dirty pink in colour underneath the sitting room window.

The cherry trees grew rapidly. Mum never liked to be crowded. A man would arrive and remove large limbs, leaving increasingly misshaped specimens.

The back garden still had its single hawthorn, under which the now complete pile of stones speckled the soil like currants in a bun. A pyracantha grew against a wall. My job was to keep it trimmed, but you couldn't control this fiend. We didn't have a compost heap. We didn't garden, we kept things neat. The only other plant, aubrietia, was encouraged to tumble down the low retaining wall by the patio. On both sides, the neighbours gardened moderately. They planted climbers – ivies, clematis and other rambling specimens – which crept up the bare concrete blocks. On reaching the top they would edge nervously into Gavin airspace. The result was always the same. As soon as the respective families had disappeared up the road on their annual holidays, Mum would waite a decent interval before becoming Mrs Scissorhands. She wouldn't offend by trimming while they were at home, but any invasion on her pristine territory weighed heavily.

Our neighbours had a gardener. He'd arrive on his bicycle and prune the hybrid tea and floribunda half-standard roses. Mum developed an idea that I'd like this career: Diarmuid's always messing around in the garden, he's always losing his Dad's implements, maybe that would suit him? Did they imagine I would be arriving by bicycle at someone's house, my trousers tied up with a piece of string, cloth cap on my head, pruning roses and walking after a lawnmower for the rest of my life?.

My ideas of suburbia were formed by walks to different schools over the years. What caught my attention walking to school wasn't the big, the beautiful, the posh or the perfectly preserved. It was a simple terraced house with a green-tiled roof. Its small front garden was decked out with hundreds of ornaments. There was a mock Victorian street lamp from which hung two hanging baskets full of plastic flowers. At its base stood a model of a thatched Irish cottage. An oriental Buddha painted pink contemplated the busy road. Snow White was there too, alongside windmills, gipsy caravans, Japanese lanterns, concrete puppies and plastic swans filled with petunias. An old lady lived there.

I marvelled at this gaiety, but the décor annoyed most people. The consensus saw the display as gaudy, garish and wrong. It was so out of keeping with an ordinary street. What did she think she was at? To me, it was a world of wonder. A loud demonstration of colour and cartoon imagery brought to life. I often wondered what she was like, what made her do this? As individual items, the Victorian lamp or the Buddha were to be found in many gardens around, but brought together they presented a strongly individual form of expression. For me, the effect was enchanting. So many different elements from so many parts of the world, so many bits of ornamentation bought in garden centres and DIY stores, each individual piece with its own social, religious or cultural history, shaped to this lady's desires and presented as a collection to the world in her garden, her stage. It was years later, as I dug through suburbia, that I'd think about the gardens I appreciated. That plot had been constructed with exuberance. I'd responded to that with wonder on an immediate level, but later the amalgamation of the essence of so many different styles in one small front garden told me how small and confused our world had become, how objects no matter where they came from were being used and enjoyed primarily for aesthetic effect, without regard for the culture that produced them.

Walking opens your eyes and suits a dreamer. I'd set out with dread. School held no appeal. Thirteen years of walks, long stretches of road passing houses, driveways and front gardens.

In my younger days, Mum occasionally dropped us off. We'd pack into the little grey car, the two girls dropped off in their wine uniforms, one blonde, one redhead, both freckled, at the Sancta Maria school for girls. They'd gallop away from the car, laughing. Just down the road, Declan and I went to Ballyroan Boys' National School and silently disappeared in opposite directions. I enjoyed neither the school yard nor the lessons. I walked home gazing at houses and gardens. Walls of griselinia hedging, a New Zealand species instantly adopted by the Irish and ignored in the UK. Later this was to be one of my first indicators of the milder, more temperate climate enjoyed on our island. It has a kind of sickly green leaf, a dull lime with round fleshy leaves, and in Ireland it grows like mad. It's easily shaped into hedging and is quite satisfying to cut. There were cordylines also, exotic little fireworks back then, usually planted in a lawn, soon shooting towards the sky with multiple heads, and then every so often flowering in ugly big protrusions from the side of their head, dotted with panicles of white flowers.

Other species used for hedging included fuchsia, a glorious freedom fighter of a shrub unused to being tamed into blocks, and dripping every summer with exotic scarlet bells.

In the summer, gardens were crammed with bedding plants, with borders and often scalloped edges of lawns crammed with low-growing colour. Orange and yellow marigolds, multi-coloured petunias, some with stripes, alyssum, lobelia, fibrous rooted begonias, red salvias and the grey foliage of cinerarea:

dazzling displays, little tapestries, piece of folk art laid out from April to September.

Patios were made from crazy paving and rockeries built wherever a load of soil could be mustered, piled up and dotted with stone. Glass porches encasing the front door would be full of geranium cuttings. Hanging baskets would dangle from twirly wrought-iron brackets beside the bell. Lawns were pristine, neat green carpets.

The inhabitants of these pebble-dashed concrete boxes had poured every penny into creating their dreams. Individualism wasn't encouraged or expressed. Achievement was measured by the purchase of a new hall door, mahogany and Georgian-panelled with brass knobs and knockers.

The arrival of a new three-piece suite was cause for celebration, and neighbours and relatives would come to examine it. Garden displays were judged one day of the week, on the Sunday morning procession to mass. Neighbours gazed over low garden walls and hedges, making mental notes far more potent than any tweed-attired judge at Chelsea would dare.

Suburban architecture was uniformly grey. Garden walls were of concrete blocks, with mortar visible between the courses, and capped with smooth and narrow angled tops. Occasionally there were pillars, painted white and topped with glossy concrete spheres, a pair of eagles or ludicrous pineapples.

On the less affluent streets, the pride, the colour and the decoration were more flamboyant. A mock cartwheel might be stuck on a wall, with concrete animals or gnomes guarding it.

The route to each school had its own special features. Just outside Rathfarnham village on the walk to Terenure, there was a wooden ranch-style house surrounded by wide verandas with flaking paint in disrepair. It seemed incongruous in this setting of row after row of brick-built houses – a hint of what must have been gentler days.

The school in Terenure was set beside another granite church in a bustling town, dead bang in the middle of a row of mid-1940s houses on the busy main road. Set fifty metres back off the street was a different type of building: a concrete synagogue, with four stained glass stars of David indicating difference and mystery. What never changed were the front gardens. Mile followed mile of closed front doors, multiple façades of homes staring neatly and benignly at a passing world. Not one brave enough to scream.

GARDENING ON TELEVISION

At home, watching television was highly regulated. Denial created a hunger. We were allowed to watch news, documentaries, and some cartoons. Our treats were *Blue Peter*, *Newsround* and *Top of the Pops*.

When Mum and Dad were out, the first thing we'd do was to gather round the box. And we watched everything. Initially we had a black-and-white set. A pub called the Captains in our local village, minutes from the house, had a colour telly, and we'd stand outside and gaze.

When eventually we got a colour TV, the black-and-white set was consigned to the attic, a wreck with some of the knobs missing. I contrived to repair it by jamming a snooker cue to a weighty object and having the set at a tilt, the lean of its weight keeping the button in, so that I could tune in to watch unsuitable programmes late at night. The tube at the back of the set took some time to warm up. All was fine until Mum went to the boiler house in the garden one night to switch off the heating, only to see the flickers emanating from the magnolia walls of the room on top of the house. War erupted.

Valerie Singleton, John Noakes and Peter Purves on *Blue Peter* were what I loved most. All thoroughly correct and industrious: children were to be educated, be good and care for others. An outdoor ethos was encouraged, and caring for those less fortunate than you an annual concern. Some things always fascinated me, such as a gardener called Percy Thrower who created the *Blue Peter* garden. Its features were an Italianate sunken pool surrounded by a low wall for sitting, and a greenhouse. Percy was older than the presenters, a grandfather figure. He wore woollen jumpers, smoked a pipe from time to time, and delivered his knowledge in a quiet and assured way.

Each week there'd be a project: sowing seeds in the greenhouse, planting shrubs, or potting something up. Gardening at its most basic, growing fruit and vegetables and sunflowers. There were competitions so we could get involved. One year *Blue Peter* undertook a garden makeover. For some charity, they dug out the basement yard of a tall, narrow building at a community centre, and created a wonderful space. I liked the community effort. I loved the change. I loved the fact that it was outside. Wheelbarrows full of grime, dirt, sand and concrete were taken away and replaced with plants, water and seating. They had created a place to be used by the people, a beautiful place. I had little idea how central gardening on television would become to my life.

At the annual St Patrick's Day parade in March, I was excited to see, on a Bord na Móna (the semi-state peat-harvesting company) float among the majorettes and brass bands, Percy Thrower waving.

Despite being shy, I had an odd craving for attention. On a family holiday in Cork, we visited Blarney Castle. To kiss the famous stone you had to lie on your back, gripping two slender iron rails as you leaned into the abyss. Outside the castle was a large green surrounded by a low wall. We were horsing around while a coachload of Americans watched us. They had cine cameras. It was a glorious summer's day. I wanted to be filmed. I wanted to travel to America on their reels of film. I wanted to be noteworthy, to be shown to friends in Ohio or Palm Beach or New Jersey. Declan was sitting on the wall in full view of the tourists. I crept up behind my brother, pulled him over the low wall and ran away. And minutes later, to make sure they'd got their shot, I did it again.

I loved being alone with my Lego, building, designing, dreaming. Hundreds of pieces spread on the heavily patterned carpet: start with a base and build. Or I'd go on walking or bicycle trips, also on my own. I'd strip a cane from a clump of bamboo in the park and swish my way through this verdant forest. I'd gaze at the graffiti and the burn marks in the shell grotto, wondering. Similarly, a decrepit concrete bandstand at the bottom of a grassy slope, a natural auditorium, fascinated me.

A HOLE IN MY POCKET

Irish school holidays last all summer. Ten full weeks free of responsibility. Time to appreciate some freedom before the call of college or work at eighteen. Word went round at the age of fifteen or so that there was work to be had. The nearest golf club, the Castle in Rathfarnham, had a plentiful supply of players needing caddies. So I joined a group of lads who broke through a hole in the fence and sat around on a wooden bench outside the club house, waiting for players to emerge and pick some of us to caddy for them.

It was easy enough work, following golfers dressed in pastel-coloured Argyll sweaters and loud, checked flat caps. I followed a group of old fogies – retired professional gentlemen who had the freedom to enjoy midday outings, some kindly, others gruff. After three hours I walked home with fifty pence burning a hole in my pocket. I placed it on top of the fridge, my first earnings, handed over to Mum. She was delighted and proud. I was dismayed at this tiny amount for such a long and boring afternoon.

Soon I had a regular, Jimmy O'Meara. I wasn't a good caddy: I had no interest in the game, and he knew it. But it was the perfect landscape for my mind to wander over – hills, contours, parts of the earth scooped out and filled with pristine granite sand. Spending time in such settings brought its own rewards.

FIRST JOB

I left school. A job came up which decided my fate. It was suddenly obvious to me. I wanted to make gardens. I wanted to make gardens that were different, that were creative. Ones for people, ones that were fit for suburbia. A week later the offer arrived. I would work from eight thirty to six, with an hour for lunch in Dublin city centre, for £60 a week. After a month, if all went well, this would rise to £70. I planned to use the position as a springboard to try and secure a place the following year at the College of Amenity Horticulture. Suddenly I felt driven.

Mackey's Seeds Ltd of Mary Street was a family firm which had been operating from different premises in Dublin city centre since the 1700s. It was a shop where Dubliners and country farmers purchased their seeds for growing vegetables and flowers, hand-weighed fertilizers, tonnes of bulbs and garden ornaments. Old-fashioned and idiosyncratic, it had a dark basement used as a vast storage area. New interns started here, weighing out different mixes of garden feeds – nitrogen, potassium, sulphate of iron, sulphate of potash and magnesium salts – into paper or plastic bags by the pound, slipping in blue or green paper identifying labels, taping them shut. It was also the storage space for thousands of packets of Suttons seeds in cardboard containers, almost as narrow as shoe boxes, identified by numbered codes.

Above this lay the shop floor, divided in two, front and back, with the counter in the middle. And on top of this again was a walk-round gallery space where two men dressed in brown shop coats would climb wooden ladders to retrieve ounces and half ounces of loose cabbage, turnip and cauliflower seed. Around a wooden walkway, with its broad sorting desk, were the offices where Brendan, an elegant ginger-haired gentleman, looked after the accounts, helped by the firecrackers Carmel and Virginia.

The shop's formidable owner, Jean-Pierre Eliet, was a thin,

tweed-jacketed and corduroy-trousered caricature of a Frenchman. His spirit was indomitable, and his mood could be judged at a hundred yards by the scowl or smile on his face. The firm had passed to his American wife through her family. He occupied a wooden cabin across from the cash desk. He'd arrive every morning at half past nine, dressed in a tweed jacket, neatly tied scarf and checked flat cap, his station wagon laden down with plants from the firm's garden centre near where he lived. He'd bark orders, call you a twit in French, march into his cubicle and slam the door, the glass shuddering behind him. Five dustbins stood outside, containing different grades of grass seed: no. 1 was for the perfectly manicured front lawn, no. 2 for the ordinary front lawn, no. 3 for the back garden, no. 4 for shaded areas and no. 5 was rye grass for rough areas. They'd be refilled from dusty hessian sacks, but for no. 2 and no. 3 you could also buy pre-packed cardboard boxes, which were stacked on the little narrow wooden ledge in front of Jean-Pierre's window. My first job was to obscure his view by building up as many of these cardboard bricks as I could fit. The shop was full of characters and had an old-fashioned feeling – a horticultural version of the department store in *Are You Being Served?*

I'd cycle into work every day. I loved my job. Phyllis, the sales assistant, wore a blue housecoat and horn-rimmed specs and had wavy grey hair. Beyond middle-aged, she was full of caustic wit and sharp asides. Carmel, in charge of the post, occupied an office at the end of the store where she sorted the post, passing each envelope through the franking machine. Sacks of mail were then dragged in a trolley to the post office every evening.

The shop manager was a redoubtable Galway woman, Josephine Keaveny. I held her in awe even while trying to escape her barking orders. She was fun, though, and in the evenings could occasionally be found pulling pints behind the bar of Dublin's oldest pub, the Brazen Head, helping out when they were busy.

She loved traditional music, and from all these colleagues I absorbed some of their passion for living. Like Josephine, Lavinia was another recent graduate from the Botanic Gardens: small, bespectacled and studious, she'd spend her lunch break in another wooden and glass cabin, going through obscure pamphlets of rare clematis species.

But nothing was expected of me. I had completed my Leaving Certificate (the equivalent of A-levels), and had a summer to wait for the results. Dad was in hospital, so there was a distraction. My brother had left school a few years earlier and gained a good position in the Civil Service. I had decided on becoming a gardener. The College of Amenity Horticulture was located within the city's National Botanic Gardens. It ran a three-year course, an academic apprenticeship that valued interest in the subject as much as previous educational achievement. Among the world's oldest botanical institutions, the gardens were renowned for their rich and varied collection of plants, their pioneering glasshouses and the knowledge of those who worked there, the gardeners of the Office of Public Works. The OPW, as it is known, does a similar job to the National Trust in the UK. It is state run and looks after many parts of our heritage. I harboured dreams of becoming a third level student here.

A year passed at Mackey's. I was enjoying myself too much. I delayed applying for college. I felt I was absorbing a lot of information. After my second year, I filled out an application form, went for an interview and was rejected. This bothered me. Having some formal education was becoming important to me, and yet I left the application form languishing throughout the third year. The closing date was a Monday morning, and it was the Sunday evening before I sat down to fill out the questions. I cycled fifteen miles with it to the Lyons Estate in County Kildare, at that time owned by the Department of Agriculture. Its grand gates were chained. Luckily, a caretaker in a gate lodge across the road took my envelope and promised to deliver it the next morning. The following autumn I was accepted as a student. After three years' working it would be tough not to have a wage, but it was the start of a new and important phase in my life. To be a student in the Botanic Gardens held an air of mystique for me and everyone I met. They were all delighted.

THE NATIONAL BOTANIC GARDENS

Dublin's Botanic Gardens sit on the banks of the River Tolka in Glasnevin, north of the city. It's a venerable institution with a mix of wonderful and innovative garden architecture. Over the past twenty years it has benefited from state investment. When I was a student working in the great Palm House, it wasn't uncommon for shards of glass to come crashing down among the cycads, resulting in whole plant collections being put out of bounds to visitors and students alike. The restoration of these houses, and most particularly William Turner's Curvilinear Range, necessitated great innovations. Cast-iron beams were X-rayed and original scrap metal from the restoration of the Palm House at Kew was purchased from a dealer, brought back to Dublin where it had been originally been cast, and used in the rebuilding of Glasnevin's wonderful structures.

The gardens are divided into seven different sections, ranging from a long herbaceous walk to alpine rock gardens, an arboretum, a beautiful reflecting pond fed by the Tolka, a walled vegetable garden and seasonal displays of bulbs and bedding. I was in a class of thirty or so, and we spent the first and third year on site, with Friday afternoon plant identity parades. The middle year was given over to practical work, with a few months in most of Dublin's parks. Duties there were varied. I particularly remember cycling twenty miles across the city on winter mornings in order to arrive at Malahide Castle by eight o'clock.

I spent a summer in the heart of the city, in the small Merrion Square Park. Laid out on the lines of a Victorian recreational ground, it lies close enough to Parliament to ensure that maintenance is always of the highest order. Office workers from all around pile in during summer lunchtimes and marvel at the vibrant bedding displays. There are shaded walks, benches, sculpture and fountains. Three or four of us from the Botanics worked there together to learn our trade, removing the bulbs from the spring displays, preparing for planting, collecting the bedding plants from the city's nurseries and planting out summer colour, and all the time keeping notebooks, storing memories.

The dedication to their craft and excitement of some people was great. The man whose job it was to run this park took huge delight in it. And the reaction you got from the park users as a new bedding display was unveiled was super. People really appreciated the difference you made. It was also a delight to have an effect on the whole city. In one park, St Anne's in Raheny, one of our jobs was to fill all the civic containers with flowers and bulbs. These would be enjoyed by Dubliners for a whole season. The Corporation nurseries grew so much colour, so many bedding plants, from seed, while shrubs were propagated by root or shoot cuttings. The practical skills then on show have remained with me.

My great ambition for this period of my life was to learn about design, to understand the process of changing space. I'd hoped that analogies would be drawn with other creative disciplines, such as architecture and fashion design. I'd hoped that within the walls of this great institution there would be people who could explain different movements, creative thoughts and significant moments, and link gardening to these and to the wider world. I wanted debate, questioning and stimulation. I had different ideas. I would have loved for those to be examined, to be prodded. None of this happened. Early on we were given paper and shown how to use our drawing equipment. We had a few challenges, were asked to design some gardens. But nothing woke me up to possibilities. My main appetite for learning wasn't satisfied at all.

However, other things took over: learning about plants and social integration, becoming part of a group, a member of a class, and immersing myself fully in parties and friendship. There was great information about the growing of plants to be had from the staff of the gardens. Some lecturers did inspire me, so I received a good grounding in horticulture.

AWAKENINGS

While I was a student I advertised my services as a student gardener, and one of the first commissions I received saw a brother and sister hand over to me a plot to the front of the house they lived in the suburbs of Dublin. My brief was that if I wanted to put a big red Dallas cowboy star in the middle of the front lawn, that was fine by them.

I spent most of my time drinking coffee and munching through packets of chocolate Hobnobs in their living room. They were intelligent, fun and sociable. I'd arrive every weekend and do a bit of work, but would soon be drawn into their wry conversation. At some point, however, I had to get on with the work. One particular weekend they were away. I gathered my materials with care. It was all straight from a John Brookes manual: a few tonnes of pebble delivered; some cobbles from the beach in Bray just south of Dublin, lifted in an illegal dawn raid; railway sleepers collected from a farm in Kildare at eight in the morning by a man with a van; and a half-oak barrel purchased from a hardware store, along with nails and small straps of steel in straight and L-shaped lengths. As for plants, there was a large rhododendron recently liberated from a friend's mother's garden, some *Phormium tenax*, grasses and a bit of bamboo. It was 1987.

At midday, I stood in the middle of this collection of plants and materials, armed with shovel and spade. A girl came out of the house and pulled a crash helmet over her head. She nodded with a distinct lack of interest and took off on her phut-phut machine. I set to work. I dug and cleared and shovelled. The lady next door with the fancy hairdo and bright red lipstick leaned out of her bedroom window and smiled. She was a bit older, a favourite aunt-type figure, and was soon supplying me with tea. But that day the tea didn't stop the work. The lawn was stripped, the unruly griselinia hedge trimmed, a retaining wall crudely built from sleepers to level off the sloping plot. By Sunday morning the gravel was spread, my excitement rising. A bolt of inspiration: I placed a sleeper protruding upright from the ground. It was barely bedded in: seven and a half of its nine feet rose starkly from a bed of clay. At its base but a foot away was the oak barrel, and in it, hovering over the circular rim, the cloud of rhododendron. Boulders were placed just so, a bit of Arizona, a bit of woodland, a strong composition. I raked the gravel flat, washed everything down with a hose and stood back. I started to tremble. Something took over my body. I had never been as certain as this in my life before. I was a garden designer.

Phut phut phut. The girl arrived back. She removed her helmet. I watched her carefully. 'Oh my god,' she said, 'that's amazing!' That's my audience.

After I graduated from college in the summer of 1988, I set out to be an entrepreneur. I imagined I would soon have a fleet of vans on the road, and I'd travel Ireland creating gardens. There were a number of obstacles in my way. I couldn't drive and I had no money. Dad came to the rescue with some lessons and a guarantee for a bank loan. It still left me short. The only grants that were available for starting up a business required that I be three months unemployed. If I wanted to add to society and create work I would have first to be registered unemployed. If I did, I'd get a grant of £30 a week for a year.

The dole queues were horrible. Signing on for twelve weeks meant not doing any work. It also gave me a taste of what unemployment is like. There was no reason to be up early in the morning. Dad was furious. Motivation disappeared. Officially, I was meant to be looking for a job. That was a requirement of collecting the dole. But I didn't want anyone else's job. I wanted to create one for myself. That's why I had applied for a grant. Every Wednesday morning I would have to present myself at the Labour Exchange and join the long winding queue of the unemployed. The building was grey; the atmosphere was that of a line of people begging. The attendant sat behind a glass partition, automatically stamped the papers and dealt out your cash allowance. Twelve weeks of this was plenty for me.

Before leaving college, I was convinced of the success of my soon-to-be enterprise. I'd had a logo designed, and soon had business cards and T shirts printed up: 'Gavin Landscaping', and another for a company called 'Trees to Please'. Side by side with transforming gardens throughout the country, I intended to develop a gift service for people who wanted to send presents. I would plant a tree in somebody's garden for £30. I dreamed of developing a countrywide network of other tree-planters, based in garden centres throughout the country. Orders would come in and planters with trees would be despatched.

After the three months I bought a van, had a logo painted on it and set off gardening. I needed only basic equipment – lawnmower, wheelbarrow, shovels and spades. The freedom of having wheels was fantastic. I toured the country. My friend Barry wrote to me from America. He was coming home to celebrate his twenty-first birthday in Galway – would I come? I drove across the country, collecting another college mate, Sean Kiernan, in Longford. Driving through Roscommon, full of beans, I missed a stop sign. The Nissan skidded sideways across the road and embedded itself into the corner of a house. We weren't hurt, but the van was almost a write-off. Not a great start. But I began making gardens. It wasn't the time to promote any new style. I developed a simple format – lawns, patios and arbours. I planted mixed borders and lots of trees. I worked hard and loved what I was doing. I found great satisfaction in transforming spaces. A by-law meant that I couldn't park the van permanently outside my parent's house. I moved once again to flat land. I was happy, in control and earning a bit of money. I had a decent circle of friends. But as I dug, the novelty of being in business soon wore

Me, a baby

Declan, Diarmuid and Conor Gavin

Me in Sligo, age 3, the original pony kid

Mum and us… at Lake Geneva, Switzerland

Dad and us… in the French Alps

First Holy Communion at Loreto Convent, Rathfarnham

Cub scouts

Emer, me and Niamh in our new school uniforms

The family in front of a prickly Pyracantha in Fairways, Rathfarnham

Drinking on the pier with Derry in Galways

Hat party in my flat with Brendan and Sean, my student friends from the College of Amenity Horticulture at the National Botanic Gardens, Dublin

Me (with my back to the camera) being presented with a gold medal for a garden design by the Irish president, Mary Robinson

*Elma, Susan, Elma, Jo and Kathy – Loreto convent
girls on our front driveway in Fairways*

Watering a new garden at Langtons in Kilkenny

Another gold. Myself and Eamonn

The family at the Royal Dublin Society gardening competition

Another year, another medal at the Royal Dublin Society

Myself and Yayee at a family wedding

Princess Anne viewing our first Chelsea garden, 1995

Discussing resiting our Chelsea garden with a buyer, 1995

Kings of the castle: me, Ed, Ger and Vincent scaling our tower as the final bell went at Chelsea Flower Show 1995

Myself and Vincent, Chelsea Flower Show 1995

Wedding breakfast

Myself and Justine in the midst of urban landscaping

Just married, Tahilla church, County Kerry, 1995

Dad, Mum, Me, Justine, Terry and Ronan at the Parknasilla hotel, 1995

Chelsea Flower Show 1995, To the Waters and the Wild

Terry and me in the days of short hair in Sneem, County Kerry, 1995

Long hair! Declan, me, Emere, Niamh and Mum in the Castle Pub, Rathfarnham

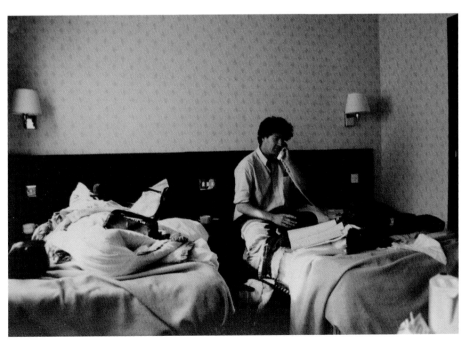

Phone bashing; still looking for sponsorship during Chelsea Flower Show build, 1996

Home Front in the Garden; *Me, John Noel (in blue) and Simon Shaw in Camden market, London, about to haul a tree over the wall, 1997*

Anne McKevitt, John Noel and me on location for Home Front in the Garden

The crew and client on an early Home Front *build, north London*

Sean, exhausted after working through the night to finish building a communal garden in Wandsworth, London, 1998

The crew visit Dublin; Jane, me and Rachel Innes-Lumsden, 1998

Book signing at Waterstones in Belfast

off. The desire to change my world of gardens came back, stronger than ever.

What was it that I loved about gardens? I think the great outdoors gave me a place to escape to. When the tyranny of suburbia or family life or conformity got too much, outside there was a freedom. Escaping into fields, across to the park, even just out the back door meant I didn't have to answer to anybody. In fact I didn't have to deal with anybody. I could retreat to my world. Without walls I could relax. Plants wouldn't ask me questions. Trees, shrubs – they all just existed happily. As I observed gardens over time, I became amazed at the lives of plants. I had learned about photosynthesis and carried out little experiments on leaves, stopping sunlight from getting to patches of green and examining the effect. We need the sun for plants to grow. But these same plants, the trees and shrubs in our gardens, could survive harsh winters and hot summers. We couldn't. Even now as I watch a plantation of birch being whipped by the wind, I am struck by the resilience of nature, how trunks will bend when necessary, gently or dramatically; how leaves cling on with tiny stalks and how they know when to drop. There is so much that we don't know about nature, so much that we can't read or interpret. If a group of trees in a plantation are being attacked by insects or disease, they can release a chemical cloud which will let others downwind know what's happening, so that they can prepare internal defences.

The colours of nature are astonishing too. I'm not a gardener who feels the need to own fifty varieties of roses or peonies, and while I understand the requirement for Latin names, I don't like the subtle vaunting of this knowledge that is often a social affectation. I delight in the simple things: a field of oil seed rape, its vivid yellow creating a patch like part of a quilt; lavender growing as it should; the upright stems of rosemary, almost oily to the touch; bougainvillea growing from a tin can on a Greek lane; even bright marigolds and tulips. We are lucky to live in an environment where we have four seasons, distinct times of the year that for me herald joy or regret. I love April, May and June, and I hate February. I am aware of the seasons because of a job that allows me to be out absorbing sunlight. The optimism of spring is like a champagne cork popping, an unstoppable build up of pressure, sap forcing its way through past the doomed months of late winter.

'THAT'S ALMOST CHELSEA STANDARD'

It was 1994, and the Royal Dublin Society was having its spring show once again: a traditional event for farmers and those with a love of country pursuits, mounted in the heart of leafy Dublin 4, where bulls, horses, and sheep were awarded rosettes by men in white coats and bowler hats. The crowds had begun to dwindle, and so a gardening show had been invented to attract the urbanites. Designers and landscapers were given small plots to create gardens. I loved showing off. I understood gardens and space. I understood what people wanted. For a few years now I had turned up surrounded by whatever band of friends I could muster for tuppence ha'penny and created my little plot. It was my annual bid for attention, a place to have fun and a place to hold a party.

I had the glorious good fortune of possessing a constant sponsor. Close to my parent's house lived the Griffiths family, an English gentleman with his Irish wife. I had done their garden, in which they had allowed a slight flourish of modern design. David Griffiths was marketing manager for, among other concerns, Impulse Body Spray. So once a year I'd be sponsored at the RDS to create the Impulse Garden. Its floral notes would waft from tin canisters sprayed by PR girls in front of my display. I'd been successful too. I had won gold medals here. I had been best in show. A few years before, in 1990, the new Irish president Mary Robinson, fresh from her dramatic victory in the polls, had presented me with my award. It was a life's highlight. And on the Friday evening the organizers of the show would allow me to have a party for the garden, where friends and family would gather. We'd eat, drink and enjoy our exclusive access to this renowned location. Congratulations on our achievements would flow. But under it all lay muted worries and mutterings: 'Well, this year is he going to do something with it? Why doesn't he get down to business?'

Unless I was continually achieving and challenging the system, I didn't seem to be happy. I wasn't young. I had to make a future for myself. The only way I figured this would happen was if I loved my work and became brilliant at it. But I wanted to make gardens that were new. This looked to be further away than ever. I could have had a perfectly good career doing respectable gardens and adapting gently to changing trends. What kicked in was the need to innovate. I wasn't doing this, and the work I had I began to mess up. My accounts were never in order. If there was money in the bank it was for spending. I found it difficult to budget.

And by spring 1994 I was homeless. I could have returned to Mum and Dad's house, but it would have been an admission of defeat. And the end of any dreams. I was perceived as a fantasist, a disaster.

With nowhere to live, even less of a business than in previous years and a bicycle as my only means of transport, I arrived at the show grounds once more. Surrounded by fleets of vans and people with mobile phones, I parked my bike against the railings and started to map out my plot. I hired some help. One college mate in particular, Barry Cotter, still had a van. So the annual trip to my parents' garden began. The trick in show gardening is to try to make the scene look as natural as possible. You want plants that aren't straight out of pots but rather great big clumps of hostas and heathers, Japanese maples more than two years old, bunches of herbaceous perennials and wafts of lush grasses. So every year I dug up Mum and Dad's garden and drove the three miles to the show grounds to bring these plants on their holidays. A week later, basking in the glow of a gold medal, with my name in the newspapers and a glimpse of the garden on a television show, I'd return them. I bet the plants were petrified when they saw me sizing them up every April!

That particular year I created a charming rural scene. The girl who used to cut my hair was from Achill Island, in the extreme west of the country. Her dad was a builder, so vanloads of red sandstone came across the country and we built this crumbling cottage. We planted it inside and out with ferns and wild flowers. It was pastoral and pretty, and despite me arriving on two wheels rather than four, and a few undisguised sniggers from the trendies of the day, we won gold again. Those weeks were always good ones. We'd stand proudly in front of our winning displays, handing out leaflets and explaining our ideas and plans to visitors. They seemed always to be sunny days. It was one week of importance where receptions and parties were held. I fitted in, I'd achieved. I'd often spend the whole of the following year looking forward to that one week.

I was standing in front of the garden with my friend Eamonn, a carpenter from Donegal who had helped me with the build, when a lady passed by. I knew her, as she'd been a gardener in Dublin's Botanic Gardens. She was with a friend. In latter years she'd become known for her involvement in Irish gardening television and media. Casually she remarked, 'That's almost Chelsea standard.' Overhearing this, I was electrified. Did she mean that I had created a garden that could stand proudly in line with others at the world's greatest flower show? If she did, that's where I had to be.

But was I fooling myself? How do you convince yourself you're right to have an idea, when all the evidence points merely to a pathetic existence? Is it right to perpetuate failure by dreaming and setting out on fanciful adventures? I can't say for certain that the route I took was the correct one. Did laziness or a fear of monotony stop me from becoming normal? I come across people now who are great at talk, excellent at getting attention, but who are forever letting people down. That was me. I was in a difficult prison. Through enthusiasm I could inspire and bring people along. I could get my friends to work with me because I talked a good line. But they'd drop by the wayside one by one. I talked a great game but couldn't see it through – except for that one week every year at the RDS.

During the other weeks of the year, without money, I had lots of time to kill. I was hungry for conversation, for warmth, for laughter, lonely for company. A friend, Tommy, lived near my parents. I had been friendly with his two sisters after leaving school and got to know the family very well. His house became another refuge. I'd turn up all the time, a few evenings a week. Tom lived with his parents. I hated knocking on the front door, waiting there to see if he was in. If he wasn't, it meant an embarrassing retreat with nowhere to go. I'd cycle around, open the gate at the side of the house and in the dark peer through the kitchen window. If he was there I'd go back to the front of the house and then ring. Within minutes I'd be sitting with a hot cup of tea and some cake his mum had made, watching family life all around me. At these moments I felt great, part of conversation, included. Tommy's mum loved gardens, so there was something to talk about. We'd skip out for a pint, down to the village, talking about television programmes, politics, messing around. We'd get chips, wander back, another cup of tea and I'd cycle away to flat land, another evening spent. The following night, I'd have to live with myself.

My final flat was in the basement of a house. Life had a routine. I had a van parked outside and was occasionally busy. A developer had some schemes with show houses needing attractive gardens. I'd hire casual labour and old mates from college. Off we'd go every morning, digging, raking and planting. I enjoyed demonstrating how people could live in the home of their dreams. And every Saturday afternoon we'd return to my base and I'd write out the cheques for all the lads. When a scheme caught my imagination there were few more industrious than I was.

I knew I wanted to create gardens that were different. I was just fed up with the whole idea of prettiness and sameness and gardens being just so or just right. You could that see for so many clients it was about social aspiration, making something beautiful in their eyes, something to show off. This is part of a garden's role. But I was interested in art, architecture, pop videos, maybe fashion design, different forms of expression. And much of what was expressed in gardens revolved around suburban tweeness, rockeries and crazy paving. Gardens needed to move on.

But Dublin wasn't wealthy. It was difficult to inspire clients with new ideas. You gave your customers what they wanted: rose beds, herbaceous borders, stone terraces, pots, tubs and hanging baskets. The doyenne of gardening remained Gertrude Jekyll. Rosemary Verey and Christopher Lloyd were contemporary names, revered in garden circles. But in suburban gardens everything revolved around rockeries and dwarf conifers. Even gravel gardens were a thing of the future.

Soon, though, there were only two of us, Eamonn and myself. Both of us were a little lost. He had left home at the age of sixteen to work on the sites in Glasgow. He was back in Dublin because he'd met a young teacher who'd been working for a while in London. We'd laugh a lot, listen to the radio either in the van or while digging, and on Fridays – if I could afford the wages – we'd have a few pints.

So Eamonn and I would dig and dream. From a pub garden in Kilkenny to an old folks' home in town, we'd plant away. In October we received a commission in Foxrock, a wealthy suburb, for a gazebo and a pond. Eamonn copied a beautiful structure from a picture book as I dug a kidney-shaped pond in front of it. The money upfront was good. But six weeks later we had little left. Christmas was approaching. Our initial enthusiasm had waned to a bored plod. There was a rush to be finished before Christmas. I remember the late evenings sticking in herbaceous plants – empty looking pots of withered foliage – desperate to create a picturesque paradise. Occasionally a steaming cup of tea would arrive from the kitchen. Late in the evening, my heavy green jumper would crystallize with frost. Eventually it was finished, but I would still have to appear and pretend to be working, hoping that the mister would arrive home in his Jaguar, so I could ask for the final cheque. Two days before Christmas and Eamonn was to head off on the long journey to Donegal without a present bought. It came right in the end. I got the cheque and the bank cashed it, but if you live your life like this too often it's just not fun.

Come January we had a fresh project for a client who'd made good selling sausages and burgers to takeaway outlets. He wanted his whole garden redeveloped. He'd a big house, money and a sense of humour. And every day there'd be a fry-up. Another friend, Vincent Barnes, had joined our little gang. Back in Dublin after years in New York, he had good practical skills. A few years later, Vincent would play a pivotal role in helping me to achieve my dreams. The client wanted a new driveway. Suddenly we were an outfit with Kanga hammers, skips and design ideas.

The months rolled by, and the garden started to come together. It looked lovely, hardly a trend-setting design but still a very pleasing scene. We had a decent budget and likeable clients. Hints that we should be finished were becoming ever more frequent and I was out of funds. The last payment was due as soon as the garden was completed. I reckoned there were five days left. My rent was overdue again and I'd no money to pay for the planting. But I could hold out for five days.

We rolled out the lawn. It tidied up everything and linked all the freshly built features. Just two days to go and a few thousand pounds due. I woke up on the last morning – everywhere was covered in snow. It was a disaster. All our work covered by a white blanket. I started raking snow, tried to melt it with tepid water with a hose. This type of garden-making was surreal and frustrating. It wasn't getting me anywhere.

Then for a while there was no work. My routine was the same one day after another. I was broke, but I knew where the landlord kept the key for the coin-operated phone box in the hall. So one or two of the lads would cycle over to me in the morning, I'd raid the drawer of the phone for shiny fifty pence pieces, and off we'd go to the coffee shop for breakfast. Then I'd idle away the day in dreams, occasionally tucking myself underneath the duvet, wishing for time to pass.

To cap it all, my Nissan Urvan packed in and was then stolen from outside the flat. Cycling around the corner the next day I found it abandoned. But that was the last I saw of it. Next day it was gone again.

That was my life. A landscaper with dreams of modern design with only a bike for transport. And I couldn't even keep a van on the road. Worse was to come.

My stereo system, bought on hire purchase from the local music shop, was repossessed. I was evicted. I owned clothes and a bicycle, the sum of my life at the age of twenty seven. I bundled the clothes into three black plastic bin liners and cycled with them to Vincent's house. They sat in a corner of his dad's shed for weeks. His dad wanted to build something in his shed again and so my plastic bags were left in a corner of the garden, rain pouring down.

I can't remember where I went to bed. It was a few nights here, an occasional evening there. I wasn't what a homeless person looked like. I kept myself clean and I spoke well enough. And if I wanted to give in, there was a home to go to. But I couldn't. This was the lowest I ever got. I am an enthusiastic character. When I was up and excited everyone around me knew about it. But when I was low and couldn't see a future I withdrew. What had the years since college given me? What had I achieved? A couple of medals from a flower show wouldn't put food on the table. I hadn't got a table. My contemporaries were buying houses and having babies. They didn't dare to dream, but they did look after their responsibilities. Why couldn't I? Should I be a gardener? Was there something else that I could feel as strongly about? I considered this for six months.

I'd always talked a good game, but I was fast becoming a joke. I owed money all round, but in the pub would imagine aloud a bright future. In the gardening industry I was easily dismissed for what I was – a failure.

TERRY

But the RDS success showed I could win prizes. Where did that leave me? How would I regroup and rebuild with so little to show for my life except for these chinks of glory? Taking part in competition was the enemy of slow, steady work. So far it had led to nothing. This year, however, things would be different. It wasn't common knowledge that I was on my uppers. All that was known was that I was now the only person in the country to have won two gold medals from the Royal Dublin Society for gardens created at their show. For a month I was the gardener to know. The widow of a German industrialist had bought a castle. Rumours had been flying around that David Bowie had been to view this massive turreted mansion in the country. Some money was seeping into Irish society and there was renewed interest in art and style. I borrowed a car, went to meet the new owner, walked the estate but wasn't up to the job. I was excited by the possibilities and tickled to be entertained to afternoon tea in a baronial hall with shag-pile carpet, but I couldn't carry on the pretence on this scale and pretend that I had a studio and a massive crew behind me.

But I didn't need to. My reputation was building in spite of my circumstances. I was the guy who'd won and the person who had been invited to design the new castle gardens. People were interested. Alfred Cochrane, an architect from a landed family, called. Would I work on his gardens? He lived in Corke Lodge in Shankill, south County Dublin. His brother Lord Cochrane owned the big house. Being an architect, Alfred designed while I implemented. He'd been developing a garden for some years and had the acquaintance of Helen Dillon, the doyenne of Irish gardeners. I planted parterres of box infilled with masses of lavender, stately dicksonias emerging from a woodland. The portico from Glendalough House, a demolished stately pile, had been erected as a distant folly. When it was finished, Alfred threw a garden party. His friend John Burke ran a garden visiting group. I began to meet people with interests in art and culture. John wanted to introduce me to someone else, a friend of Helen Dillon's, Terry Keane.

I knew the name. Terry was a formidable gossip columnist, fashion journalist and bon viveur. She occupied a unique place in society, scandalizing and exciting readers with her tales of the Irish at play on the back page of the country's most popular newspaper, the *Sunday Independent*. Separated from Ronan, Chief Justice of Ireland, Terry led a colourful life. The easiest picture to paint of her would be a perfect mix of Jennifer Saunders' and Joanna Lumley's characters in *Absolutely Fabulous*. And then exaggerate the dramas. She lived in a town house, with her children either living with her or nearby. It was a salon where Ireland's cultural elite and opinion makers gathered, and champagne and red wine flowed.

John informed me that Helen had designed a garden for Terry on the back of a cigarette packet. Would I be interested in implementing it? I was intrigued, scared and pleased all at once. What would this person make of me? How would I pull this together? I was to meet her at a party at John's house. 'If you get a chance,' he said, 'introduce yourself and talk gardens.' I was nervous and spent most of the evening avoiding contact. In the early hours we were both heading for home at the same time. Terry was looking for a taxi. I was driving a small, borrowed, rusting Peugeot van with puddles in the foot well. Would I offer her a lift? We lived just a few minutes apart. Why not? We chatted animatedly all the way, and the following day I arrived to see the garden. This encounter would change my life.

The Keane family home was a hive of activity. John arrived. I was to be interviewed. I was shown the sketches, my opinion was sought and a quote was requested. Within a couple of days, Vincent and I were digging. I knew the job had to be a good one. At last something positive would come out of winning an award. To be the chosen, to have a commission, to create a garden at a beautiful Georgian villa was wonderful.

Her desire wasn't for anything contemporary. I just had to make sense of Helen's sketches and make over a triangular-shaped plot. An old French wrought-iron balcony was to be turned into a garden table, set at the base of a sycamore as a focal point, with box hedging and herbaceous planting leading up to a big gravel pathway. Three quarters of the way down this path another would shoot out at 90 degrees to lead to a garden room, and at another 90 degrees off this path a rondelle was to be created, a circular cobbled room surrounded by trellis, edged by box and planted with roses.

I'd arrive at eight in the morning and work till nine in the evening. Vincent and I kept our heads down, lifted the existing lawn by hand, wheeled everything out to a skip in the side car park and excavated the pathway. We dug over the beds and added well-rotted humus material, listening to the radio, working steadily. In the morning we'd look up at the conservatory. Built on the second level, it had access to the garden through an awkward side stairway. A window was thrown open. A blonde girl in a white towelling dressing gown was drying her hair. 'Did you see her?' I asked Vincent. One day she would be my wife.

That evening I was still working, alone. If I was lucky enough to have a job, this was normal. I worked hard; I had nowhere else to go. Terry shouted out, 'Come in for a beer!' A few days later it was lunch. If it was me on my own, or if Vincent was with me or anybody else, everyone was invited. There were no airs and graces, conversation was lively. This wasn't normal. To be included, to be invited in, and as a tradesman to eat at the table with the family, especially one so well-known and influential, was striking. Any feelings of intimidation melted away. The sense of fun and drama enveloped me.

Terry had three daughters, Madeleine, Justine and Jane, and a son, Timothy. They weren't shy. There was often a battle going on, possibly about washing up or maybe a difference of opinion about the government of the day. During a typical week, Terry might disappear to Paris for a couple of days and then go on a trip to New York. You might arrive on a Saturday morning to find guests wandering through the house who had arrived for lunch the previous day. You'd never know who would pass you on the garden path – artists, painters, politicians, movie stars. If the man on the moon walked by, you wouldn't blink. Buzz Aldrin once came for dinner.

Being useful held great currency. Soon it wasn't only the garden that needed my attention. Terry, followed by quantities of Louis Vuitton luggage, went off on a Caribbean cruise. The house needed painting. Tommy and I took on the job.

Terry's kids told us that when she returned from long trips abroad their mother's mood could be tetchy. They giggled as they suggested the painting needed to be perfect. In her bedroom she had requested Regency stripes. We toiled late into the night. People would come in, gaze, and leave. We had no idea if we had got it right. She arrived home, loved it; everybody relaxed. There were parties and dinners at the drop of a hat, to celebrate everything. It had only been four or five months, but because we were around so much we had become friends. Things weren't going well where I lived, and Terry noticed. I was arriving for work on foot. Her kids had moved out, and she didn't like the fact that it was just her and her elderly mum in this large house. Would I move in? It suited everyone, and what was more she had a new car. From Tuesday to Friday she worked in the newspaper office in the city centre. If I dropped her in for ten o'clock and collected her at not a minute past five, I could have the car for my business.

That's what happened for the next six months. I'd bring her to work and then go to a quarry or a paving warehouse, fill the boot with stone, the back seat with plants and any spare place with compost. I'd deliver these materials to site and dig, and at half past four make a dash for the city. As long as I was on time, she'd look at the straggled remnants of foliage draped over the steering wheel but say nothing. Life was always interesting. Hugh Grant was in town, the hottest movie star on the planet. She'd bypassed the premiere of his movie, but was keeping a promise to go to the after show party. Nervously, he was led over. Her opening gambit was,

'Young man, I believe you can't kiss.'

He flustered his way through the conversation.

'Why did you say that to him?' I asked.

'I just wanted to see his reaction.'

He bored her. We spent the night chatting to Alan Rickman, and Hugh never made her column. A week to the day later, he was found with Divine Brown.

The back garden had been completed successfully, and I moved on to the front. I had another idea. The conservatory had been converted into a kitchen. It seemed remote, though. Access to the garden wasn't easy. Houses of this period didn't have a great relationship with the garden. I talked to Terry about creating a deck made from heavyweight railway sleepers, supported by steel RSJs, and incorporating some wide steps right down to the garden. We'd open some double doors and create a definite flow in this house between inside and the garden. Terry was always one to be enthused by a new project, so Vincent and I calculated the cost, and within a week we had created an elevated wooden platform. We finished at ten o'clock one evening. Doors had yet to be installed. Terry propped a ladder against the structure, ordered a Chinese takeaway and the three of us dined in some style.

In the evenings we would all sit around the kitchen table or in the drawing room. Anywhere else this set-up might have been unusual, but Terry held open house for anybody interesting, daring or creative. I began to talk about my dreams, knowing that I was surrounded by people who were interested and had the ability to push me. A place like the Chelsea Flower Show enthralled Terry. She loved gardens, was amused by society, and cemented in me a determination to go for it.

Terry's daughter Justine was sharing a house with some friends in Heytesbury Street, not far away. When she moved out she had left behind her dog Poppy, a beautiful but haughty Cavalier spaniel. So she'd drop in every day or two. Justine was a psychologist, blonde, beautiful but reserved. Her character was very different from her mum's. They shared a love of art and culture. Justine played the role of an amused onlooker at some of the more rambunctious goings on.

I hadn't turned into a social butterfly. I was still quiet and reserved, but I suppose some fun. We began to get to know each other. When I was first building the garden we had both found ourselves in an embarrassing situation. Yayee, Terry's ninety-four-year-old mum, who lived downstairs, had invited me to come back to the family home one evening for dinner. I didn't know that she had also invited her granddaughter Justine. Just the two of us, and at ninety-four Yayee wasn't the best cook. If she was alone in the house there was a constant fear that firemen would have to be called or the police. She certainly wasn't a pushover though. Walking down the main street one day she had been knocked over by a guy on a motorbike. He was the one carted off to hospital in shock. She bounced back home muttering something about that poor young man! Terry, being a fashionista, had a wardrobe that was bang up to date, and Yayee wasn't going to be left behind. And much to Terry's annoyance, she would kit herself out in colourful leggings and go strolling up and down the main street. She would snoop around the house, opening every drawer, examining anything different. She'd tut tut over empty champagne bottles and sides of smoked salmon that had been abandoned on the table after a late evening. She'd open the front door to accept a stream of floral bouquets sent to her daughter, muttering to confused delivery men, 'Who are these from? What is she up to now?' She had a wrath like few others. If she liked you, you were fine. If she didn't, it was better that you never set foot in number 62 Ranelagh Road.

Despite having been a second mother to her grandchildren, she had sort of lost the ability to cook. I arrived; Justine arrived. The table was laid haphazardly and plates of fish fingers were produced. Yayee disappeared. She'd been matchmaking. After about seven minutes, Justine made a polite excuse and left. I remember the front door banging loudly. A month later, at one of Terry's parties in the drawing room, we found ourselves laughing about it. After that we would laugh together a lot.

Why did we click? I think we were two lost souls who'd found each other through the din of very different lives. Together we seemed to understand each other. I was astonished. I was still on the edge of going nowhere, not young at twenty-nine. I had one foot in a life that was isolated and dark, a place where I continually let people down, a world where I couldn't achieve anything. And another in a place full of light, love, humour and creativity. And of course turbulence. With me, there was always turbulence.

In life there are distinct points that you never forget: achieving something, winning something, something obvious. The most momentous in my life was about to happen, in the gentlest of ways. When I was looking at failure, feeling a fool and realizing there was no place left to go, Justine told me one evening that she believed I could achieve anything I wanted to. I was astonished. Why would this amazing person have any sort of belief in me? It was all I needed to continue.

Yayee lived with Terry. Her quarters were on the ground floor. Her real name was Ann. She had looked after her grandchildren when they were young, and when they tried to pronounce her name Yayee was what emerged. It stuck, and everyone from doctors to the prime minister knew her as such. Through my time making the garden she'd peer out of the windows, smiling broadly, eyes shining manically, creating a T-shape with both index fingers. I'd go the side door.

'Would you like a cup of tea?'

'That would be great, Yayee.'

I became friends with a ninety-four year old. While Terry swanned around the world dipping in and out of continents and social scenes, Yayee lived at home. Upstairs anything could be happening – parties, rows, quiet family evenings. Yayee's diminutive presence moved through all of this. Originally from a large family in County Cork, she had moved to London at the age of eighteen, worked in a bank and married an Irish doctor, Timothy O'Donnell. Terry had been born in London and lived there till she was eighteen, and when Timothy became ill, Yayee came back to Ireland with Terry, who started to study medicine at Trinity College, Dublin. And now Yayee and Terry lived together in this Georgian house on Ranelagh Road. They adored each other and fought like cat and dog. Yayee was pious and neat, conservative and reserved, with a twinkle in her eye. Terry was the polar opposite. As I built the garden, on my own or with Vincent, Yayee was ever present, fascinated, always peering out and always with a cup of tea on offer.

You never escaped from Terry. When one project was complete, you were always either in the middle of another project or waiting for a new one to start. If you had an idea to create, to make, to plant, it stood a good chance of happening, and whoever you were, if you were on the orbit of the Keane family you were included in everything that happened. Here was another home where I could call in to just to say hello and be assured of conversation and comfort.

Yayee and I got on famously. I'd sit on a chair by the bed, she'd be in the bed, and both of us would be watching television, munching cake that had been found in a cupboard upstairs, drinking tea. There was an Irish cook, Darina Allen, who had a programme called *Simply Delicious*. Darina wore exaggerated glasses. Yayee would have to talk about them. Darina cooked using lots of butter. Isn't she terrible, I love her! Yayee would say. And then we'd watch the evening news and I'd say my good night, slip out, leaving Yayee gazing in my wake. I think I was viewed as being really sweet, calling in on this elderly lady. In fact it was the opposite. I was getting more from these encounters than anyone could imagine. Someone to sit with and talk to, tea to drink, silly conversation, and my own life successfully avoided.

My meeting with Terry and getting to know her family marked a positive turning point. It was almost as if I was entering a new phase of my life. I had been brought up to conform, to work hard and achieve through study and dedication. Since their marriage my parents had had little time for fun. They'd instilled a good work ethic and manners in their brood. Through circumstance I became a dreamer. Genetically I must have had some in-built artistic leaning. And now, at a time when I should be well set on a road of stability, I was unreservedly welcomed into an environment where artistic creation and fun were lauded. I hadn't abandoned my background, but my ambitions and dreams were being listened to and encouraged. I felt fortified by new optimism. A new chapter in life beckoned me.

PART
TWO
CHELSEA
AND
TELEVISION
FAME

CHELSEA ON MY MIND

I began to think, 'What if, what if?' I had nothing – only minor gardening notoriety and no possibilities. Other than showing off, things had been a failure. I had no place to live. I had no clothes. What if I did a garden at the Chelsea Flower Show? What was the Chelsea Flower Show? Could this be my redemption? Could something happen?

With the Irish economy gently warming up, there was at least some work around. By bicycle and then in a borrowed van, I picked myself up. I got together the deposit for a flat in a large house overlooking a park. I started to dream again, set up a little desk for myself and wrote notes and lists. I was asked to give a talk in Dublin's central library on gardening. Twenty elderly ladies sat in a room and listened. I soon set up my own institution with the grandiose title 'Dublin School of Garden Design', and I thought about Chelsea.

The school offered a series of afternoon, evening or weekend courses, and it worked. I trawled through books, took notes, had them typed up and photocopied. In the Botanic Gardens I took photos of the plants, and had slides made. I put advertisements in local and national newspapers, and a steady stream of housewives, retirees and garden devotees signed up. We got a cash box, a duplicate book and a rubber stamp. I started to teach the basics of how to design gardens. Soon I could afford the rent and put food on the table. I began to live, a little.

I ran the courses in a language school two doors from where I lived. My slides would inevitably arrive from the developers five minutes after the students had taken their seats. I'd disappear into the hallway, slotting them into the cylindrical wheel which I would then click into the projector. I'd put them in upside down or the wrong way round. The photocopier would run out of paper. Midway through the class I'd leave to heat up a large kettle for the tea and coffee break. It was manic, but somehow it worked. People were enjoying themselves and I realized I could teach.

I began to read more and photograph images from books. My library of material developed. I started weekend courses. I was surprised at my ability to stand up in front of people and talk. I had grown up shy, instantly turning red if anybody looked at me. I was polite but had few social skills. But it seemed that when it came to gardens, things were different.

The final part of an eight-week course was always on a Saturday morning. We'd fill a coach with our participants and drive to wonderful gardens in County Wicklow. We'd spend a morning walking through ideas that we had talked about in the previous weeks. And in the early afternoon we were all dropped back to Dublin. As the empty coach pulled away and the last of the students' cars disappeared, I'd shake my head with astonishment. Something I had started was working.

That flower show in London niggled at me. I didn't know much about it. It wasn't a big television event. But I knew that every year it seemed half the world's gardeners got together to gaze at the latest must have, the latest big blooms, vegetables and trends in garden design. Two guys in the year above in college would travel to visit it each year, so that they knew what was happening in the bigger world outside our gardening village.

I had a belief that something was going to happen to me, that things would be OK. The boost of winning gold again at the RDS show was enormous. To achieve some sort of credibility after years in a desert of doldrums meant there was hope, and the possibility of a future.

When you have nothing, you often have nothing to lose. I recall standing at a bus stop and making a decision to take small steps And the steps also meant not being scared of walking down the street and meeting somebody I'd let down, somebody I owed money to, somebody whose garden I had never finished.

Eamonn was back on the sites in London. I had an address for him in Cricklewood. I gathered together a couple of hundred quid, some photographs of our work, and myself and Vincent got on a boat. We sailed to Holyhead and took a train to London. It was late when we knocked on his door. He was living with nine other Irish émigrés, squeezed around a kitchen table, enjoying a feisty game of cards. The Chelsea Flower Show, what's that?, he asked. I slept on the floor, Vincent kipped somewhere else, and having tracked down an address the following day the three of us headed off.

RHS HQ

I remember it clearly, a lovely sunny day, warm red brick buildings, mansion blocks and discreet offices surrounding a cricket pitch. Wide granite steps led to the imposing front door of number 80 Vincent Square, HQ of the Royal Horticultural Society. A pleasant porter at the desk asked us what our business was. I told him:

'I want to put a garden in next year's Chelsea Flower Show.'

Without blinking, he sent us up the grand staircase, one floor, two floors, three floors and finally the shows department.

'Can I help you, sir?'

'Yes, I'd like to build a garden at next year's Chelsea Flower Show?'

He spluttered. 'Sorry? You can't just walk in off the street and ask to put a garden in the Chelsea Flower Show, it doesn't happen that way.'

I reddened. The two lads fidgeted behind me.

'What do you do?' I asked.

'You address a typed letter to Ms Mavis Sweetingham, outlining your previous awards at RHS shows, and including examples of your work and what your intentions would be if producing a garden at our foremost event.'

We slunk out of the building, away into the afternoon sunshine. I felt stupid. What had I been thinking? Why didn't I just listen to everybody? Get a job, work for the parks department, design pretty gardens for pretty ladies. Why did I have to be different? This didn't last long, though. I asked Vincent to find a typist. I pointed at a café, that's where I'd be. Eamonn and I sat with mugs of tea and scribbled a letter:

'10th March 1994

Dear Ms Sweetingham,

I'd like to submit a design for next year's Chelsea Flower Show. I am a garden designer based in Dublin. I have won gold medals at shows there. I have worked for both private and commercial companies. Our next client lives in Beirut and wants us top create a rooftop garden on her penthouse. I'd love to do something modern at Chelsea. This is my address. Thank you very much.'

Fanciful though it was, it contained a grain of truth, fully embellished by me.

Vincent arrived breathless. He had a found a woman who was prepared to type a letter at short notice. We jumped in a cab and headed to Elizabeth Street. Vincent pressed the buzzer at the address he had been given.

'Come up, second floor,' a voice said. The three of us bundled up. She took my notepad. 'I can't read this,' she growled. 'Who wrote it?

'I did.'

I read my letter to the RHS aloud. She started to smile, charged a couple of quid for a beautifully typed page, and sent us on our way. Back to Vincent Square. It was closed for the evening. I slid the envelope under the door.

A few days later we were back in Dublin, digging, teaching, living. The road to Chelsea now looked bleak. It was a nice summer. My sights were no doubt set once again on the following spring festival at the Royal Dublin Society. Till then I'd get by, and then some more fun.

A month went by, then two. I called at my parent's house. There was an envelope, addressed to me but without a stamp. Inside was an application form from the Royal Horticultural Society, inviting me to submit plans to their selection committee for the following May's Chelsea Flower Show. I was ecstatic. I was being invited to submit a design for a garden at the world-famous flower show. Surely this would be my redemption.

What should I do? What would I do? Questions flooded my brain. First things first. I'd never been to the show. Someone sent away for a video. I sat in front of the screen and memorized each second as the camera panned across garden after garden. My mind kept going back to what that lady had said as she passed my last show garden: 'That's almost Chelsea standard.' If she thought it was, well, there must be hope. I had two months to get my ideas together. There was a date after which my plans and filled-out forms would be put before their first committee.

Was I going to shock the world with a contemporary garden? What did I mean by contemporary anyway? I thought long and hard. From the video, Chelsea was full of pastiche. Let's give them what they'd expect.

I picked a Yeats poem, 'The Stolen Child', and took a phrase from it: 'Come away, O human child!/To the waters and the wild'. 'The waters and the wild' – that conjured up an image for me. I had an idea for creating a garden with a backdrop of a crumbling stone tower house, a still pool of water with bog iris and rushes to the front and low stone walls: a rustic rural scene. I borrowed a car and drove around the country – over to Galway, through Clare, down to Limerick, and on to Dingle at the very southern tip of the country. Along the way I took photographs of water, ponds, hedgerows, and stone walling. I looked for crumbling towers and found a few. And I sketched.

Back in Dublin, I sat down in front of a blank piece of paper and slowly planned my vision. I had a strong idea of what this garden should be. I could picture it in my mind, and with pen and pencil I transferred that image to the page. I filled in the form, wrote about the inspiration behind the scene, made a list of species I planned to use, estimated a budget of £60,000, and fabricated a potential sponsor and contractor. It looked OK on paper. I sent it off in the post, recorded delivery.

Weeks passed, then a month. A letter from the Royal Horticultural Society arrived at Mum and Dads.

'Dear Mr Gavin, It is with regret we have to inform you ...' I didn't need to read further. Signed, Mavis Sweetingham.

I walked out of the house, down the driveway, dreams dashed, feeling stupid, again and again. I was an idiot; it was never going to happen. Why didn't I just get on with things?

THE ANGRY YOUNG MAN OF GARDENING

Time slipped away. We were heading towards another autumn and I fell back into bad ways. The courses were going well, that was something. We'd had to leave our first premises, but had moved into new ones, an auctioneers' in a Georgian building just off Merrion Square. A few nights a week myself and Vincent would cycle in and, when the office workers had left, transform the bidding room into a classroom. Vincent would do the teas and coffees and I'd talk about gardens. Afterwards we'd go for a couple of pints and talk about life passing by.

And I was resigning myself to a life of dreaming and digging. I'd go out into people's gardens early in the morning and work at a steady rate through the day into the evening. I was popular with clients; it was obvious I liked to work. And I would debate with myself, voices in my head. Why did I want to be different? Why did I want to make gardens that were different? What was it that bugged me so much about beautiful herbaceous borders, broad limestone terraces, stately urns, cherubs, archways, and rockeries?

I'd go to a few garden meetings, designers gathering together debating their issues of the day. I'd go to bookshops and devour the writings of the American landscape architect Thomas Church, who designed gardens in the 1940s and 50s, and John Brookes, who espoused the whole notion of the garden as a room outside. In college it had been revolutionary for me to see different materials being used, dramatic euphorbias rising from plains of honey-coloured gravel, low dishes of water set under trees to make mirrored focal points, arbours and barbecues. All mild stuff, but dramatic for me.

Helen Dillon was writing articles in the newspapers at the time. She was an incredible plantswoman, and the articles contained a fiery spirit and sense of humour. As for Gertrude Jekyll before her, plants were her palette. She used colour beautifully. Her husband

Val was in charge of keeping the rectangular lawn snooker-table perfect. I appreciated the craft and recognized the genius. Why did I want to be different? What was it about outdoor spaces that I wanted to change?

I'd dig away listening to talk radio. I could get Radio 4 on long wave. There was a show called *The Afternoon Shift*. They had a gardener on called Paul Cooper. He visited the presenter's house, took a look at her narrow London town garden and made it over in contemporary and magical style. She had been sent away for a few days and when she returned she squealed with delight. He revealed the new garden in the evening. Projectors shot images of rural French scenes out onto the walls, stone terracing was swapped for bouncy rubber matting, and a vertical bed had been built, allowing visitors to climb up a tall wall at secret rendezvous points for illicit get-togethers. But the twist was that it was courtesy of the BBC sound effects department: it didn't exist, but Paul Cooper had painted these images in the listeners' minds. I wrote away for a recording. In my evening classes I would switch off the lights and play the tape and listen for the gasps of reaction.

The following day I would go to another garden and dig another herbaceous border. I'd debate in my mind, and in time I came to a conclusion. The traditionalists weren't wrong. They enjoyed their pretty borders and their beds of hybrid teas and floribundas, their rockeries, and their rectangular reflecting pools. What was wrong with that? But I wasn't wrong to dream of something different. It wasn't wrong to seek something new, it wasn't wrong to take other inspiration. It was a funny debate raging in my head.

Mum and Dad's answer phone was bleeping. There was a message from Mavis Sweetingham. Would I ring her urgently?

Would this be the moment when things would change? It was late September. The call to London was a blur, but went somewhere along the lines that spaces for the following year's Chelsea had been allocated a long time ago. They had always liked the design

I had sent in, there hadn't been room for it, but now someone had dropped out. With little notice, would I consider building my garden? I was light-headed. Yes, yes. Could I come over to see her? Yes. Did I realize that it would be extra difficult for me given the time limitations? I would have agreed to anything. My design had (maybe by default) been accepted by the Chelsea Flower Show.

Next year the world famous flower show would feature an Irish garden, designed and built by me. I was ecstatic. I cycled away, my bicycle powered by rocket fuel. Things were about to change. There were loads of forms to be filled, committees to please, and most importantly funds to be raised. Technicalities, I thought.

I planned a strategy and started talking to people. I had a matter of months to prepare. I examined the plans that I had submitted – an Irish garden in the middle of London, based on a romantic, sorrowful Yeats poem – that phrase again: 'Come away, O human child!/To the waters and the wild'. So what did I need? Stone, and lots of it, to build a crumbling tower. The waters – what did that require? A pond of some sort? The scene would be rustic and very green, a wild green picture encapsulating images of travels around the country, a lazy scene, unkempt and very romantic.

A week later I was back in London, at 80 Vincent Square, this time with an appointment. I felt important but somehow out of place. At an off-licence around the corner from the Georgian square I bought a bottle of Baileys, and with this as a gift I presented myself in front of Ms Sweetingham. She smiled at that, but most of the meeting was matter-of-factish. Did I realize what I was getting into? Did I know that everybody else had such a head start? Was I sure I would be able to pull a design out of my mind, and less than eight months later be ready to present it to thousands of people who would travel from all round the world? My mind raced silently, of course of course of course. I left the wood-panelled office with a skip in my step. It was for real. It would be happening.

A business consulting client offered to raise the funds for me, in return for 10% of any sponsorship funds he raised. I commissioned drawings of the garden from an illustrator. A brochure developed. I talked and talked to anybody who'd listen. I rang radio stations and newspapers. No one cared. The furniture retailer Habitat was due to open in Dublin. I wrote to them. I needed sponsorship in the region of £60,000 to step into Chelsea. It was an enormous sum. Nobody was interested.

Time passed. Nothing was happening. Nothing. People who'd offered to help raise funds fell away. I took to bed for two whole days. What was going on? It was fear. The stark realization that nothing was happening. I'd talked so much about the possibility of creating this wonderful idealized landscape, and here I was in a familiar retreat.

I felt my withdrawal, my hibernation would shake those around me into action, would make them realize the importance of the quest in hand, and would make them do the work for me. It wasn't long before I received a brutal kick up the bum and strong advice to get on with it.

I had a sense that it might not happen, there would be no garden. I'd be left at the starting block, no further forward, but no further back.

I decided I wouldn't let it happen so easily. Blind faith is a dangerous thing. It's a recurring theme in my life, being carried away by the excitement of possibilities, the 'what if' situations, the imagining of scenarios. I'm not much good at the detail. I can be good at exciting and enthusing support in others, but it often ends up with a flagrant disregard for facts and situations laid out in front of me. These situations have tempered with age, but the possibilities for new and ambitious scenarios still tempt me.

KERRY RETREAT

Fate intervened. I had a friend in Dublin, Noelle Campbell-Sharpe. She was an entrepreneur with many magazines to her name. A larger-than-life figure who drove a vintage Rolls Royce through the city and whose hobby was satisfying a craving for anything to do with Napoleon. At one of the furthest extremes of Ireland, Ballinskelligs in County Kerry, on the south-west coast, she had built a house. Designed by Alfred, an architect friend of mine, it was a fun, elongated thatched cottage with a secret medieval hall and her own barn. Perched on the side of a windswept mountain, it had a panoramic view over a majestic scene – the expanse of the Atlantic Ocean with the Skelligs, wild rocky islands inhabited a thousand years ago by monks who eked out a spartan existence in beehive stone huts, dedicating their lives to prayer and God. This is a magical place but a ravaged one. Its haunting beauty hides hundreds of years of tragedy, poverty and emigration. The land, though beautiful, is tough. Some sheep and goats survive on its craggy hills. The fishing industry is but a distant memory.

As her contribution to the local community, Noelle created a remarkable arts centre, and she purchased a series of abandoned stone rooms, a row of cottages, and converted them magically into artists' studios. They are perched on the last road in Ireland. It's a difficult place to get to, and the weather can be savage, or it may be still, calm and beautiful. Artists apply from all around the world to visit for a week or a month, tempted by the wild, seduced by the light. They live in the cottages and paint their imagination.

Kerry is rich in culture and folklore, and has a temperate climate. It may be wild and wet, but it never gets too cold. In summer, for thousands of miles along each of its peninsulas, hedgerows of fuchsia flourish. And below them another introduced species, crocosmia, sends up lime green stems with drooping bright orange bells at their tips. Matched with the red and pink of the fuchsia, it can make the countryside look as if it's on fire.

Nearby are landmarks such as the Killarney National Park and the wonderful maritime town of Dingle on the Dingle peninsula, famed for its scenic beauty as well as its Hollywood heritage. *Ryan's Daughter* was filmed here and it became a safe haven for Julia Roberts when she fled a Californian marriage. The long beaches are glorious and, like many parts of Ireland, empty. Summer or winter, they are exhilarating places to immerse yourself in the wild sea. This has always been my place for retreat, for holidays, for a swim, for a bowl of soup with some warm fresh brown bread, butter melting, followed by a pint of Guinness. Noelle invited me down for a weekend in February, three months before Chelsea.

A month later I was still there. Ballinskelligs in Kerry had become my temporary home. For the first few days I had the house to myself, but I was soon joined by Vincent. We had a little battered van, again lent by a friend. And nothing else. My proposal for the Chelsea Flower Show revolved around wild Irish planting. Most designers pick out their plants from foreign nurseries years in advance. Specimen trees costing £20,000 or more are shipped in from abroad. And even the daintiest of flowers are selected with incredible care. Everything that flowers and is to be shown in a garden is expected to perform and be in prime condition during show week. Plants are held back or forced by means of trickery and vast refrigerators to satisfy the voracious appetite of the show visitor. Perfection, whatever that means, is key.

In County Kerry, perfection was all around me. Nature in all its forms. The landscape and everything we regard as natural changes all the time. That may be from day to day or seasonally. But it's also by the century. The landmass of Ireland would not so long ago have been full of deciduous forest, little of which now remains. The demands of agriculture, tribalism and politics saw to that. The introduction of alien plant species, plants from around the globe, has contributed greatly to our perception of both what is beautiful and what is natural.

So in March, armed with spades, shovels and forks from Noelle's shed, plastic gardening crates and fertilizer bags, we drove around. Day after day, up hills and down boreens, digging up nature itself. We dug flag iris and rushes from dark bog pools, gathered moss in glens from beneath dripping oaks, stripping it away like orange peel. Wonderful *Euphorbia hibernica* was dug by fork to produce luscious sulphur-coloured clumps and laid gently in the black latticework plastic trays.

CHELSEA NO. 1, 1995:
TO THE WATERS AND THE WILD GARDEN

I couldn't buy plants – I had no money. With two months to D-Day, I was driving a borrowed, battered old Peugeot through the green lanes of rural Ireland looking for plants to dig up and bring to central London.

Dublin flower shows had been very easy. I'd submit a design, pay a £100 deposit for my space, arrive and create a garden. I'd cobble together a motley crew of friends and classmates, and work from early morning to late evening for a week to create a small garden. Every experience was different. Sometimes I'd have a car or a van. More than once I arrived to direct operations by bicycle. It was my annual moment of pride through the years. In fact I probably I lived for it.

With two months to go before Chelsea, if I wasn't digging I was driving up to Dublin and sitting outside offices, begging for more support. I'm not a forward planner. A deadline that is a month away can seem very distant to me. I have a great belief in things just happening, coming together. The day came when Vincent and I had to fly off to London, into the unknown. Two people were never going to build a main show garden. Flying away meant leaving everything behind – equipment, plants and materials. We didn't have a network of friends or helpers in London, and we certainly didn't have a team of contractors. Was it irresponsible, or just blind faith in our own and each other's abilities? To find ourselves a week later still shovelling soil from one part of our plot to another was dispiriting.

After a few days, our money had dwindled. Soon we had no place to stay. There was an Irish club near by, in Eaton Square. I went round there and asked if they could take us in. I'd have to ring someone on some committee. I could never get hold of them.

Back and forward to the garden – more digging. Next door a Japanese garden was being constructed. A massive hydraulic crane was lowering weighty stones into position under the watchful eye of Koji the designer, who'd flown in from the orient. Their plants had arrived. An eye-watering collection. The crew building the garden were a friendly bunch. Someone from another garden came over to us, asking if everything was OK. 'Ask her for help,' I was told, 'her' being Mavis at the RHS. 'If you let them know you're in difficulty they will help out, but you have to ask, they're not allowed to offer.' I pondered this. Yes, we were in trouble, but were we not over here (as I thought) representing Ireland? And even if very few back home showed any interest, I didn't want to let ourselves or the country down.

Around the corner there was a large barracks which housed the Irish Guards. Maybe I'd go and talk to them, maybe they'd help. But what would they do? Even we were running out of things to do. Someone at home had set up a meeting with the Irish Tourist Board, Bord Fáilte. They would help us to the tune of £6000. I went immediately to Dublin. My base was Justine's mum's house. The moment I arrived in the door the phone rang: it was Vincent calling from the showground. There was a problem. As it was Friday and the start of a long weekend, most of the other contributors had left site. To hurry things along and to get a day free at the weekend himself, Vincent had 'borrowed' a mini-digger from the next-door garden. Moving soil to the highest point on our plot, he'd smashed through a water pipe, and now the Irish and Japanese plots were flooded. There was no water anywhere else in the grounds. I laughed, glad to be hundreds of miles away.

That afternoon, off I tripped to my meeting, a very happy man: happy to be back in Dublin on a lovely spring day and to be about to get £6000 for our London dream. Nowhere near what we needed, but since we had nothing it was a fortune. We sat in our benefactor's wonderful corner office with views over a bustling

Baggot Street and the canal. I told him of our endeavours. They like to encourage gardening, it's one of the main reasons why people visit Ireland. So we talked and he confirmed the grant. I said thank you, that's great, we talked some more. I've never been very good about money. But here was a man promising real cash, saying goodbye to me. So I asked, where was it? He looked startled! 'Oh, you don't get it now. Send in the paperwork when the show is over.' I left, devastated. All that money, so near yet so far. What to do?

Back at the house, we sat round a bottle of red wine. Friends were called, a plan hatched. I was due the money if the garden was completed. I was committing myself to completing, so let's try and borrow it. A friend of a friend volunteered. I'd have a cheque first thing Monday morning. I could cash it straight away and make the half past noon flight back to London.

Monday morning, twenty past nine: an envelope plopped through the door. No note in it, just a lovely rectangular piece of paper with £6000 spelt out. I saw it was an Allied Irish Bank cheque. I used to do business with them at their branch in St Mary's Road. I'd had a credit card with them a few years back. I still owed loads of money on it and I'd ignored letter after letter. They were stuffed in a drawer unopened. The cheque had been issued at the St Mary's Road branch.

By quarter to ten I was in the queue. It moved slowly. A neat row of tellers worked behind a glass curtain. My turn. I approached the girl and slipped the cheque under the slender opening. My passport for identification followed. 'Cash please,' I said. She tapped the keys on her computer. After a moment she looked up at me and said, 'Could you hold on for a minute,' and disappeared. Then, 'Mr Gavin, the manager would like a word.'

'We've tried to contact you so many times, Mr Gavin.' My head was blank. Her voice wafted through a void. I heard myself talking, telling her about shifting soil over in London, about plants packed in fertilizer bags in Kerry, about piles of old cut limestone sitting off the Dublin ring road. I was a thirty-year-old schoolboy in the head's office, being berated. Tears rolled down my face. Embarrassing for everyone. She took the £1400 I owed on the cards but let me off the interest. And I caught my Gatwick flight.

In London we were now ten days behind every other exhibit, but at last I was able to make things move with some funds in hand. Most of what I needed to complete the garden was back home, plants in County Kerry and stone in Dublin. I hired a truck to collect the plants, as well as what we'd manage to scavenge. I'd been to a local nursery that grew the most fantastic *Dicksonia antarctica*, the hardy Tasmanian tree fern. This place was located in the most picturesque of places, a secluded cove reached by a steep road from the coast route. The nursery also had a wonderful selection of ferns and a euphorbia that I absolutely loved, *E. hibernica*. I figured I'd done a deal with the owner to pay sometime in the future, so the transport was despatched to load up. What followed, though, was a six-hour ordeal. A stand-off.

Mr Vogel, a German, wouldn't let go of his plants until he'd had a ream of faxes from me and everyone I knew to guarantee money on my return. The truck got stuck going back up the hill, and arrived at Noelle's to collect our main plants at midnight.

I could only imagine the scene, with plastic fertilizer bags filled with mosses and flag iris being lifted in the early hours of the morning on to a flatbed truck. At Chelsea itself, I was meeting plant suppliers and people dealing in pond equipment.

I met a great lady who specialized in wild flowers, and with renewed belief that things were on the up and that our planting was in transit, I ordered a host of goodies: *Viola tricolor*, red campion, purple aquilegia and foxgloves in flower. I started hunting down some trees. A friend had told me of a nursery in Ely, Cambridgeshire, which had wonderful field-grown multi-stemmed birches and gorgeous willows. So off I went to spend more money

I arrived back to an amazing sight. Our stone had just been

delivered from Dublin, and hot on its heels was our Kerry plunder. And there was help. A few friends had arrived: Phillip and Eddie, pals from college in Dublin, and Ger had travelled with the plants from Kerry. They arrived with the story of a cow invading the enclosure where our stash of wild plants had been stored and treated herself to a floral breakfast. And sure enough, there was evidence of a strong pruning. To much hilarity, a frog hopped out from one of the sacks and away up the embankment. From the wilds of Kerry to the mania of SW1 by way of the night ferry from Cork: that must have been one confused amphibian. But our problems were not over.

We were pretty much out of money again, and though we had much of what we needed to make the garden, now we had nowhere to stay. I walked around to the Irish Club. OK – at this stage they'd do a deal, and I was put on the phone to a member of the committee. We could have beds in the attic, no food though, if we promised to fill the window boxes and hanging baskets. Done! A very grand new home.

Back on site, another problem. Vincent had been overheard by our wildflower supplier talking about our predicament. He'd made a joke to someone about doing a runner from our lodgings. She came to our site and told me she couldn't supply plants as there were rumours circulating about our credit worthiness. It felt like a punch in the stomach. I was gutted. I'd almost gathered together the ingredients for a garden, we were within five days of completion, and my credibility was being called into question. However shambolic things appeared, I was an honest individual. She relented.

Our heap of stone needed building into a tower. Vincent had been back to Travis Perkins and had pulled a cement mixer behind him along the Pimlico Road, Chelsea Bridge Road and finally down the Embankment to the Bull Ring entrance. The foundation was poured, but who would build the stone walls? We were all good for manual labour, even rough block work, but I wanted this tower to look authentic. Kilburn in north London was the area where Irish people had gathered over the decades as they crossed the sea seeking work. On Wednesday evening a couple of the lads went up and started asking around for stonemasons. A woman behind the bar in the Crown Pub in Cricklewood told them of two brothers from County Mayo. If they went across the road, down a lane and knocked on the kitchen window of number 6 they should have some luck. Within twenty-four hours these boys were on site and we formed a chain gang, passing stones and mixing mortar. One more problem – we'd no pond liner.

The garden was based on the phrase 'To the waters and the wild', which called for a pond in the foreground of our scene. So I needed something to retain the water. I ogled beautiful rubber liners as they'd been installed in other plots, and we tried to blag one. No luck. We improvised by using plumbers' tape to stick two pieces of heavy-duty polythene together, placed this large sheet over a bed of sand, and filled it up. I waded in and carefully created a couple of tiny islands, planted with birch and yellow iris. We were tired and filthy, but smiling. Three days to go. By the Friday evening we were broke: not a penny. So we didn't eat.

I loved what was happening. I even loved the garden. It was scrappy around the edges but it had passion. RTE had a crew turning up on Monday to follow our story. The production assistant, Carmel, took me to another part of the site for a coffee. My stomach rumbled, which gave her a clue to our situation. Quietly she told me that there would be an appearance fee, it wouldn't be much, £60 or £70, but I could have the cash now. I watched as her hands opened her purse. The three of us, me, Vincent and Ger, were famished – that money would mean food. In a few days the show would be full of our family and friends, breakfast and dinners in restaurants, but this felt wrong. We would survive. I told her we were grand and I'd been exaggerating, and quietly walked back to the waters and the wild.

On Sunday evening we worked late. Most gardens had finished; we were nearly there. I knew we'd make it. We fitted in. We'd come from Ireland and built a garden at the Chelsea Flower Show, and at half past ten we left the site. At eight o'clock the following morning the show grounds would open to press and previews.

We walked down the streets, tired, and arrived at the Irish club at quarter to eleven. The doors were locked and the building looked big and dark and empty. We rang bells and threw stones. No one answered. We laughed to ourselves – this was ridiculous. We had three hours' work left to do and we'd planned to go into Chelsea at five o'clock the following morning to do it, yet here we were, tired, filthy and locked out. I suggested going to the local police station and asking for a cell for the night. Anything would have been better than being stuck out in the open. We settled on knocking on the door of a pub. Vincent and I had previously enjoyed a pint there, and the landlord was Irish. He opened the door in his dressing gown, and let us use the spare room. There were a couple of mattresses and we took down the curtains to use as sheets.

The automatic irrigation system for the pub's hanging baskets had turned on, and dripped on us as we crept through the doorway. But there was another problem.. The royal family were due to make their official visit to Chelsea that day, so security passes were needed to get into the show grounds. The police would be patrolling with sniffer Alsatians, and all our passes were locked in the Irish Club. We each kept watch as the others scrambled over the cast-iron spiked fences onto our plot, and dug and planted. By eight o'clock the adventure was over.

In turns we wandered back to our lodgings, showered, changed and presented ourselves for duty to explain this garden that we'd created. A friend, Mary Skelly, got a message to me. She had a garden centre in Tipperary, I'd worked with her in a garden shop in Dublin, and she was over to see what we'd created.

'I'll see you tomorrow,' she said.

'No you won't, I replied, 'We've not eaten in three days.' She crossed the city to buy us fish and chips, the best meal I've ever had.

And then Justine and her mum arrived from Dublin. All three of us had been through hell on this adventure, but now the garden was built. We stood there gazing. A man approached. He was the husband of the wild flower woman, and he told me he wanted payment. If I didn't pay him immediately he'd take the plants back – in front of the gathering throng. I excused myself for a moment, and ran away. Justine and Terry looked at each other and followed. I was hiding behind a tree. I'd given up, that was the final straw. Someone was going to start demolishing our exhibit unless I could produce £800. Justine's mum wrote a cheque.

By two o'clock everybody had to clear out. Only one ticket was allocated per garden for the royal visit. I was at the end of a row right beside the press tent. The royals came down, and just before they got to me were led away around the corner. The Queen and the Duke of Edinburgh disappeared and I felt like I'd been kicked. I don't know why, but the moment had really been built up. Then Princess Anne, who was also being led around the corner, turned and came over to have a look, and we had a chat. The security girl, Audrey, who we'd made friends with in the past week, stood by and took photographs. Once the royals had left, the gala evening was on, and glasses of champagne and trays of finger food were being passed around. I stood in front of the garden and explained our little piece of Ireland to the black-tie-and-evening-dress throng. I hated it. People were there to be seen and enjoy the exclusive access, but often didn't care and were getting slightly tipsy on bubbles – this wasn't what we'd worked for.

The rest of the week was enjoyable. We had food and lodging, and those who travelled over were amazed at what we had managed to achieve. My brother Declan arrived to surprise me. He has no interest in gardens, and we are very different people. During the build I poured out my angst and frustration in reverse-charge calls to his office from public phones in Victoria Station. I caught sight of him in the distance, part of a river of hundreds of people walking towards me. I stood still as bodies washed by, astonished that he would leave his job and come over to see what we had done. Within seconds he was upon me, disappointed he had been spotted. He had wanted to surprise me at the garden. That single moment was my Chelsea highlight.

There was a warmth and generosity in the air for the rest of the week. Our garden was the only one sold that year. A second-generation Irish family wanted to install it in St Albans. When the bell went on the Friday evening we relaxed and partied. We scaled the tower, put seats in the pool and drank beer. We camped under tarpaulins in the show ground that night. Then on the Saturday we went to see the garden's proposed new home and got a cheque for a few thousand pounds. The buyer sent trucks to collect the garden. We were late leaving Chelsea, but we went home with some money in our pockets. And I took time to consider our exploits.

I'm not sure how much Chelsea had impressed me. I'd been looking for answers, answers to the direction of my own life, but also ones about gardens. For that week, Chelsea was certainly the world centre of horticulture. But for all the possibilities as it opened, for all the adventures as it spawned, there was part of it I found uncomfortable. I had managed the system and looked to my inner resources and friendships to pull through. But in terms of the show itself and some of the people involved I felt some disappointment.

The only certainty was that I wanted to create gardens that were different, gardens that took on contemporary influences, gardens that meant something to me.

There was a slow realization that to do anything new, especially on the suburban canvas, would be going against the *status quo*. People were becoming interested in design, in the context of clothes, cars and even buildings. But this new awareness and education was still slumbering in garden circles. My desires in this area were reactive. I didn't know what new meant. I could devour the books of John Brookes and Sylvia Crowe, and yet they were written in a different language. Maybe it's that there wasn't a lot of fun there. Design was pious, self-regarding and occasionally too intellectual. But between the twee, the pompous, and the classic styles that were being continually reinterpreted, there seemed little that was new.

Things were changing elsewhere. I'd asked Justine to marry me. And she'd said yes. Justine and I had been going out for some time, and I'd tested the water with her about a month before a celebration of the publication of Terry's book, *Consuming Passions*, at a restaurant in Dublin. As the evening wore on, spirits got higher and higher and I whispered to one of Justine's sisters, Madeleine, could I borrow her ring? She agreed, and I got down on bended knee in front of the other guests and asked her to marry me. Luckily Justine said yes, and we were engaged – albeit using her sister's ring. Her other sister, Jane, spent the evening constructing a ring for Justine from the wire champagne cork cages

I was excited and astounded. Somebody who believed in me so much would now share my life. I had little to offer, but she gave me renewed motivation to sort out my act. There were going to be two of us continuing the journey. We set a wedding date for mid-summer. A new mood of optimism blew through my life. I did a few interviews with newspapers and wrote a new garden design course. It was successful: lots of people wanted to know how to take control of their plots and turn them into urban Edens. Two women in their twenties arrived together every week – Anita Notaro and Ursula Courtney. Anita was a producer for RTE, Ireland's national broadcaster. She had read something about me, loved gardens and felt she might be able to develop an idea for a television series. After class, Vincent and I would have a pint with them. One evening I told them the story of the previous May, of our adventures at Chelsea. The following day Ursula rang. She revealed that she was a researcher on *The Late Late Show*, the world's longest running chat show. Would I come on and tell Gay Byrne, the host, about our adventures in London?

Ursula did have one caveat. On the night she had in mind, they had another guest booked, the Prime Minister of Newfoundland. She'd have to convince the host that he had no story to tell, that he was a bit boring. I was extremely nervous. The interview got the green light. Ursula took me to lunch to conduct a research interview. We talked about Chelsea, family and life. A crew was sent to film a roof garden I was building on top of a video shop,

Driving around Dublin nervously on the day of the programme, I listened to the premier of Newfoundland being interviewed. He was fascinating, funny, and full of brilliant anecdotes. That evening I sat in the hot chair, with family and friends in the audience, and told the stories of our adventures in London. It was the highlight of a sputtering career. In Chelsea they had given away four or five bronze medals, of which we had got one. Then there were shoals of silvers, silver gilts and golds. And there had been a best in show. I talked about getting a bronze medal. People assumed it meant we had come third! After *The Late Late Show* I become a name in Ireland.

Not everyone was overjoyed. There were some classmates who I didn't hear from for quite a while. Eventually a close friend told me there was a feeling about that by appearing on the show Gavin had got above his station. It was disappointing, but it was not to be the last time I would get such a reaction.

All sorts of interest followed. A multi-millionaire rang me and asked me to design a park for the impending new millennium. After months of working on it, he got bored with the idea. I was approached by a holiday park, Butlins Mosney, who had some sponsorship to offer for a second garden at Chelsea. More importantly, wedding plans preoccupied us.

113

We had a big engagement party in Justine's mum's house. Our parents met and our friends mixed. It was too big, though, and made us opt for a very small wedding. I'd come to know County Kerry through the Keane family. We were fond of a hotel, the Parknasilla, outside of Kenmare. Justine's mum would take a house for the summer nearby, so we went searching for a little country church. We found it in a place called Tahilla. It was simple, not overly ornate, perfect for us. Justine's granny Yayee was overjoyed. Her dreams had come true. We walked down the aisle surrounded by our immediate family and a few close friends. Justine was dressed beautifully in pink, and outside the church a white Rolls Royce appeared from nowhere. The driver took a wrong turn down the country lanes. We wanted to disappear, just the two of us, but eventually had to tell him he was going the wrong way. We had a lovely day and took a short honeymoon touring the country. There had been one condition that Justine had set to the marriage – that I would never do a garden at Chelsea again. She had seen the stress at first hand, and didn't want that to be part of her life.

CHELSEA NO. 2, 1996:
A VIBRANT CITY GARDEN

But it was too late. I was already a Chelsea addict, and was determined to show what I could produce if I was allowed exhibit a second time. My primary aim was to create a contemporary garden, a garden influenced by what was happening in art, architecture and music at the time. I had given the Royal Horticultural Society what they might expect from somebody coming from Ireland the first year, but now it was my turn.

The breakthrough in 1995 had been the big stepping stone. Returning to Chelsea seemed easier. We knew the lie of the land. But this time I wanted to create something that I really believed in.

Home was a rented ground floor flat in a small Georgian house, one bedroom, bare wooden floors, £25 a week and a bargain even then. We loved it. I'd had a lot of the structure for our next London adventure made in Dublin, and we packed the van with it, and with our tools and equipment, and set off on the long drive.

This was to be my first outing as a contemporary garden designer. So what did I regard as contemporary? What was I going to unleash upon the gardening public? How did my dreams and ideas manifest themselves in my new scheme?

Here goes. A curved glass-brick wall with water rippling down its concave shape. In front of it, a stainless-steel etched border with zantedeschias in flower, a small *Dicksonia antarctica*, myriads of grasses, hostas and a small *Trachycarpus fortunei*. There was a lawn, and a glass patio illuminated from underneath by a series of spotlights. I had seen a Michael Jackson video for 'Billie Jean'. As he danced on the sidewalk the paving stones lit up. On each boundary I cut up lengths of wood, painted them blue and knocked them together to create an abstract fence. This was my revolution.

The build was tough, with loads of mud because of constant rain. I was pleased with the curved glass-brick wall.

As usual, there were television cameras and press everywhere. Word was sent to me from BBC *Gardeners' World* that they were doing a feature on young (relatively) designers at Chelsea that year. Would I be available to film something?

Family and friends were again over from Dublin. There were lots of distractions. We hung around the garden and just enjoyed the circus.

Our garden wasn't great. I had tried my hardest. I remember the excitement of using different materials, potting up a kumquat in a metal bucket, and using galvanized dustbins as planters. Maybe with better training, more experience or a better eye it could have been wonderful. Maybe with a client base back in Dublin who were interested in things that were different, I could have launched myself into the heady world of the gardening elite with a revolutionary style that would have caused jaws to drop and people to mutter reverentially. Lots of maybes.

Our achievement was being there. It was a step towards what I wanted to do. After years trapped in a gardening wilderness, I had understood that it was important for me to move forward. I was reacting against tradition while trying to understand the new, but I was badly educated in both genres. And I had created a garden that posed more questions that it answered – but at least it had been built.

I watched famous faces go by, and from a distance spied Monty Don. He was a gardening correspondent for Richard and Judy's *This Morning* programme. In the run up to that year's event I'd written a page for an Irish newspaper on my feelings about returning to the show. I talked about what I felt the realities of doing at garden at Chelsea were: a lot of the joys and some of the falseness. The *Independent* had seen the article and asked if they could reprint it. I hadn't been entirely complimentary. Monty came over to me. 'I really liked your article,' he said, 'but you'll pay for it.'

A producer from BBC Birmingham came to see me. Her name was Annette Martin and she told me what she wanted to film. Alan Titchmarsh, would come to the garden and would seem a little bit bewildered by it. He'd ask me questions about my inspiration, and would talk to me about the garden having another life, after dark. Echoes of a nightclub: strangely, the glass wall had been inspired by a feature in the men's toilet of a Dublin nightclub!

That evening was gala night. Justine, her mum and some friends were with me, and we all just wanted to go out and leave the grounds behind and have dinner, but I had to wait.

Annette and her cameras came back and we waited for the light to fade. They had brought a jib arm – a camera crane that flies way up into the air, and can get the whole garden in one single frame.

'Where's Alan?' I said.

Annette said, 'No, he won't be coming back; he's gone off somewhere to dream about Chelsea.' I said my words and the camera flew up into the air. I was free to go. I hadn't enjoyed my moment of television. I left the grounds and went to party in a bar on the King's Road.

The following morning, Vincent went to the show early. I rang him. How had we done? I asked.

'What do you mean?' he said.

'What award did we get?'

'We didn't get any.'

I was stunned. There was a letter from the judging committee pretty much saying they hadn't a clue what this garden was all about. An hour later I slunk in the main gates. Embarrassed about what was to come. Chelsea is like an exam. If you put a mark on your paper, you get a point for turning up. At my second attempt, rejection and humiliation. Where to from here?

On Wednesday evening, a group of us got together in a friend's hotel room in Kensington. Chelsea didn't receive the wall-to-wall coverage it gets now. And this hour-long special of *Gardeners' World* was to be the BBC's highlight. As we watched, we saw a non-committal Alan in my garden, asking me about it and then disappearing. The programme ended with Alan wandering into another garden, a traditional one, finding a bed of camomile. He lies down on it, falls asleep and begins to dream of everything he's seen that year, all the delights that have been paraded in front of him. And then there am I lonely in my little plot, all lit up with no place to go. I'm waiting for Alan but he's elsewhere, asleep. 'Where's Alan?' my voice said, 'He'll never know what he missed.' We went for a few pints. It had been funny seeing the garden lit up and on the BBC. No amount of Chelsea judges could take that away.

On Thursday morning I walked back in the gates. A security guard stopped me. 'Hey, you're that bloke from the television last night.' I was taken aback. I walked to our plot. There was a crowd gathering there, a photographer and another camera crew. I was confused. My life was about to change forever, all through the power of television.

TV STAR

There was something in the air. Following my second Chelsea, particularly the TV skit with Alan Titchmarsh, the world and his wife seemed to want to contact me. A call came from London. Would I like to be a team leader on a pilot for a show, a comedy gardening quiz, to be filmed very shortly at Kew Gardens in London? I'd be a team captain, the other one would be Alan Titchmarsh. I was shocked, bewildered. What was that all about?

But two weeks later I found myself in the studio – timid, shy and I'm sure wholly unsuited to the task at hand. Sitting on my left was Penelope Keith and on my right the comedian Jeff Green. And there we were, doing battle with Alan. It was a beautiful summer's day, and it disappeared in a haze.

A week later came another call, BBC Birmingham, Pebble Mill, the home of Alan's former chat show – I used watch him every lunchtime. They had a programme that they wanted me to guest on, Stefan Buczacki's *Gardening Britain*. Would I be an expert on a particular Sunday in Suffolk? So within weeks I was off on another trip, this time a huge production, an outside broadcast in a gorgeous part of England. There were big trucks, catering, and cameras everywhere. We were to stay in a hotel and there was a young production team.

Gardening Britain was a televisual version of Radio 4's *Gardeners' Question Time*. The main question I had to deal with was about gunneras. Some lady wanted to grow one in quite a dry place, and it was up to me to put her right, to tell her of its marginal preferences, and to describe how big the plant could grow. The afternoon was spent trying to keep a gunnera leaf from wilting.

Back in Dublin a week later, another call. Could I go to Birmingham and work on programme ideas? And then a production company in Manchester rang. They were called Action Time and dealt in quiz shows. They had a makeover formula programme already in production in the regions: their first one was for Granada. Would I join that team as a garden designer? It was bewildering. In my life nobody had ever asked me to do anything. It was I who did the asking, and yet the phone kept ringing. My earnings in Dublin were probably in the region of £4000 or £5000 a year. Now I had people offering me £300 for a day's work as a garden designer in a different country.

Another call. A production company called Catalyst: would I come over and see them? They were based in London's Shepherd's Bush, and they made *Gardeners' World*. This was an exciting trip. I was unknown and untested. *Gardeners' World* was one of the longest-running series on British television. Broadcast every Friday evening, it taught people their gardening craft. The presenter was the much-loved Geoff Hamilton. I'd never been a wild fan of *Gardeners' World*, but I knew Geoff from a different series he'd done, about making cottage gardens. He was the ultimate in do-it-yourself. He laid the pathways, put up the boundary fences or trellises and planted from cuttings or seeds. He built summer houses, seats, pergolas and retreats.

I travelled over to Shepherd's Bush. The production offices were an incredibly busy hum of activity, with people sitting by banks of telephones and computers, whiteboards on the wall, weeks of the year mapped out. I had a meeting with the programme editor in his office. Geoff was a brilliant man whom everybody loved, he said, but he wouldn't be there forever. His health wasn't fantastic, and they were looking for somebody to ease in gently with an eye to becoming his replacement. I was shocked. I had a life in Ireland, I was married and this was a different country. Everything else had been fine, but now all of a sudden somebody was talking about what amounted to a job – a proper job, maybe even a career. As a gardener in those days it wasn't what you aspired to. There might have been one or two people on the telly, prominent people who might be well known, but no one set out to be on television.

It was an alien medium for me. I was clever enough, I was passionate about my stuff, but I wasn't Mr Everyman. Through years of living a relatively solitary life, I wasn't easy to get on with, and I certainly didn't have the knowledge of Britain that gardeners would require. But I said that I did, and I went back to Dublin a very confused person.

In the meantime, I started working for Action Time, making programmes, doing cheap and cheerful makeovers, travelling around the northern regions of Britain. The show was called *Surprise Gardeners*, the presenter was William van Hage of the renowned Van Hage Garden Centre family of Ware in Hertfordshire. He had done a couple of series. My job was to do design, and to lead the construction throughout the day. The way it worked was this: William went to a garden centre, hopped out from behind the shrubs to ask shoppers about their gardens, and offered to bring his hit squad to their garden for a day for free to transform their outdoor room. It was a magical concept: we'd start by spending a few days doing hits in garden centres, the people would be checked out for suitability, and then we'd be on the road for two if not three days in a row, doing gardens in different towns and villages. We spent the nights in restaurants and pubs, filthy and exhausted. And although very new for me, it wasn't particularly terrifying. All I had to do was design the gardens and talk about what I had done. I didn't understand the camera but I had no fear of it, and on a schedule like that there wasn't time to worry.

Back in Dublin, looking at the news one Sunday evening, I was shocked to learn of Geoff Hamilton's early demise. I'd never met the man, but he was revered. Like Percy Thrower, he'd been a good solid pair of hands, leading the nation assuredly through its favourite pastime. Alan stepped in, almost instantly, to fill those big boots, and did it brilliantly. Soon I was called back to Shepherd's Bush by Catalyst, this time not to talk about *Gardeners' World*. A new project had been commissioned. A brand new channel, Channel

Five, would be taking to the airways a year later, and Catalyst had been asked to make its first gardening programme, a thirteen-part series called *Virgin Gardeners*, in which two gardens would be created in each episode. Already cast was a lovely girl called Bonita Bulaitis, and they wanted to screen test me for the other presenter's role

So back over to London. If it hadn't been for Ryanair's sponsorship of my second Chelsea garden, which included ten return flights to the UK, I would never have been able to pursue these different dreams. This trip was to be particularly eventful. It was the last flight into Stansted that night, and it had been delayed by about an hour. I had very little money, despite working more regularly than ever as programmes can take many months to pay. I caught the last train from the airport to Liverpool Street Station, but all the tubes were closed. I arrived at Shepherd's Bush by cab at two in the morning, tired, cold, hungry and with nowhere to stay. It was too late to knock on doors. Just seven hours later I was to present myself for my first important screen test. I walked up and down the street. There were no signs of life. I considered rolling under a car and staying there for a few hours.

Eventually I saw people arriving back at a Bed and Breakfast. They let me stay in a family room in return for all my funds. It wasn't in a great state that I presented myself to a director and researcher at nine o'clock. I was sent into the back yard and asked to prune a buddleia with a pair of secateurs. I was told to talk about what I was doing and why. It was a disaster. I remember calling home that afternoon, fairly sanguine about the process. I could never be annoyed about not getting chances again, and I could never say I wasn't listened to or that I hadn't had opportunities presented to me. It seemed to settle a lot in my head. I had messed things up, that's why they weren't to be – but that was grand, as the television part of things hadn't been an ambition, and anyway it had felt good to be given a try-out.

Within weeks I was told I had the job! My first proper television series. I was thirty-one and back on a flight to London, this time for a proper role. I was scared of the city and naïve in the extreme. Once again it was into Stansted and into the tube to London, then a taxi driver took me to Acton and a horrible Bed and Breakfast. For a few days every two weeks over the course of a year, this would be my home from home. The director, Gavin, would collect me outside Acton tube station each morning in his vintage sports car, and we would drive to Rickmansworth. This was the location of a brand new suburban estate, where a fireman and his nurse wife wanted a new garden. The process was to be recorded in the old-fashioned BBC way, slightly monotonous and with no flash handheld camera work. Bonita was designing a garden elsewhere. She was allowed to design. They mustn't have trusted me. Someone else did mine. It was a nice production team. Here was another group of people that I began to feel a part of.

I was living in a bubble. One minute I was busy with a large crew, spending nights in bars drinking, early mornings digging. The next I was on my own in a train or cab on the way to something different. I'd temporarily left my life in Ireland, but I wasn't sure for what. I was getting to design gardens with tiny budgets, to use some ideas, but all the time there were hints of something big about to happen. I didn't know if the type of gardens I wanted to create could ever be made on a television programme. Too much commitment would be needed. The big change for me was earning money. For the first time ever I had a healthy bank account.

It was May and I was in Dublin Airport on a travelator when my mobile rang. I was on my way to London for something, a quick overnight trip. It was Barry. Eamonn had been involved in some type of accident, the details were unclear. Barry was on his way to the hospital. He didn't think it had been that serious. I returned the following day to devastating news. He hadn't made it. The simplest of accidents, crossing a road in the middle of the day, and

Eamonn was gone from us. It didn't make sense. So much was happening for me, everything was changing, and he'd been such a huge part of that. There I was in 1997, gathered with his grieving young friends and family at a hospital. The fun we could have had together: he would have come back and joined me, he would have made stuff for me, and we both would have experienced some success. He'd laid part of that foundation. But it wasn't to be. The death of those close to me invades my being. You deal with grief and you feel you move on. But it takes a long time. I don't know if this is a particularly Irish thing, but when during long nights I dream of those who have passed, it's very real to me.

HOME FRONT IN THE GARDEN

Simon Shaw, a series producer at the BBC, contacted me. He was producing a magazine-format interiors programme, *Home Front*, which encouraged people to change their homes to suit their personal style, offering inspiration and DIY for interiors. They were thinking about doing an outdoor version. I had been spotted on coverage of that year's Chelsea. Would I be interested in talking to them? I jumped at the chance. Within a week I'd met up with Simon and Daisy Goodwin. Daisy is a legend in the television industry. Working for the BBC and then the independent producer Talkback, she has been responsible for the development of a host of lifestyle programmes and is renowned for talent spotting. They both quizzed me. Would it be possible, did I think, to make over gardens on a quite a grand scale within the life of a television programme? Yes, I said. Here were people with ambition, creativity and a budget who wanted me to join the team within the Beeb *and* I'd get to design gardens. Simon and Daisy felt I had a fresh approach, uninhibited by tradition. They decided to make a pilot. This is when an episode is made in order to test both the practicalities of the programme idea and the onscreen presence of the presenters.

On the first morning of filming the pilot, in a garden in Shepherd's Bush, I was introduced to Ann McKevitt and Kevin McCloud (who later went on to present *Grand Designs*), resident designers on the indoor programme. Tessa Shaw, the main presenter of *Home Front in the Garden*, would oversee the introductions, and I would be responsible for the overall design and the planting. I wore cobalt blue jeans and a lime green shirt. My hair went past my shoulders. I thought this was a good look. Everything for television had to be exaggerated, I felt. I completed a rough design for a circular lawn, a circular railway sleeper deck and a lookout tower for children in this awkward angular garden.

I saw in the newspapers that at that year's Chelsea there was to be a garden inspired by La Majorelle, the garden owned by Yves Saint Laurent in Marrakesh. One of its defining characteristics was the use of cobalt blue as its primary backdrop. Maybe because it matched my jeans, I wanted to bring this dramatic imported colour into the garden. Vincent came over from Dublin and took on the role of project manager. And we created a somewhat garish but very different and exotic Eden.

Sometimes these pilots aren't for broadcast. Ours was. This pilot episode of *Home Front in the Garden* was broadcast on Monday 16 June 1997. The format was an instant success. Our garden show added nearly a million extra viewers to the interiors show. A series was commissioned, and *Home Front in the Garden* was born.

It was an exhilarating but tough journey. Out of the blue I had a job that challenged me to explore and create gardens that were different, gardens that asked questions, that entertained and that embraced outdoor living. It was quite revolutionary: not the designs, but the concept. The first series involved a roof terrace in Camden, a tropical city garden for a couple of Indian extraction, a family garden and a fantasy garden. The projects were divided up. Kevin and Ann would often work with colour, and I'd try to incorporate ideas such as I'd used at Chelsea – glass brick walls with water pouring down, a lot of stainless steel, trachycarpus and other broadleaved architectural plants, huge metal containers made from pieces of ducting pipe, and even televisions in the garden.

I enjoyed myself enormously. Vincent took a lot on his shoulders and found the builds very tough. We didn't have great back-up. There was no contractor with crew as such, and of course we wanted to achieve an awful lot. Our gardens had to be dramatic and challenging. I was very earnest about my work. I took it all very seriously and was eager to make the most of every opportunity. My style wasn't that similar to Ann's, and this occasionally caused conflict. Maybe at a different time in life I might have been more relaxed, but I felt some annoyance about the insiders moving outside. I was trained as a gardener, I understood plants and soil, and these will always be the essence of a good garden. Ann's work was more about smashing tiles and cementing them onto concrete walls, or creating bubble-effect water features. It wasn't her fault. I am sure it was great to get the gig, and for the viewer it was interesting to see somebody they felt relaxed with and knew from interior transformations working in the garden. These other designers helped create a new audience for gardening programmes.

Simon was very kind to me, opening up his home and his social life. He and Daisy contracted some great crews and directors. The programmes we were doing – some good, some not so – felt pioneering. Tradition was being thrown in skips by the bucketload. Anything traditional, suburban or twee was swept away. I was a new broom. I was also insanely busy. When I wasn't in London making *Home Front in the Garden*, I was working on *Surprise Gardeners* with the Central Television crew, or off with Channel 4's *Collectors' Lot* looking at twenty different tractors in a field.

My life had changed. Justine was back in Dublin living in our flat, with the occasional visit to London. I was very lucky if I saw Ireland. After a busy day, in the evenings I would lug a suitcase onto a train somewhere and travel to the next location. I've never had any interest in clothes. All of sudden I needed different outfits – different shirts, different jeans for different programmes. Sometimes shows would provide them. Occasionally there would be a stylist, but I would always end up lugging everything from one location to another.

I was very lonely and confused. What was happening to me? I'd found myself living in England, but I had never really made any decision to move there. All my reference points had changed, and at the end of the day wherever I was working I found myself alone. The odd evening I'd go down to see my aunt and cousins in Billericay, but mostly it was a bit of television, sometimes looking at a script or specifications for the next job, and then bed.

The second series of *Home Front in the Garden*, a longer one, was commissioned. Vincent had had enough. He had been brilliant, and really he had built my dreams, but so much had rested on his shoulders that it had stopped being fun. Kevin McCloud also left, so it was just me and Ann. But we worked on separate gardens. She got two and I got four.

SEAN AND PAUL

In the gap between series I went back to Dublin for a few months. The programmes hadn't been broadcast, so it was a bit funny: I was in no man's land, not sure of what would happen next. I was asked to design a garden in the south of Dublin at Blackrock. Helen, a girl I had taught in my evening class, told me she had two brothers working on a dramatic project. Would I be interested in doing the garden?

The location was a Georgian house that appeared small from the outside but metamorphosed into a palace beyond the front door. Sean and Paul Cunningham, Helen's brothers, were there. They eyed me suspiciously. Who was I? What did I want? I was here to do the garden. They worked inside, while I started planning beds and borders. At eleven o'clock we'd stop for tea in a garden shed that was fitted out like a kitchen. It turned out they were brilliant crafts people, and the lady who owned the house had asked them initially to build a rabbit hutch. She left them with a pile of money, and they had built what could only be described as a wood and brass cathedral-style hutch. It was fantastic. Working together was great fun. Soon we were having pints on a Friday evening, and then eventually I asked them would they think of coming to London to do some jobs?

There was definite reluctance. They had recently returned from spending years in New York, fitting out a pub on Time Square, so they had done their time away and were ready to settle. The pride they took in their work, their commitment to it and their sense of fun, tinged with a quizzical approach to life and a definite sense of rebellion, told me we could work together and enjoy it. They didn't 'get' gardens, but they admired anything creative. In the pub we talked about possibilities. What if this or that could be achieved?

The Cunningham family is from County Leitrim, an oft-forgotten part of rural Ireland. It's not a small place in terms of space, but to this day I'm sure it still has just one set of traffic lights. The family's farming background meant they had a variety of practical skills. Landscape didn't threaten or mystify them. Machinery was second nature, and spending long hours completing a task, often till late at night, was never a challenge.

In London, Simon the producer was worried about finding a replacement for Vincent. He'd seen that the job of project manager had become a tough gig. And my gardens weren't about to get easier: I was just beginning to have fun. After a month of gentle persuasion, the boys agreed. The three of us headed back to London for the second series of *In The Garden*.

ON LOCATION

The popularity of the show meant that we now had a budget to move around the country. We'd established that we were taking a different approach, and applications flooded in. People were desperate for something new, something different, and we seemed to fit the bill. Looking back, some of the projects become a blur. Our brief was to explore the potential of what a garden could be. I was now a designer on my own with a crew. My friends were creating the gardens with hard work and humour, and we had clients who were eager for change. The BBC was looking after us all. We had flats and wages. For the first couple of years Tessa presented, but by year three the show was given over to me.

The BBC2 had a new controller, Jane Root. She loved my approach and made it clear that she was a fan. After fighting for years to get to do anything, it seemed the world was my oyster. I had a pass to BBC Television Centre. I would wander through the production office in East Tower when no-one was around, picking up recce tapes (videos of gardens that we might do), letters from people applying for makeovers, and tapes with half finished edits of what we had done. I felt part of something, a member of a team and a bigger organization.

The show received a lot of publicity. Through my agents, fan mail appeared, first in dribs and drabs, then in gushes. We had to produce postcards with my photo on them, and I would sign bundles of 500 at a time. The publicity might have been a distraction, but every minute of the day I thought and talked about gardens. The excitement of scribbling designs on notebooks, beer mats or a drawing board, of developing ideas and then seeing them built, was all consuming.

Our crew, led by Sean and Paul, would take over gardens, typically for two weeks. The garden owner might help with the clear-out process. We'd track down specialists working in glass, steel and wood around the country to seek their advice. The researchers would wait for my ideas and then get on the phone to find craftsmen to turn them into reality. I'd give the directors of individual programmes a brief of where ideas came from and they would develop stories. Every programme needed a film of an 'inspiration trip'. Sometime we would go down to Cornwall, visit gardens whose planting was dominated by large-leaved architectural specimens, and scale down the concepts for smaller suburban plots. We travelled to the Eden Project to see glasshouses, to the roof terraces at the Rockefeller Center in New York to view gardens in the sky, or to a bubble house near Cannes to see architecture inspired by organic shapes..

The process was always the same. I valued the opportunity of making a new series, but didn't really comprehend how lucky I had become. A series would mean eight different gardens, very varied in size, budget and story. A team of researchers would have gone out and filmed potential locations, while evaluating the passion of the contributors. I would be sent a selection, and pick a number that I would like to take a close look at.

We'd spend a few weeks on these recces. I would arrive at an appointed time at someone's home. The first five minutes or so were always awkward. You're the bloke from the television, a celebrity coming into their home. They were excited and nervous. I had to try and see through all this and examine their reasons for wanting a garden and what type of garden they would like. Generally the inappropriate ones had been weeded out, so when you arrived in somebody's garden you really wanted to do it. But what would I do? Listening is very important. Settling people, asking a few questions, understanding their desires and then trying to figure if there is something you could offer. Because my gardens were seen as new and radical, people often felt they hadn't the vocabulary to explain. We used mood boards, pages ripped from magazines or holiday photographs stuck on cardboard to create a feeling of what would they would love.

I'd scribble away in my notepad, listening to everything, sketching as I went. I would put down the book and begin to create shapes in front of my eyes with my hands. Hopefully I would have left the family indoors. It could be a funny sight, me charting out shapes in the air. Later I would translate those shapes on to photographs with a felt-tip pen. The idea was always to create movement, mystery, direction and beauty within the very fixed boundaries of suburban fences or hedges. I could imagine things, see things. I'd use a disposable camera to take my own snapshots. I might instantly have an idea of what could be appropriate or what I would love to do. Or I might be perplexed, uninspired by the location or the materials, by the house or the people. As I drove away, my head would go into overdrive. The design process would start.

Sometime I wouldn't sleep. Too many ideas. I travelled with notebooks and biros. Every page started the same way – the day, date, time and place, followed by the project. I'd scribble unintelligible lines and shapes, marks on paper that only I could understand. I'd leaf through hundreds of clippings that I had collected from magazines and newspapers. My eye for the unusual made me hoard inspiration.

I would form a concept and scribble again. Before I could pass over any ideas for a garden I had to be able to visualize it myself. The planting schemes people wanted were usually the same. Britain was in thrall to the so-called new exotics – broad-leaved, green and architectural, with drama from palm trees, the rustle of bamboos, the white bark of a *Betula ermanii*. I didn't rely so much on colour, save for the odd accent here or there. I used lots of grasses and sedges, and my main focus was always on mature specimens.

These programmes were a reaction to years of *Gardeners' World*. To some extent they rebelled against the craft of gardening. This was instant gratification, reflecting the fast, furious and style-conscious lives of people today. And this is what inspired most of the criticism we received: 'It's not real gardening.' It was reactive. I think it was also of its time. We made television programmes that welcomed people who otherwise would never have sat down and watched anything to do with gardens. We brought idiosyncratic style outside, and along with *Ground Force*, a massively popular BBC1 show with Alan Titchmarsh and Charlie Dimmock, we lent gardens a new popularity.

The next stage was always the same: meeting Paul or Sean somewhere for breakfast, in a pub, in a car, wherever, and explaining what I was thinking. If my proposal excited the boys, who had little interest in gardens but a great love of challenging convention, if they wanted to build the project, that would push me on to formalize the presentation. I would work late into the evening, at the BBC or whatever kitchen table I had commandeered, to draw something up. I would present the plans first of all to the producers and directors, hoping my enthusiasm and descriptive powers would result in a green light. We'd schedule filming days, and then with full crew arrive at the location.

The first day held its own frustrations – there was a lot of hanging around. The crew had to get the 'before' shots, interviews, what the people would like from their garden, how worried they were about the design, what they thought I would come up with and how much would it cost. I'd be somewhere in the background, pacing and picturing the garden. Sean might be there: at that stage we weren't allowed touch a blade of grass, but I would be telling him where I expected things to be, and he would be making his contacts locally with skip contractors, local labour and suppliers of sand and cement. We'd be checking to see if the hire companies would be delivering on time, waiting for mini-diggers to roll off the back of trucks. We'd be chatting about the team we had, what the director was like, whether Sean's researchers had been up to the job, if he was staying somewhere good – all the ingredients that were involved in bringing a garden together.

Then it was my turn. On the first and last day I needed to be clean and presentable. Had I got drawings? This was always the big question. The directors worried if there was nothing to shoot. I'd go into the kitchen or the living room and reveal the designs in an artificial situation. Generally a husband and wife would sit at the kitchen table and I would be positioned to one side. Lights would shine warmly on foreheads, and then action. Before I revealed anything, I would talk through the plot, describing what I had found and what I had been excited by, and then I would open the presentation. This part of the job I have never found easy. I have never felt relaxed, or been able to present an idea with the confidence of someone who knows they've hit the nail on the head. I have been planning gardens for over two decades, and most often my solutions are welcomed. But I never count on it.

Once the clients said they are happy, then we could start. I would leave the kitchen and go out and walk the plot with Sean. My job at this stage was to draw out shapes on the ground. We used a white line marker in a spray tin, and I tried to translate into reality those tai chi shapes that had become lines on paper. A mark on the ground can mean setting something in stone. In creating those lines, I was translating a plan from paper, working out proportions, showing where patios or decks would be, what shape they would be, how a lawn might curve and the shape of the beds on either side of it, and finally I'd lead down to a pavilion. This was the usual formula, with weekly variants. Once Sean had the shapes painted on the ground, he'd calculate the amount of materials needed and immediately get somebody on the sourcing case. I'd walk through the garden with the client, demonstrating the proportions, trying to bring it to life. I'd do the same with the director, letting them know what to expect two weeks later.

And then I'd look into the camera, sum up the situation and leave for the next location. The following day, maybe a hundred miles away, I would repeat the exercise with Paul and his gang. The builds would begin, and there would be constant phone calls. My planning would always be erratic. I preferred to be on the ground, so I would drop in as often as possible. A director might take me away for a day or two to film a background story – on roof terraces, on broad leaf planting, on metal cladding, anything remotely appropriate. And then I would return, always exhilarated by the prospect of change.

Every build had its proportion of new faces. I'd be given the low-down by Sean and introduced. If people were good at digging or plastering, tiling or planting, we'd never let them go. They became part of our travelling circus. The weeks involved temporary offices, shipping containers plonked outside somebody's semi-detached home. Endless skips, sub-soil, old concrete and garden rubbish continually on the move. And deliveries non-stop. Work would continue late into the evening under arc lights. Neighbours and passers-by were always fascinated. The project manager always tried to keep things happy. After a few days, a judgement was made as to whether things would be on time. We would see if final filming would have to be rescheduled. Had the weather held us up? Had I asked for something to be built that was far too complex, needing more time, more money, more skills thrown at it? At nine o'clock there would be a delivery of pizza, and then work would resume for another hour or two. The small teams bonded fiercely. There was little time for a pint in the evening. Everyone would stagger to bed and arrive not quite refreshed the following morning at seven for more of the same.

I approached each series as though we were a rock band making tracks for an album. What gardens did we have, what were we doing in each, how did they relate to one another? Midway through, I would start looking for the planting. Here, I was on my own. I'd usually ensure that a few thousand pounds were left in the budget for this. The planting brought everything together, and I'd found nurseries that specialized in larger plants – a notion that was uncommon back then.

Plants much prefer to grow in a single location, to get used to this spot when they are young, to be looked after and to be allowed to prosper with a little bit of food and drink along the way. But if you have the budget for bigger specimens, the ability to handle them and the commitment to look after them until they establish in their new home through watering, staking and feeding, it's perfectly feasible to move them to a new plot.

In continental Europe it was commonplace to purchase specimen plants to create instant impact. The practice wasn't unknown in Britain, but had generally been reserved for commercial landscaping and the well-to-do. Garden shows such as Chelsea would not have evolved without the availability of trees and shrubs that were seven years old and upwards. In the contemporary age, with people often moving home every three or four years, using these specimen plants meant they could achieve an instant sense of maturity in a brand new garden.

I would try to keep half of my planting budget for these bigger specimens which would cost anything from £200 upwards. Through my years of living in the doldrums in Dublin I'd kept masses of gardening articles. Dan Pearson, a very good plantsman, had mentioned Tendercare in Denham, just outside London. This was a convenient supermarket for plants, just a half an hour from the BBC. For more exotic species, maybe ones that reflected our warming climate, I would go to Architectural Plants in Sussex, and Pantiles in Surrey was also good for a whole range of plants.

Inevitably I'd overspend. But I'd play on the idea that nobody would notice until it was too late. Every series went over-budget, sometimes substantially, but with such strong ratings much was forgiven. A letter would be sent to my agent. I would be called in for a meeting. I'd cite the brief – to make gardens that were bigger, better, wilder – and I would be sent away after being told not so politely to try and do better next time.

It was imperative that our gardens looked great for the final shots, and planting always changed the nature of them. After weeks of mud, foundations, concrete, metal and timber, our roll-out lawns and truckloads from nurseries would arrive in the last seventy-two hours. I'd arrive alongside them. This was when I took charge. For most people on site, the green things were a mystery. But I was in heaven. I was completely and fully organic by nature and aware of environmental concerns, ensuring all compost was peat-free, and that we never used weedkillers or artificial fertilizers. I encouraged the boys to prepare the beds by digging in tonnes of farmyard manure when available. I hated seeing the trucks unloaded, with all the potential damage that could be done to the plants, so I would wait in the garden as our super-sized trees were brought in on trolleys, or even swung over the house by crane.

On my visits to the nurseries I photographed everything I was buying, and for a few days I would spend my time planning exactly where I wanted to put it all. Decisions on the ground, on site, had to be faster. The work was hard, and people didn't want to stand around as I scratched my head. Once I was happy with the location, four or five lads would arm themselves with forks and spades, dig a hole, line it with fresh compost and manoeuvre the beast into position. The final placing was very important. I would look at it from every angle, gesture that it needed twisting this way or that or that it was leaning slightly towards me, and then give the signal for backfill.

The transformation really took place in these precious hours. I'd identify one or two people who were good at digging and get them to work with me. Everybody who loves gardens has their own way of doing things, and I would jealously guard my control at this stage. The lads would be very happy. They liked someone else taking responsibility and really appreciated the extraordinary effects achieved.

We battled against time and the weather, often working late into the night, sometimes right through the night. Because the gardens were built in pairs, once I'd finished one and cleaned myself up for the final shots, I'd hop in a car and start the process elsewhere from scratch. We worked hard. By the time the series ended after eight seasons, our commitment hadn't faltered. We were still doing long days and long nights. And being rewarded by the dramatic changes that could be achieved in fourteen days. Full crews were only employed for three days – at the very start of the process, in the middle for an update, and then at the end. Because the client had often watched the garden progressing through their kitchen windows, our true reveal was often to the returning camera crew and the jib arm operators. My secret pleasure was seeing the face of the cameraman as he came in to the back garden. Knowing what we had set out to do, he would break into a smile: 'Wow, this is amazing, you've done it again boys!'

The final series was our most adventurous. There were interdepartmental changes. We'd already been shifted from Arts to Lifestyle, and now we were to be moved once again, to Birmingham. It was difficult and frustrating all round. We had a new series producer who we had worked with previously, Patrick Flavelle. I felt the programme didn't travel well, and maybe our new team didn't understand the extent of our ambition and commitment. Through frustration I drove Patrick mad. The happy days on this series were behind us. This was ironic, as the work was never better. It had been difficult to tempt Paul and Sean back. Paul was now married and happily settled in Dublin, with a child. Sean had married too. His days of roaming another country making gardens were soon to be at an end.

Pushing the boundaries again, I explored the notion of gardens that moved. Near Epping Forest we created a huge pavilion at the end of a garden, but on tracks. In reality it was a cable car. It would trundle up and down the garden following the sun. It was magnificent and expensive. In Birmingham we installed a car lift into newly built walls, so creating a patio (planted with a mixed border and set with tubs containing birch trees) that could rise in the evening, revealing an outdoor evening room underneath. There were problems with planning and grumbles in newspapers. Our overspend was becoming ever more dramatic. Jane Root was about to leave to take over the reins at Discovery in Washington. It was charter renewal time for the BBC, and some newspapers were quite rightly taking a closer look at how licence fee money was being spent. I might have felt that the series and the gardens were stronger than ever. The ratings were still good but the mood had changed. The party was over.

LAURENCE LLEWELYN-BOWEN
AND HOME FRONT

I used to watch Laurence Llewelyn-Bowen on *Changing Rooms*. I found him the strangest creature but fascinating, off-putting and intriguing at the same time. Like most viewers I didn't know what to make of his flamboyance, and I certainly didn't realize that we would soon be in a long-running partnership.

Lifestyle shows were hugely popular. The chefs, the gardeners and interior designers would often find themselves banded together at events. BBC Worldwide would run the Good Homes Show and Gardeners' World Live. *Home Front* was a brand that appealed to all sectors, so I would be hired for a week to lecture a few times daily at the NEC in Birmingham, or even at the Dubai equivalent. And all the television people hung out together. So I bumped into Laurence and his wife Jackie, and we spent a few hours having pints. By the end of the few days I still didn't know what to make of him. Jackie and Laurence were heading to London before I was, and Jackie left me a note backstage: 'Come around for dinner, we really mean it.'

I was apprehensive, I don't know why, but I accepted, and so within a week I was in a cab to Blackheath. As usual, I was nearly an hour late and arrived in a sweat. There were no worries. We were getting a simple takeaway, with a chance for me to unwind in a family environment for a few hours.

'It was very kind of you to ask me, Jackie,' I said.

'Oh don't worry, you're over from Dublin, you won't know many people – we just wanted to look after you for a while.'

We became good friends.

Laurence's over the top persona reflects who he is. At that stage in his life he'd exploded into view and was enjoying the notoriety normally associated with pop singers. He revelled in the attention, and had probably felt that it was only a matter of time before others appreciated his gifts. *Changing Rooms* fast became a BBC1 programme and so had a mass audience. I was in a different place, vaguely known by people. He was assumed to be an effeminate dandy – well, dandy he certainly is, but there was an assumption that he was gay – though this couldn't be further from the truth. He is a strong character, both physically and emotionally. And on site, while initially an object of curiosity, he soon had the whole crew, builders included, wrapped round his little finger. He can be quick-witted and funny, but also very cutting. Everybody loved him. I enjoyed basking in his reflected glory whenever we were out, and I liked the fact that the whole family were very open. You were welcomed as a friend into their group, and this was before we had worked together.

In the second series of *Home Front in the Garden*, the producers were trying out other designers, moving people from homes to gardens to create some projects. Laurence wasn't part of the *Home Front* team, but because we got on well I suggested him. In north London I created a small family garden. It was Sean's first project managing job, and Laurence was invited to be the guest designer. The cameras arrived, and within minutes I'd asked him why he'd come wearing the floral family curtains. That was our relationship. He'd slag me off about new ideas or outlandish design, and I'd have a go at him for being…well, him. Simon the producer liked the chemistry. And after about a year, the two of us were invited to take over the original show. *Home Front*, with Laurence doing a few rooms inside and me redesigning the garden, made its television debut.

Even though I'm a bit older than Laurence, because of his personality I adopted the role of a naughty younger brother. We travelled the country and went abroad on inspiration trips. Laurence hammed everything up and I took the role of garden designer far too seriously. We had a laugh, but behind it I was compulsively competitive. I felt his approach was maybe too lighthearted. He worked on a practical level, arriving on the back of a sleek Virgin Limo motorbike; I'd be spending days digging with the lads. I pooh-poohed his presentations. He was rarely that unkind about mine. Our reference points were miles apart. I brought a naïve, child-like and maybe sometimes impractical approach to my projects, in my zeal to discover the new at others' expense. He appreciated decoration, flamboyance and effect. Consequently our styles differed greatly, and it was an odd kind of mix. We had clients who might like one or other of us. It would be strange if they liked us both, because we were so different. Maybe they didn't like either of us, but they just wanted to have their homes and gardens transformed cheaply.

Laurence and Jackie's place became something of a home from home. Jackie is a brilliant cook, and we all enjoyed a social drink. The ratings for the first show were enormous and the Controller of BBC2 sent us a bottle of champagne each. I believe there was a wrestling match to see if the series could be brought to BBC1 and be granted an even bigger audience. Happy and successful days. In one year I completed one series of *Home Front in the Garden*, consisting of eight programmes, and two series of *Home Front*, making another ten projects. It meant I spent all my time travelling the country. But each and every opportunity to create a garden was brilliant. And whenever Laurence arrived on site it was always fun.

I explored different notions in gardens, including raised terraces inspired by aeroplane wings; Miami-style Art Deco pavilions with wide paths and glass bricks and beautiful ferns; sunken outdoor rooms to create privacy in built-up urban areas; and a purple Art Nouveau terraced staircase garden, tiled in Welsh slate complete with a mirrored grotto. Fun, wonderful, over the top projects that needed thousands of man-hours to construct our hare-brained notions.

I remember a December in Luton at the end of a very busy

143

year. We'd been asked to design a solarium on the flat roof of a modernist house called 'Blue Rails'. With a garden down below. Laurence worked his magic with carpeting, a bed that folded out of the wall and Lloyd Loom furniture. The garden was another story. I expected modernist lines to appear: rendered white walls, concrete and lawn, something quite harsh. But whenever I sketched, a glitzy Hollywood type garden emerged: think ostrich feathers and Las Vegas dancers. In truth, more Laurence than me – a symmetrical splayed lawn and delicious curves stepping down level after level, all edged in brass, and blue mosaic pools on other side with jets of water. It would have been a perfect stage for a Busby Berkeley dance routine. And then, at the end of the top lawn, a mirror-ball egg, two metres high, that rotated at the touch of a button. When it stopped, doors opened to reveal a mirrored cocktail cabinet. We filmed at the American Bar in the Savoy Hotel. We sipped Black Velvet, Guinness and champagne, from pewter mugs, and we laughed as the revolving egg shone in spotlights and sprinkled its twinkles throughout the neighbourhood. In one fell swoop I had out-camped anything that Laurence had ever tried. This, our final garden of the year, was our most flamboyant. Sean, Paul and I drove in a convoy to catch the ferry from Holyhead to Dublin, home for Christmas. When the programme was aired a few months later, Nancy Banks-Smith gave the egg its own television review in the *Guardian*: it shone and shimmered, she said. This egg was auditioning, looking for an agent!

For a BBC2 special on Islam, we went to Marrakesh to seek inspiration. That was quite a sight: Laurence dressed as normal in a duck-egg blue suit with wide cuffs walking through the souk, oblivious to the stares of the locals. We looked behind the mysteries of Islamic design in homes, gardens, furniture and fabric. I found it exhilarating. Laurence, on the other hand, left for London a little early.

On another occasion we went to Venice. We had a couple of days, and Laurence was due to be joined by Jackie after our filming. He'd arrived before me and was tucking into the Prosecco in a bar on St Mark's Square. I hadn't touched alcohol in four months. When things are really busy, work and drink don't mix. Laurence complained that it was going to be the most boring trip if I didn't, and so – sensing a few days that would be more relaxed than usual – I joined him. Two hours later we were floating down the canals in a gondola, pissed as coots. The director must have been overjoyed by the gibberish I came out with, berating Mr Bowen for the lack of passion that I perceived in his designs. Utter waffle and embarrassing to watch – especially when I found I was part of an invited audience at Television Centre when it was played as one of the year's daftest television moments.

The madness wasn't always inspired by drink. Doing a garden on the south coast, Laurence and I devised a maritime theme. When I come to think of it, we used to get away with murder. We decided that throughout the programme I would appear to swim everywhere. The first shot was of Laurence having breakfast on the beach, with full silver service and his own butler, while in the distance this figure (me) emerged fully clothed from the sea, as if I had swum across from Dublin. I joined him for breakfast. Then I swam to Cornwall to join him at his holiday home, as he whizzed past in his speedboat, *Ladyboy*. Finally, we rowed down the Liffey in Dublin. The room Laurence had been creating was a bathroom. When the cameras followed him and the client into it to see the magic he had created, I emerged from the tub, fully clothed again and covered in suds! What were we on?

People took a passionate like or dislike to Laurence. We wrote a book together, and hundreds of people queued in out-of-town shopping centres for our signings. Laurence was particularly hip among the Goth crowd, who must have sensed a kinship. I was pretty much along for the ride. He would refer to me as his chubby or hairy Irish friend. Charming. If his online fans, who took part in his chat forums, were getting out of hand, Jackie might turn up to give them a piece of her mind. She could be quite formidable. Nothing was going to even hint at threatening family harmony. They both enjoyed their fame. At some stage Jackie even had a column in *Hello!* called 'My Life as the Wife', which dwelt on how she became invisible if they were out, and how people just wanted a piece of him.

I learned a big lesson. I was becoming more popular and finding it difficult to handle the attention. To Laurence and Jackie it was water off a duck's back – you got on with it, it was part of the job, but you never let it interfere with your real life. And whereas people's reaction to me on the street has always been warm and friendly, it wasn't always so with him. One day we were in Soho in London, about to film a lunch with a new television client, Fiona Ellis. We went into an Irish bar, O'Neills, to wait until the crew were ready. At midday the pub was almost deserted. A man walked in, saw us and walked on by. A few minutes later he approached our table on his way out: 'I always wanted to call you a c…, so you've made my day.'

Laurence didn't flinch. I was angry. Laurence said:

'What's wrong with you? Don't be such a wuss!'

'That guy,' I said, ' He was so bloody rude.'

Laurence didn't care. 'What did he say to me?' he asked.

I repeated it.

'Well, I've made his day. I don't care how I did it. I don't care how I did it, so that makes me happy.'

Later I told Jackie the story. Her reaction was the same.

Only once did Laurence and I have a falling out. We were working for a lady in Essex. He was reupholstering her boudoir and I was digging. Over a cup of tea I told the lady I didn't like what Laurence was doing. This was typical me, being pally wally with the client because I spent so much time on site, and stupidly having a go at him in his absence. Just for fun. A couple of days later we were filming at the house. I arrived by car, Laurence was already there. He saw the car arriving in the driveway and ran. I had never seen him run. I opened the door. He was livid.

'What did you say to the client about my work? It was so unprofessional.'

His face was red with temper.

I had blown it.

'Laurence', I said 'I'm sorry. I made a mistake.'

He looked at me, relaxed and said, 'Oh, OK, that's fine then. You've done exactly the right things, apologised straight away.'

He forgave me.

The irony was that of the two of us I was the bigger drama merchant on programmes. He was generally well prepared (well, he had a team of assistants to help him), turned up on time and amused all. One newspaper described us as the biggest pair of bitching queens since Elizabeth and Mary. It says everything.

The attention I got crept up on me. I wasn't an instant personality, but after a while I found it overwhelming. I couldn't understand the extras that came with the job. I never understood why people would want to get to know the person behind the persona. It troubled me, and I talked to a few people about it. My family in the UK became the *Home Front* team – some researchers, some directors, Sean and Paul and Laurence and Jackie. People saw that I was vulnerable and shielded me. I talked to one of the researchers, Cynthia. Invites were coming to parties and stuff was happening. I was being sent gifts. I couldn't understand how it was that all of a sudden I was earning good money, and yet never had so much been available. Clothes shops wanted to kit me out, people wanted to give me cars, lots of different scenarios. Cynthia listened patiently. 'You remind me so much of someone,' she said. 'You mustn't tell anybody, but my brother was in a similar situation. He became very well known.'

I was intrigued. Who was this guy?

She wouldn't say. All she'd say was that she understood. Eventually, when I had promised never to breathe a word, she revealed that her brother was Billy Ocean. I fell around laughing. And as I was never one to keep a secret, the following day the whole *Home Front* office was surreptitiously humming 'Suddenly' and 'Caribbean Queen'. She was livid, but years later she was to sing these songs brilliantly, unaccompanied, at our kitchen table in Kensal Rise.

Laurence and I had the opportunity to continue with a sixth series of *Home Front*. However, it too was to be moved to Pebble Mill. The garden programme hadn't fitted in well there, so we talked and decided to leave things where they were. It was 2002, and we had had a great run, we had enjoyed ourselves and while we were still a popular team we reckoned it was a good time to say goodbye.

It wasn't goodbye to television. Far from it. But it was an end to our manic contemporary garden building.

What had I learned? I'd fulfilled lots of ambitions. Firstly, I had got to create gardens, which was exactly what I had wanted to do with my life. I had been allowed to challenge convention, and I'd had an influence over the way people regarded their outside space. I'd set out to understand myself and my capabilities through gardens. And through some misadventures, I'd been able to effect real change. My gardens weren't to everybody's taste, but they were refreshing and showed that choice was available. At last garden designers had permission to look for influence from other creative disciplines. I had been among a group of people who had inspired others through television programmes. I'd managed to create some beautiful gardens, some that were thought provoking, and some that were dubious. I'd always tried my best, and now we belonged to an age where the suburban garden mattered. The craft of gardening and the art of garden design had been the exclusive preserve of the passionistas. It had been difficult ten years earlier to find anything contemporary, especially in suburbia. The pendulum had swung the other way.

Thousands now wanted to be garden designers, and many garden designers wanted their own television shows. In Ireland the floodgates opened and it was as if a new industry was born. More than ever, people saw the Chelsea Flower Show as a way to make a name. What had happened to me, however, was relatively unusual. The gardening industry is still a tough one, and these days garden design is tougher than ever. My email inbox and postbag are full of messages that show the palpable frustration of others who'd love to create – young designers in the States or Poland looking for answers, needing clients to believe in them and their new ideas. My experience was a freak one, perhaps a one-off. I'd got lucky.

Looking back on those years, our work was quite revolutionary because it was different. I made mistakes, and some of the design wasn't very good, though some was excellent. I can say that I always wanted it to be brilliant, and I always listened to the client to hear the brief, to examine the rules. I wanted to present something new. Most of the architecture I worked against was bland: nondescript brick, concrete or pebble-dashed house exteriors. Almost all the gardens were in suburban situations. Occasionally there would be one in the country. Almost all the projects were middle class. The client would initially pay a nominal £500 towards the build. The BBC had a budget, so we would encourage suppliers to give us a good deal, citing, if we could, subtle promotion.

Some of the designs were certainly outlandish, but broadly I stuck to the traditional elements of gardens and gardening. I wanted to encourage greater use and more enjoyment of outdoor spaces. And I wanted the garden to appeal to all members of the household. The wow factor became a big issue. After a few reveals this was the word that I would hear most often from people on seeing their outdoor spaces transformed. I believed in lawns and terraces, planting, greenhouses and growing vegetables. I needed to include practical aspects – pathways, garden sheds and, if desired, washing lines.

My belief, developed over many years, that there were new ways, new ideas, new shapes and other plants to be explored became the programme's *raison d'être* – but I never believed we were as bonkers or radical as some of the reaction from the press suggested.

TELEVISION LESSONS

The first person to point a camera at me told me I was perfect for television. I came across well. I looked right, I had an accent, a twinkle in my eye and a sense of humour. More importantly, I was passionate about my subject. These must be the secrets to my success. But it was very confusing for me. What was it I was supposed to be good at? I was scared in front of the camera, but I appeared relaxed and not intimidated. I like people, but often I am not good in company. Developing another skill, television presentation, was rewarding. I learned on the job. The ideas I produced for various programmes were exciting and visual and different, so I was able to provide content; and I could enthuse people, members of the team, to make things happen.

But the very passion that proves successful is sometimes often my biggest impediment. I deal with situations on an emotional level. I have a deep response to design. I am highly affected by aesthetics, my surroundings, objects. Beauty or good design sparks my imagination, makes me content and feel good. When things go wrong, it can be very difficult. Television is an industry that can chew you up and spit you out. It's ruled by finance and by schedules. I have a strong sense of right and wrong, of the importance of not abusing people, and of loyalty. When things are going great on a programme, everybody loves me: I'm a character, with charm and ideas. When I feel things are wrong, I get dragged down into a swirling blackness. I argue passionately and I disappear. Few people know how to handle me.

But that's not what people see when I'm on television or making public appearances. When you achieve prominence through television, your life changes. Possibilities open up, doors open and you become a commodity for the media, for industry and for charities. All of this crept up on me gradually. I have written nine books, and with book launches come tours and publicity. In Belfast, three hundred people queued at a bookshop for a few hours. I was led in the back of the store. It was quite a vision. I had people stand in front of me crying, not quite believing they were getting to meet a curly-headed gardener in a T-shirt. *Home Front* had some very passionate followers. I was confused by this. Whatever I had set out to do was for me. I was sorting out, initially in my own mind and then in people's gardens, why I wanted to create gardens that were different and what they would be like. For it to result in such strong excitement was a bit intimidating. I acted the part of a person happy to be in the public eye, but really I just went through the motions.

Along with the signings came lots of press interviews. I'd go into a studio and talk to twenty radio stations around the country in a few hours. Interviewers were allotted sessions of five or ten minutes, somebody would plug me in and the questions would start. The front cover of the *Home Front* book had a picture of the shark's fin garden. Most conversations started with, 'Why would you do that?'

Newspaper interviews and chat show appearances can be interesting. You learn fast to be on your guard. I had no true perception of my popularity and was unaware that things I'd say on television or in a radio interview could make a headline. It's a journalist's job to create interesting pieces. If I am fascinated by somebody I want to develop an understanding of the person behind the image, and it is strong opinions, ways of life and backgrounds that contain these nuggets.

Justine was very private. She'd grown up in the glare of publicity: both her parents were prominent for different reasons. As a journalist, her mum often would set up shoots with her children. Justine never appeared. It might be a colour supplement piece about Christmas dinner, say, and how glamorous it was in the Keane household, but Justine was always absent, wouldn't play ball. She married the penniless gardener, the guy who to the outside world might have appeared hopeless, and within a few years here am I appearing on television in different countries, creating inevitable interest in us. Her family thought this was hilarious. And Justine appreciated the irony. She revelled in my success, but didn't want me to talk about her. She enjoyed being on the outside looking at the circus, but always concerned for me. And for her I tried to be as reserved as I possibly could. It's a delicate line, but my public character and openness have certainly been tempered by the person I married.

Only once was this to change. When Eppie was very little, I was invited to open the Southport Flower Show. In a radio interview in the months leading up to the event, I had said how thrilled I was to be able to bring my family to this flower show. Eppie was banned from Chelsea. It wasn't personal: no really young children were allowed. To celebrate Eppie's presence, it was decided that a rose would be named 'Eppie Gavin'. We were overjoyed. Terry Wogan, Alan Titchmarsh and a host of others had roses and sweet peas christened in their honour. I had been bypassed, but with Eppie aged just two, *Rosa* 'Eppie Gavin' was to be unveiled. On a beautiful sunny day, Justine and I stood in the centre of the showground in Southport and were both happily interviewed by ITV and the BBC. We rushed back to the hotel room to watch it on the evening news programmes, the two of us proud as punch.

This was a major exception to the rule. I have to accept that lots of people around myself, my wife and my family are reticent about the media. They don't seek publicity in their lives, so I try where possible to keep to the work, to working relationships, inspiration and how things happened for me. I never became a gardening superstar, I wasn't in the Alan or Monty or Laurence category. I could be interviewed by Jo Wiley on BBC Radio 1, Jonathan Ross on Radio 2 and on any number of Radio 4 shows. I was viewed as somebody who enjoyed fun and was a good laugh, as a person people would like to have a pint with. Any turbulence in the gardening world, any time I stand up to people having a go, doesn't matter to those who like me. In the world of flowers, people are always set to take offence. Beyond that I am considered normal, cheerful and interesting.

In Ireland we'd always listened to Radio 4 on long wave. In the early days, from my second Chelsea on, I'd ring my Mum and let her know that I was to be interviewed on *Woman's Hour*, *Start the Week*, or even the news. In Ireland it has always been a privilege to sit on a Friday evening on the sofa of *The Late Late Show*.

In Britain my highlight was appearing on *Loose Ends*, Ned Sherrin's lighthearted end of week celebration on Radio 4. The first book, with the shark's fin cover, led to an invite. Emma Freud was to conduct an interview as part of the show. It was recorded on a Saturday morning, and Sean, who was working on one of gardens in London, had a day off and was staying with me in our flat on Kensington Church Street, accompanied me. We took the tube from Notting Hill to the studios at Portland Place. It didn't start well. We hadn't got the correct tickets, an inspector stopped us and we were fined. We arrived at Broadcasting House. The nature of the programme was that all guests were in the studio together. Sean went out for coffees as I waited in reception. Things got a little surreal. It was the eleventh hour of the eleventh day of the eleventh month, Remembrance Day. I was waiting to be collected. Another guest walked through the revolving door. At eleven minutes past eleven, the bells tolled as Dom Joly stopped in his tracks and stood silently in the foyer. I gazed at the surreal scene. While steeped in remembrance, it was like being in one of his off-the-wall comedy shows. Sean came back with the coffees, Emma was there, and Sean whipped out for another for her. I had met her before and I was smitten. She had a twinkle in her eye. She'd asked me around to have a look at her garden. The builders were in. I was madly busy working on programmes and had never followed up. All was forgiven. I can remember nothing about the interview, but loved being at the centre of this institution. Ned was the perfect host, polite, theatrical and professional, steering his ship. By coincidence, Dom's dad lived in my block of flats and there were other Irish guests, a comedy troupe of bespectacled singers called The Nualas. After the show, Ned brought everybody to a pub around the corner for refreshments. This day sums up lots of my media experiences in England – humorous, gentle and amusing. I had been welcomed by the establishment.

CHELSEA NO. 3, 2004:
THE CAMELOT 'LOLLIPOPS' GARDEN

A familiar setting beckoned. May 2003 saw me back at Chelsea with Alan Titchmarsh, but this time co-hosting coverage of the Flower Show. I had created two gardens there that few had noticed. I had exhibited at Chelsea with Vincent in 1995 because I felt something might happen there. I didn't know what. I expected to get some clients who would appreciate gardens that were different.

That is what happened, but in an unexpected way. The hunt had been on for fresh gardening presenters and I had fitted the bill. I worked hard, had ideas and was presentable. Initially it was Channel 4 who had the franchise to broadcast Chelsea. I worked on the coverage with Monty Don, a new face with an established one. Monty had been working in television for years. As a passionate and innate gardener he had opinions. He was also a generous person to work with. On our second day he told me that his best friend had said the combination of the two of us was brilliant. He played it straight, and I was the enthusiastic cheeky one.

The BBC then signed a multi-year deal for coverage of the show, and I retained the role of second-in-command, this time sitting next to Alan. Production companies saw gardening as being the next big thing, taking over from cookery programmes and they were desperate for any type of new format. Alan was always warm, generous and professional. He seemed to know everything about television and had also met everyone. The contract negotiated with the Royal Horticultural Society meant loads of programmes. The BBC paid for the substantive access. There would be preview shows with day and evening teams on the Sunday, and then Monday to Friday live afternoon and evening shows. A variety of people, some non-gardeners, hosted the afternoon coverage. Alan and I anchored the rest.

Alan stared into the camera as the autocue rolled... 'Good evening and welcome to the Chelsea Flower Show.' We had enormous fun. It took a while for me to settle into the studio set-up and live television. Our base was a square box built on the site of my first garden on the Rockery Bank, held up by scaffolding poles. On top was an open terrace. I would wander in from whatever other programmes I had been doing around the country, have a run around the show, make a general assessment and then get down to work. My interest was specifically in the garden designs, always searching for a move towards the contemporary, very passionate about what I saw. I disliked the twee and the overly intellectual. I wasn't mad about themed gardens, but loved anything that had some soul. Alan dressed in pinstripes; I was generally on the scruffy side, in trainers, jeans and a T-shirt.

The programmes were packed with little films following the progress of gardens and exhibits from Britain and around the world. Daytime was spent being grabbed by a director and a crew. Chelsea hadn't yet opened on the Saturday, so the crowds were enormous and getting through them could be difficult. It was like negotiating Oxford Street on Christmas Eve. Alan was on *Ground Force* as well as *Gardeners' World*. I was on *Home Front* and a myriad of daytime programmes. Both highly visible, along with Charlie Dimmock and Rachel de Thame, we would have crowds gathering and hanging on our every word as we delivered pieces to camera.

Visitors to the show were passionate. They're well behaved and intoxicated by the great world of plants. They want to see the biggest leeks, the longest carrots, the brightest chrysanthemums, the rarest orchids and the oldest bonsai. They are looking out for cottage gardens and oriental ones, olive trees that have made the trip from Italy and anything that has made a stir on television or in the newspapers. The presenters added to this circus. Three or four times a day, Alan and I would join up to record pieces in gardens or at plant displays, such as an auricula theatre.

Crowds would gather. You didn't dare fluff your lines, and this became the entertainment. In the evening, during live transmissions, I never held back, whether it was having fun with Alan or revealing strong views about what was on show. This could be difficult. The following morning some people loved what you'd said about their display, while others made complaints to the BBC.

Some years were more relaxed than others. Garden styles were changing, and there was a lot more contemporary work around. I loved the position I was in, with access to everybody and all areas. The atmosphere behind the scenes was brilliant. On the Friday evening, when our last broadcast was finished, everybody working on the programme would gather behind the Portakabins next to the catering truck. Alan would step up, and talk for a few minutes about the magic of making television in such a spot. He would thank everybody and give presents to those who'd looked after him, and then he would come and hug and kiss me. And every year a tear would run down his face as he did this. We both loved this week together.

I knew how difficult it was to create a garden in these situations. I felt removed from all that now. Occasionally people enquired if I would ever do a garden again at Chelsea. I felt I had the opportunity to create up to twenty gardens a year on television between all the shows I was involved – *Home Front, Home Front in the Garden, Planet Patio* and others. On the other hand, there is nothing like presenting ideas to a live audience and having instant feedback.

I rang Sean. 'I'm thinking I would like to do another garden at Chelsea.' 'Brilliant,' he said, 'go for it!'

The next morning I told Alan. 'Why would you do that?' he asked.

'I just feel I should be down there with everybody else, reminding myself what it's like.'

That evening, live on BBC2, Alan announced I was returning the following year to build a garden. My most notorious trip to

Chelsea was about to begin.

I had breakfast with Jane Root, the Controller of BBC2, at the Electric Restaurant on Portobello Road, just a few doors from the studio. We were reviewing my programmes. On the way out she said she'd been watching the coverage of Chelsea, had heard I would be going back to do a garden. Could they make a series following the journey? I figured it would be a bit boring, but it was work and it might make the trip easier. She thought it could be fascinating to see how things happen from the garden designer's point of view. It was given to BBC Bristol, and I was introduced to two directors, Steve Poole and Robert Letts.

Steve came on board first. I met him at a hotel in Bath. He'd made programmes like *Jamie's Kitchen* and *Life of Grime*. He was interested in people's stories, but was there a story here? To him I was a jumped-up gardening presenter. He loved his small town garden. Robert was more straightforward. They would follow the garden's progress from the summer of 2003 right up to the its debut. They'd need full access at the studio, at home, and then at Chelsea. I didn't even know what type of garden I wanted to show. It was fly-on-the-wall/reality television. It was about to become *Diarmuid's Big Adventure*.

There was nothing much happening in Portobello Road. The studio had remained quiet since we had moved in because I was making too many television series. I had set it up to gain some independence from television. Our programmes were being transmitted throughout the world, and because of this we had requests to design gardens in lots of different territories. But I didn't have time to actively develop the business.

I started to wonder what it was I should do at Chelsea. I was having fun designing gardens on television shows, and in Derby I had just completed a garden where I had made an abstract sculpture using coloured discs welded to the top of black rods, like spinning plates. This had come about through an interest in

1950s design, especially the Festival of Britain. I sketched and developed a notion of different coloured spheres on black poles like lollipops, wandering through a green landscape. I wanted to explore this idea of imported colour against a verdant background. I wanted to create a futuristic garden pavilion – a room in the shape of a pod, again covered in coloured metal balls, one which would open automatically by means of hydraulics.

Often Chelsea gardens are years in the planning. Occasionally it's just months. For Chelsea careerists, the planning and building of a garden is an obsession. I had a busy life and not much time to get obsessed. I scribbled the drawings of the garden down, had the concept illustrated and sent off an application to the Royal Horticultural Society. I'd no sponsorship and no time to look for it. The garden wasn't going to be cheap. Like a lot of applicants for space I was economical with the truth in some of my answers. I was positive about receiving financial support for this undertaking, but I wasn't yet sure from where. Sitting in the studio, the director would ask me had I got the money. I'd reply no, but I wasn't worried and laugh the situation off. And then days later they'd film while the RHS committee considered my application form, which probably indicated I was fully funded.

I was figuring out how to make the garden. I was searching for plants and paving slabs, and talking to a company, Elite Metalcraft, about building what would be the prominent features. On top of all of this, Justine discovered she was pregnant. We were a busy and happy household. Our imminent arrival meant more to us than any garden being built anywhere.

I was also writing a book, called *Ten Steps to Designing Your Own Garden*. Selfridges and Harrods both asked me to take over windows of their flagship stores for a month and design some displays. In the midst of the mayhem, Mark who was now running the studio, reported a few funny phone calls. Bunny Guinness, who would be creating a garden next door at Chelsea, wanted to know who our sponsor was. It seemed an irrelevant question. Not having one, we palmed her off.

Sean disappeared back to Ireland and wouldn't answer the phone. Stuff was going on in his head, he was also about to be a dad, priorities were changing. I didn't want to let the cameras know I now had no sponsor and no project manager. The crew flew to Dublin to try and find him. I had a row with Robert on the phone as I wandered around an airport somewhere. Things were difficult. Bunny had been on the phone to the office again.

I rang and wrote to all the usual suspects, companies who I felt might have an interest in sponsoring a garden. Nobody did. I had left it late for corporate financial planning. I didn't know what would happen but was sure that something would turn up. Having tracked down Sean and his brother Paul and got them back on board, we filmed on their family bog in County Leitrim, as I identified gnarled and twisted birch trees that we planned to lift – specimens that I thought would look great in the garden. I went to Crûg Farm Plants in Wales to meet contemporary plant hunters and search for exotic species that mightn't be seen elsewhere. And I visited and revisited the metal factory in Perivale, Middlesex, where we tried for months to figure out the complexities of attaching five thousand enamelled steel balls on to an outer shell. I went to the Isle of Wight to examine the enamelling process. It was great fun seeing everything happen, although being followed around so often by a crew could be difficult.

'Where do you like to escape to when things are tough?' asked Steve, the director. I described Ballinskelligs in Kerry.

'If we book you tickets will you go there?'

'It would be lovely to have a little break.'

And that's what we did. I went back to the place where I had gathered the plants for my first Chelsea, swam in the roaring sea, and once again marked out the garden on a beach. In the programme I believe this was portrayed a bit differently – as things are really hotting up, with no money to be found and the intricacies of the design still to be figured out, I disappear.

I'd become friendly with Lawrence Dallaglio through creating a garden for him and his wife Alice in Richmond. I talked to him about Chelsea and my difficulties in finding a sponsor. Within a few weeks he had invited me to his testimonial dinner, where I sat between Zara Phillips and Stuart Higgins, a former editor of the *Sun* who now runs a communications company. 'That's the man who'll help you,' said Lawrence. And he was right. Stuart loved the concept of the garden, and immediately saw a connection with one of his clients, Camelot, operators of the National Lottery. A meeting was arranged. Camelot were about to celebrate an anniversary, and our multi-coloured balls would fit in perfectly with their message. I was introduced to their inspirational chief executive Dianne Thompson. A deal was agreed. We had a sponsor. We would produce the Camelot Garden at the 2004 Chelsea Flower Show. Things were progressing at last.

We managed a trial run with the Irish lollipops when we were commissioned by the Irish government to create an installation for the opening of the Irish State Guest House, Farmleigh, in Dublin's Phoenix Park. Our multi-coloured balls, set by Sean and Paul and myself in green parkland, created quite a sight. Lots of people loved them, especially children. They made one or two people angry. I was delighted with the ways things were progressing. We had a team, the technical issues were sorted, the lollipops and the pod were being built and plants gathered.

There was another call to the office. Bunny Guinness again. As well as being an exhibitor she was a panellist with *Gardeners' Question Time* on Radio 4. Could they interview me in my garden on the final Wednesday of the build? No problem. Every Sunday in my childhood GQT had been on the radio in the kitchen as Mum prepared lunch. To be mentioned on the programme would be an honour.

Arriving on site to set up the build was a big moment. There was huge relief. It looked as if all the elements would be ready on time. Mark, Hester (from our office, who had previously been the production manager on a television series *Gardens Through Time* which I had presented along with Jane Owen) and I arrived from the studio in Portobello Road, Sean and Paul were over from Ireland, and Dave and Eavsie, two brilliant lads from Blackpool who had done all the heavy work on the *Home Front* series, were also there. The Bristol TV crew seemed to be an extension of our team, charting everything and often disappearing to find out the Royal Horticultural Society's view of things, going down to the judges, interviewing them in their homes about me and having lunch prepared by Sir Terence Conran in his country mansion. I wasn't aware what they got up to when they weren't with us. I was amused and a little embarrassed that I was being talked about. But people could say what they liked.

Sean and Paul had built the boundary wall. There was discussion with our neighbour, Bunny, about the proper height. In the goldfish bowl of Chelsea, with two sets of cameras pointing (Bunny's garden was being filmed for local television), this quickly became a magnified issue. I let the contractors sort it out. It wasn't a big deal either way for me. But soon I had Bunny rabbiting on. With nothing else to film yet, this five-minute drama became the gossip.

The following morning I left a bottle of champagne and a neighbourly note in Bunny's shed. A lot of good it did me. Three times in the first week of the build she came over to confirm that I was happy to appear on *Gardeners' Question Time*. And then the moment came. The garden was taking shape. That final week, after the main construction work is complete, you are trying to knit your vision together with plants. Lots of energy is invested in achieving your dream. You go through periods of loving and hating what you are creating. You examine it too much. There's a camaraderie on site and within your team. You work early mornings and late at night, you're filthy and tired, always with an eye on that clock that is counting down to eight o'clock on Monday morning, when the garden must be finished,

I'd been nervous about coming back to Chelsea. I was now a name in the gardening world, I had a camera crew with me and I was concerned that I would be seen as a show off. *Diarmuid's Big Adventure* was being broadcast every Wednesday. However, there was an excitement about our garden. People had been able to see that we were going through the same ups and downs as every other exhibitor. I'd been welcomed back as a garden designer. I felt part of the Chelsea community. I was really grateful for this.

Bunny arrived. *Gardeners' Question Time* were early. Could I do the recording now?

'No problem,' I said

She and a producer, a lady wearing an embroidered waistcoat, and a sound technician arrived. They started to throw questions at me about my garden. In my description of it for the catalogue I had said I planned to create a beautiful suburban Eden.

But what was beautiful about this? they asked.

What place did *Geranium* 'Brookside' have in a garden at Chelsea? And if it was suburban gardening, how could people in the suburbs afford specimens of *Dicksonia antarctica* at up to £150 a time?

I could feel the atmosphere was changing. The questions seemed hostile and as the interview continued I began to get a suspicion about what was happening. The producer started stirring things up by going on about how I had once been critical of Bunny's gardens. Bunny interrupted:

'No, he didn't say that! He said I made theme gardens!'

So this the nub of why she wanted me on the programme. Next door, she was building a garden to celebrate the Boat Race. Her fences were criss-crossed oars, and there had been talk of her putting a boat up on the dividing wall. Bunny was brilliant at creating gardens based on dragons and picture-book tree houses, and exhibits depicting children's tales. They were always executed beautifully. I enjoyed looking at them, but design-wise they weren't my thing. I'd obviously said this in a broadcast, and her way of getting back at me was to confront me mid-build on a radio programme.

I was livid and asked them to leave the garden. They seemed delighted. They had riled me. This was the part of Chelsea I hated. I'd met Bunny the first year, back in 1995, when I was nobody. Maybe my success had piqued her. She was also in the media, but not to the same extent as me. I was astonished that the stuff that usually remains unsaid, that people hide behind, had emerged with such clarity. No more nice neighbour. It had all been caught on camera. Immediately, she retreated to her own plot. She asked Robert, our director, not to broadcast it. I'll never know her true motive but that said it all to me. I shouted at her across the wall, was she happy now? And twenty minutes later, the producer and sound man walked by my garden towards the exit gate, laughing together. I wanted to get away. Bunny later gave a quote to the press saying she wasn't elitist, she had even designed gardens in Peterborough!

I sat and swayed in a hanging metal seat among the planting. Sean and Paul gathered round. Everybody tried to buck me up. Charlie Dimmock came over. I was astonished and wanted out of the showground as fast as possible. It was the following afternoon before I returned, still completely disheartened. It had been a bad decision to build a garden again. There's always someone to pull you down. I limply continued the bedding in of *Geranium* 'Brookside' on my knees.

The following morning, a friend came up to me. Nicki Chapman was reporting for BBC *Breakfast News*, a live transmission from the show. The producers had been following my big adventure on television: would I give her an interview? It was set up for

8:15am. She asked a question, 'So how's it going?'

And I said everything I wanted to about my neighbours.

In Nicki's earpiece her producer was saying, 'Just let him keep going, don't interrupt.' And I talked about why Chelsea was the last place in the world I wanted to be at that moment.

Twenty minutes later the show ground was crammed with press. All the drama that could possibly be required was being generated by two gardeners at war. Yards from each other, Bunny and I would stand in front of our respective displays having a rant about the other. Something that was very special, the wonderful experience of creating a garden at the Chelsea Flower Show, had been taken away.

You never stop seeking the approval of your parents. It was Thursday of Chelsea week. The final programme of *Diarmuid's Big Adventure* had been broadcast the evening before. Millions had now seen the completed garden, which at times had looked as if it would never be made.

I was photographed countless times, sometimes looking angry, sometimes laughing. And I played the part of a rebel with a cause. Alan came by: judging was about to begin. Loyally he shouted last-minute instructions to the team about sweeping some of the paths and clearing fallen leaves. He grabbed me to begin my real work for the week – preparing our BBC coverage.

After the many months of build up, panics about money, sponsorship, finding plants and hiring a team to build the exhibit, the garden was finally there. Being part of Alan's gang seemed like a doddle. I was glad it was all over. Tired and filthy, but looking forward to the week ahead.

The garden proved to be a magnet. It seemed everyone arriving at the show knew its story. For weeks it had been, 'Will he/won't he make it?', 'Will it be ready on time?' I hadn't watched the soap opera that was profiling my efforts, but when pensioners start sending you their winter fuel vouchers, children their pocket money with notes willing you to succeed, and housewives £5 and £10 notes – well, you know something is up! My Mum in Dublin had taken to ringing Justine in a worried state. Obsessed by my own self-created trials, I never realized the effect the process was having on others. What did strike me, however, was my acceptance by most of the other exhibitors. I'd feared that being a telly person, I'd be treated differently. But I think what they had seen, week after week, meant I was one of the gang.

Of course not everyone liked the garden. There was a diversity of opinion. But I always find that interesting. And swept away by Alan, leaving my colourful suburban Eden to do its own thing, and requiring some sense of normality in front of the cameras, I set my mind to other things. Nothing prepared me for the week ahead. By eight o'clock on Tuesday morning the crowds were ten deep.

Laurence Llewelyn-Bowen and his wife Jackie came in. It was a tradition that Laurence and myself would wander around, filming for a few hours on the first day while bagging a bottle of champagne from some stand. Our over-indulgence continued. Sir Terence Conran came to visit. He didn't like our garden. Well, he didn't say that, but I knew that was what he meant when he said children would love it. I found myself strangely low about that.

My family had always arrived from Dublin for the start of previous Chelseas. They were livid when they found out they'd got their dates wrong. The annual trip my mum and sisters made to New York to visit my brother had coincided. However, they were due to arrive on the Friday – the final day. So that left Dad at home alone in the suburbs. He'd been going through a rough time and wasn't in the best of health, but quietly he'd always followed my career, and he'd watched the process as we tried to raise the money to build this garden, glued to the box every Wednesday evening at eight. Through the years he's been amazed at everything that's happened to me, and has squirreled any articles or features away up to his office. With mayhem all around me, I called to make sure he was OK.

'I'm coming over,' he said.

'You can't, you're not up to it.'

I'm coming over,' he said.

I was concerned about his health, but more selfishly I was concerned about me. I was the only one he knew in London. I'd have to look after him during a very busy week. But that was it, he was arriving, flying into Gatwick on Thursday morning. How was this going to work?

On Wednesday evening the final programme went out. People knew the garden was complete. We'd made it. Dad would have been watching.

Thursday morning arrived. At seven o'clock I rang Dad in Dublin. He was up. I tried my hardest.

'Would you not take a cab to the airport?'

'No I won't.... I'm fine.'

He saw taxis as an unnecessary luxury. It didn't occur to him that he could hardly walk, it didn't matter to him that it would take two buses to get to the airport, one from his village to the city and another for the seven miles out to the airport. And that's what he did.

The week was mayhem. If I wasn't recording something I was signing autographs, or being grabbed by members of production to go to the next set up. Occasionally I'd visit my garden, where it was hard to get through the crowds. Visitors knew it intimately – they'd followed the series and they wanted to see it in person. I'd try and creep in around the back, get someone to lower the door of the oval building and hide out for a while. I loved looking at their faces from a distance and listening to what they were saying and hoping for smiles. And most people were smiling.

The design was an experiment. A contrast between the vibrant, imported colours of the lollipops and the soothing green planting.

Occasionally I'd reach for my mobile phone and check on Dad again.

'Where are you now?'

'I'm at the airport'

'OK – can you check your flight number on the screen?'

I admire his stamina and persistence.

'Where are you, Dad, are you OK?'

'I'm on the train.'

'What train? Where's it going?'

'The Gatwick Express.'

'That's brilliant. It will bring you into Victoria. Will you get a cab from there?'

'I will,' he said

'Call me and I'll go outside and meet you at the Bullring Entrance.'

Sure enough, a black cab soon pulled up with Dad sitting in the back. He looked smart in a linen jacket but was obviously tired.

'You OK?'

'Yes,' he said. We went through, taking things slowly, with mayhem all around. Dad was silent.

'Well, did you see the programme last night?'

'I did,' he said.

Each step took an age. We moved on in silence.

'Well, what did you think of the garden?'

Silence. Then: 'I wish you wouldn't do things like that.' I was devastated. We walked on, my mind racing. I figured I'd lead him right through that garden – he would be so knocked out by it.

We ducked under the rope. In front of hundreds of people, I led Dad up the winding futuristic flying saucer garden path, right into the pod. As we approached, I pressed the sensor switch hidden in my pocket. The doors opened automatically. That's it, I thought.

I sat him in one of the circular hanging chairs and said,

'Now you've seen it, what do you think?'

He said, 'I closed my eyes.'

My return to Chelsea as a garden designer had been an interesting but turbulent experience. My ambition had been relatively benign: to step down from the commentary box and create. Because of the television series, however, it had become a story that millions had followed. After years of making television programmes and gaining a gradual acceptance and increased recognition, I found things had changed. I'd gathered some information about the content of the series from friends, families and strangers, but I couldn't have known how much it would affect people. Maybe I had been naïve.

People had connected with what I wanted to do. For some it was a David versus Goliath scenario, me tackling a conservative institution. Cheekily. And they liked it. For others, it was me simply having a go at the British establishment.

There was a fascination with me and a warmth towards me that I was grateful for. People saw I was complex, but also honest I think. And they didn't like to see me being put down, by committee members or by the establishment. After the Bunny episode I received mound of letters and postcards telling me to ignore her.

I didn't see it as others did, however. Like so many other people, I had had an idea. I had built a garden. I didn't know and didn't care what people had said about me on screen. I hadn't set out to make a statement, or to incense. I wanted to create something that was fun, using colour. I wasn't campaigning. It was my own experiment.

And to be honest I got it wrong. The individual elements were great. I loved the planting. There was one little area – a collection of box balls with some soft grasses growing in around them and a white-stemmed *Betula ermanii* rising against this background – that was beautiful. There were other trees, a maple with a peeling bark and an almost mahogany colour underneath, for example, that were fantastic. The building itself, our pod, was fascinating – beautiful, I thought, different, and technologically complex. It had opened and closed on command. The background colour, that deep aubergine, looked good with the different shades of green against it.

The paving was great. It had been beautifully built by a dedicated team of people from Marshalls. It had been a difficult task to create smooth concrete cream flying saucers, but they had done it. The pavers had been set on a wonderful line, describing ever-decreasing circles, snaking up through the planting and hovering over the lawn. But. As the discs were being lowered into position by crane, in an operation of military precision, somebody from Marshalls let slip that they hadn't been sealed. Sean came over to tell me this quietly.

'This is going to be a nightmare,' he said.

And it was. We spent hours on our hands and knees scrubbing this beautiful porous surface, battling to keep it free of marks. In the final two or three days this was to prove debilitating.

The lollipops were great. We had worked long and hard with Tom Gallagher from Elite Metalcraft, who had been in charge of making all the metal features. They had ended up being very expensive, but were exactly what I wanted – bright, shiny and quite tactile. In the strong sunshine, they cast clear shadows. I used them badly. I wanted to create a ribbon of colour wandering through the space on tall and slender black stems. I hadn't succeeded. The garden was fun, accomplished, verdant and experimental. But it wasn't what I wanted. It takes time for things to settle.

But when I strip away all the hysteria, at heart I am interested in making gardens. Though this one created a stir, on reflection I am disappointed. I had all the materials, all the ideas, all the people and all the support to pull off something that, while still being fun, could have and should have been more.

JUDGES

The RHS is a broad church. It has hundreds of thousands of members. Submitting an application to design a garden at the Chelsea Flower Show means abiding by many strict rules and subjecting your display for judgement. There are many judging panels swarming around, both inside the floral marquees and outside. The show garden panels are a mixed bunch of eminent figures, many with gold medals to their name. Some are wonderful, interested in excellence and in promoting the world of horticulture and garden design. Others are judges because it makes them feel good about themselves. It allows them to be important and to play god. So it's not a perfect formula, but I doubt I'd arrive at a better one.

I had stepped into Chelsea again and cemented a certain notoriety: I had the bug again. My circumstances had changed. I was known now, someone to watch. If I could follow through with my idea of creating gardens that were different and show them to people who loved gardens, this would be rewarding. Years earlier I had wanted to destroy suburbia, to experiment. Now I had the ability to design gardens as theatre.

Within my industry, I receive an interesting response and a mixed one, ranging from deep suspicion to adulation. And I have designed and planted gardens of varying quality, from terrible to beautiful. So I have certainly done my bit to lend credence to differing opinions.

The Chelsea judging panel is made up of past medal-winners. It is a necessarily incestuous relationship. Those passing opinion on competitors come from the same world. And the participants, the competitors, aren't the best designers in the country. We are the egos. Chelsea is a select club. And the gardeners who like to achieve and want to progress to the highest echelons in the club are the ones who will conform to the rules, written and unwritten.

The serial offenders are designers who find the attention and the process intoxicating.

Why don't I win gold? I'm not good enough. And I don't believe the myth. I don't have the eye and the skills for perfection and detail that others possess. It's been my luck to gain acceptance into this forum. Over the years I have managed to skim around its perimeters, creating the impression that I'm different, bolshy, and that the normal rules don't apply. The show gardens at Chelsea are elaborate flower arrangements created under artificial conditions. The RHS has sustained a tradition that celebrates achievement, that promotes our craft and a great gardening heritage.

The trouble begins when we perpetuate the myth and believe the hype. We are allowed to borrow these plots of land and encouraged to think cerebrally. We entice vegetation into flower or hold it back. Soil is heated up or cooled down. There are strict rules on structure and height. In the real world, however, nature doesn't decide to flower all at once in the third week of May.

What is perfection in gardens, in any case? Plants grow at different rates, and like ourselves they can be odd-looking. Dew can scorch leaves. Bees and insects, slugs and bugs, work with plants. We strive for something that is not real. Through Chelsea, and all the other shows, we, the 'elite', create and perpetuate fairytales.

Any amount of artificial coaxing is acceptable behind the scenes. Plants are commonly grown in peat-based compost, the best base for them but officially and ecologically a material whose use is frowned on. Many chemicals are used to preserve, protect and enhance.

You are judged against your own brief. You say what you want to achieve and this group will assess its success. Being a judge is a thankless task.

Showing my first garden at Chelsea in 1995, I was probably hoping for a good medal. I was embarrassed with bronze, but it hardly mattered because few noticed me. I had been quite influenced by others arriving to build gardens like me for the first time, who were determined to achieve gold and who were obsessed by the judging system. The following year I got no award, but I gained a career. And by the time I went back to Chelsea in 2004 there was some jealousy among judges who were affronted by me and my prominence. I am judged fairly. I bend the rules and create gardens that I'd like. When I'm told what standard I have achieved, I may be satisfied or embarrassed, or feel stupid, angry or wronged.

My attitude has always been: arrive, build your garden, tidy up, leave and always say thank you very much – nothing else. Pre-judging groups arrive wanting your scheme explained, and they'll make a report and recommendations to you, the main party. I don't engage. Post-judging groups arrive to explain patiently where you fell down. I don't need to know. Some would love to let me have it, to tell me how terrible my attempt has been. There's one judge who makes a point of disagreeing with everything I say at other RHS meetings. I smile to myself through gritted teeth. The decent ones come and chat later and explain what they like.

Nothing is expected of me, so I use this as an invite to enjoy myself and have fun.

When I joined the panel for the RIBA Stirling Prize for Architecture in 2008, I realized how difficult judging can be. The onus of responsibility is heavy. If my career had depended on favourable judgements at the Chelsea Flower Show, I would have had cause for concern. The baggage I carry has an impact. I've never curried favour with the garden design establishment. These people are not my clients. The people who I create gardens for privately or through television are my concern. I developed a certain independence of thought during my college days. Once I had the confidence and the belief in a different approach, I realized that striking out on your own doesn't make you popular, but it does gain you some freedom.

174

Tom Stuart-Smith is a name known to many who visit the show. He's a decent, 'posh' English garden designer. Chelsea is full of gold medallists who pretend to be the real deal. Tom really does produce beautiful gardens – contemporary, well-considered and sharply implemented. At Chelsea Tom is always 'in'. Crowds in tweed jackets and panama hats gather round in clusters to revere his work, sponsored – inevitably – by a champagne house. Groups of garden design students huddle and murmur. He is blue chip. His plants are bred in a crèche, his specimens chauffeured from European nurseries where they collect you by car from the airport and stand you lunch during visitations. His hard materials are carved by laser from granite blocks abandoned by Michelangelo. Tom wishes them into position effortlessly. Occasionally he puts on his judge's hat. Joining the brood, he rambles from one plot to another. With his tall curly head and furrowed brow, he's easily picked out from the crowd. He takes Chelsea seriously, but you get the feeling that it doesn't rule his life. I like him. For a long time I was too shy or possibly felt unworthy to have proper conversations with him. If my critiques on the television were too pointed, he certainly never let on.

On the last day of my last Chelsea, in 2008, I was perched in the second-floor tented restaurant overlooking my garden, whiling away the afternoon. This vantage point gave me a place to hide while surveying all beneath me. I saw Tom and his wife, Sue, standing gazing at the garden. It hadn't done well – a bronze. Tom stood, stared and chatted. I sent a text to Paula, who had been handing out leaflets. My design was a café garden complete with espresso machine. Would Tom like a coffee? He turned round, spied me, smiled and waved me down. The three of us sat in that odd situation, surrounded by an ever-changing crowd who gazed on as we sipped on our coffee. Tom explained his annual ritual. On the Friday morning he comes in as usual, then come lunchtime he says goodbye to that year's garden for the last time. They stroll out of the gate as a couple. The conversation turned to my bronze. It had confused them. So they had decided to come back to Chelsea to stand and gaze. 'It's interesting being a judge', Tom said, 'A kind of mob mentality can form.' A couple of years earlier when he was on the panel, a garden had been picked as best in show. And it wasn't, he said, it was hardly a garden, it was an exhibit. The judges had been influenced by a pre-judging panel led by a particular individual who had insisted it be so. 'It's probably what happened here,' he said, 'but in the opposite way. I think I'll write to *The Garden* about this.' I don't know if he did. But the fact that he said it was decent.

Mind you, this attitude isn't exclusive to Chelsea. Not long ago I was doing a similar job for Moscow City Council, judging some pioneering work by young Russians. Everything was polite and pleasant until one woman arrived, blustered into the room, planted her ample bum on a creaking seat, and proceeded to railroad the slowly deflating panel. It was her way or the high way. I had nothing to lose, so with a smile I argued relevant points. I can't remember the outcome, but I enjoyed the encounter. And then when I am told that Bunny Guinness has judged some of my gardens, ah well now, as my father-in-law would say, ah well now.

THE GARDEN DESIGN COMMUNITY

For the garden design industry I seemed to have exploded upon the scene. I'd been visible at a couple of Chelseas, but within a relatively short space of time I was doing programmes for all the major broadcasters. And understandably, many people didn't know what to make of me. Some of them had been toiling away for years, trying to achieve recognition, producing endless show gardens, writing articles and joining associations. It's probably the same in other disciplines, but garden designers like to build a myth about themselves. And so you can join clubs and societies, read or write in magazines and journals. Too often I have felt these were forums for hot air, for people talking to themselves about themselves. I am not a joiner. The last club I was in was the cub scouts. I am a member of a dinner club, but that doesn't really count as it's only Guinness, food and a late night once a month.

The best way to achieve prominence, if that's what you want, is to do extraordinary work quietly. Simple as that. You build a solid foundation. Too many get addicted to the idea that they are very clever, with little to back it up. And then they spend the rest of their careers desperately hanging on to a fading notoriety.

So I arrived over from Ireland and I got a lot of the gigs. I have a different accent, so I couldn't be placed class-wise. I was making gardens that are different and gaining an audience. It was time to be held to account.

I was invited to give the keynote address to the Society of Garden Designers. The invitation came logically through my agent, John Noel. I said yes. I felt honoured. I don't claim great things for my work, but it's nice to be given the chance to explain my adventures. Sometimes it's a roller-coaster ride but I find the possibilities of gardens fascinating, and I love to share my enthusiasm.

With a month to go, they forwarded me the latest issue of their journal. The editorial read: 'Diarmuid Gavin has agreed to appear for the princely sum of £250... what's he going to be like justifying himself in front of his fellow professionals?', and so it went on. I rang John and said, "I really don't want to do this, I can't be bothered.' John doesn't deal with garden designers in general. Sorting out Russell Brand's scrap with Jonathan Ross, possibly; supporting Davina through difficult times, definitely; plucking Jade from obscurity, yes; well let's just say it is a different life that he has. He rang them. 'Diarmuid, just go and do it. They just don't know how to deal with your world. Yes, they are being rude. Go, give your talk – just get on with it.' I did.

The venue was Olympia and there was a large audience. One of the other speakers wouldn't look at me. Through the day, as speakers were being announced, whoever was in charge started sniping again. 'Oh yes, of course the big event later to come, can Diarmuid Gavin prove that he is this, that or the other?' I sat there, ever more embarrassed: rather than making me feel comfortable or welcome, there was a constant attitude of, 'Who do you think you are?'

My time arrived. I don't remember much about it. I probably spoke for forty or fifty minutes. It went well – the audience were with me. I explained my gardens, why I did them, who I was and what I wanted to achieve, I wondered why it was that fashion designers and indeed architects were expected to be different, and yet garden designers weren't. I talked about this new motor car I was driving. I couldn't remember what it was, but it was black, low, sleek and automatic. It was precise and responded to the engineering of the day, the style of the day and the desires of its client.

'What is it?' someone cried.

I hadn't a clue. Someone ran outside to check. It was a black Jaguar XKR convertible. Laughter. On that note the session ended.

Julie Toll, a great Chelsea trooper whose *London Evening Standard* garden I had admired on my first trip to the show, collected feedback forms. She told me I'd had the best response of the day. The committee invited me to dinner. I thought no, let's leave this elegantly. I'll go to the drinks reception and say thank you. I was happy, I walked into the reception and there were handshakes, smiles all round. The first person to approach was a guy called Ryan, the head of the society's sister operation in Ireland. His words were, 'Great to see you, Diarmuid. You know, personally I think you're great, but there's very bad feeling about you at home.' This was news to me. His little mate joined in. I clasped a glass of warming white wine as I listened to an explanation of why I was apparently so disliked, smiled and as soon as I could said my goodbyes.

I would next hear from this character when he thought I was producing a garden at a festival where he'd also be exhibiting. An email out of the blue said he'd look forward to locking horns with me. Maybe people make themselves feel important by trying to cut you down to size. It's best to keep away and not give them the opportunity.

I love meeting friends at the show, people you wouldn't otherwise see. In the last day or two, when you are down on your hands and knees possibly doing a final planting, there will be a booming American voice, carrying a witticism that would make Dorothy Parker jealous – Gordon Taylor! And somewhere in the background will be the more refined Guy Cooper. A pair of gardening Miss Marples.

'Well, you've done it this year,' Gordon will bellow, flinging out his arms in an exaggerated manner. Then he'll dart a finger at a piece of furniture, 'But I'm not sure about that thing.'

And then Guy: 'Yes, I was wondering about that myself.'

'Well, how are you?'

The conversation continues. Exploits are traded. I give them a nugget; they come back with a bigger one. Gordon and Guy are always upping the ante by working for some industrialist or other. It's a dance we have of the impressive. Lovely to see them.

And then the perky Jane Owen, with her delightful eyes that scan the view and instantly appraise the triumphs or failures. She will probably have a notebook; she writes wonderfully for the *Financial Times*. I think she is proper posh and dines with the dons in Oxford. She brought me to her club once, where a Dame Somebody-Important gave an interesting talk on family law in the middle of Chelsea week. Jane had forgotten why she had invited me and was mystified as to why I accepted.

I always like seeing Monty Don. The first time I met him was during my second Chelsea. I knew him from the telly. He was the *This Morning* gardener, trading tips with Richard and Judy. I inherited his mantle. Other peers I greatly admire include James Alexander Sinclair, the English rose Rachel de Thame, James Wong and Matthew Wilson – a wonderful promoter of the art of gardening. I've had my petty jealousies, disliking some newer presenters maybe because I felt threatened. But overall gardening television is stuffed with crashing bores. And the audience doesn't care. Ratings have plummeted. The contemporary way is to play a role and not let your personality good or bad be seen. It's banal.

Our first Chelsea pond had been made by taping two bits of polythene together and was looking a little messy. A contractor working down the avenue, Peter Farrell, gave me a bucket of duckweed. These tiny specks of green floated over the water surface, hid the joins and completed the scene perfectly. So seeing Peter in those early years would make both of us smile with memories.

Arabella Lennox-Boyd, also in my first year, insisted to the RHS that the white plastic marquees behind my garden be covered by green netting. She was adamant that I would have all the help I could get. She is always ready with a jolly smile.

And then there's Koji, the famous Japanese garden designer who was the expert on next door's garden that same year. We have a huge welcome for each other and then the language barrier kicks in. I never have a clue what he is on about, but it is always good to see him.

There is a Chelsea Pensioner who spends time in our garden every year we are there. Originally from Ireland, he trades stories of war and stories of London. He is delighted when we are around, because stepping in the display we've created means he's one step closer to home.

And there are those that I started out at Chelsea with. Fiona Lawrenson premiered at Chelsea at the same time as me. She retired from showing gardens but jumped to the position of judge, peering over her secretarial spectacles, tall and beautiful.

Jeff Morey travels every year from Florida, where he produces magazines for the garden centre industry in the States. He makes a point of keeping up with new trends that he can report back to his readers. What's happening in London makes a big splash worldwide. Early in the week, Jeff will always leave a message on my mobile. We make a point of meeting up, having lunch or going for a pint.

Warren Lange is a garden designer and television presenter from South Africa. He'll often be around with the cameras for his programme *Top Billing,* and will as usual extend an invite for me to visit that wonderful gardening country. Soon our family will visit his and go on safari in Grahamstown, South Africa. And there's Natasha Hopkins, who makes the trip from New York to work with the crew who record the official Chelsea video; it's always great to see her face, and she's even hosted a dinner party for me in her building overlooking the Hudson River. Richard Wallace, a television director who works with the same production company based in Portsmouth, will definitely make the trip to London. We've had lots of adventures over the years and Chelsea is our place for catching up.

FRIENDS BY DESIGN

I was born on 10th May 1964 in Honeypot Lane Hospital, Middlesex. The registrar for my birth was the wonderfully named Pete Townsend. The following day, ten miles away, a young designer called Terence Conran opened his first Habitat store. Having worked at the Festival of Britain in 1951, his ethos was that good, simple design can change your life.

Terence was excellent at spreading his message, so even in Ireland I was aware of his influence. His portfolio was soon huge, running past Habitat to British Home Stores, Next, a publishing house, and then a design museum. His restaurants, carefully chosen, were always an immediate hit. Terence sold the ideas of good food, fine wine and great utensils, as well as stylish furnishings throughout the home and workplace.

I was eighteen and travelling solo to London. When I told Mum where I was going, she immediately had a request. She gave me £15, and asked me to go to Habitat on Tottenham Court Road and purchase a chopping board she had seen in a magazine.

It was my first port of call. Her money would disappear if I didn't get this quest out of the way straight off. That block of wood was large and heavy. I put it in my haversack and it travelled with me for ten days. I left London from Paddington, taking the train to Holyhead and the slow crossing to Dublin. I handed over the purchase. 'That's not the one I wanted, that's much too big!' When I got married it was a gift from her to us. It sits now on the work surface of our kitchen in County Wicklow. Good to look at, great for chopping, and even better for making me smile.

By the time I started to work in London on a regular basis, Terence was a Sir. He was working on a hotel development in Dublin. He'd had connections with Ireland in the past, promoting the work of a government initiative about craft in County Kilkenny. I'd been asked to design gardens for the roof of his development, and I worked with his team. Proper contact came at the Chelsea Flower Show. He'd done a garden in association with another designer. I was doing the commentary and interviewed him. Terence and Lady Conran couldn't have been nicer. A friendship began.

I'd begun writing gardening books, and had signed a new contract for three with Dorling Kindersley. 'Terence would love you to do a book with us,' said Lorraine Dickey, boss at Conran Octopus. I was hugely flattered but I couldn't, not for years at least. 'Have lunch with us anyway' she said. We met at a restaurant on the Embankment. I was half an hour late. We chatted about gardening, life, Ireland. Terence was quite picky about his cheese plate. There were grapes on it:

'I can't abide it when they do that.' His hand shot up as he summoned a waiter. 'Could you take these things off my plate?'

I said, 'Terence, you can't do that – it's rude!'

Lorraine turned to me: 'You can if you own the restaurant.'

As soon as I was out of contract I had my first production meeting with Lorraine. 'Terence has done one gardening book before, many years ago, a large format with Dan Pearson. How would you feel about joining him for the next one?' I was astonished. One of the most prominent designers worldwide would put his name next to mine on a heavy tome. His previous collaboration with Dan had become a classic. And I'd get to bring my thoughts and ideas to the next one. In a life full of recent adventures, this was a new high.

A big book means a long process. There was a surprisingly small team. Once we had sat down and agreed the basic principles, the form of the book and the division of labour, we set to work. Even with only half the text to write, because of its size this meant lots of words. The title was *Outdoors*, and the book was to be a look at contemporary work in gardens around the world. Garden books don't often cross borders, owing to different climatic zones, so in our case studies – the parts of the book where we would illustrate principles of design through examining individual schemes in detail – we'd make sure that northern and southern Europe were covered as well as Scandinavia, Asia, Africa and America. A lot of time went into picture research. Tens of thousands of images were gathered. I would make regular trips to the publishers in Canary Wharf and look at endless images of gardens. The book would be published in ten different languages worldwide so we needed to reflect the freshest and most vibrant work being done.

Through Terence I felt welcomed into the heart of the design establishment. Acceptance isn't something I pursue, and I wondered why Terence would be bothered with me. I think he enjoys the same fun that I do. He saw that reflected in the gardens I made. I pretend not to be too impressed by him or his life, but I am in awe – of being treated as an equal, of being listened to, of having considered conversations about what's happening, of sitting so to speak at the feet of a giant.

Our lodgings for our second Chelsea visit were on Elizabeth Street. It's a long road, with the Victoria end inhabited by cheaper hotels and guesthouses, but it eventually morphs into an exquisite Chelsea shopping street. It was on this part of the road that Sue, the Canadian lady who had typed our first Chelsea application letter, lived.

Across the road from her is Philip Treacy's shop. He is a milliner from Galway, and the displays in his window change regularly. Wandering past on my way to or from the showground, I'd stop and spend five, ten minutes at a time with my nose pressed against the cold glass pane, examining his work. I've no interest in hats, but these creations awoke me to the world of possibilities opened up by design.

Genius is a term bandied around far too loosely. But what Philip creates can't be described as anything else. Using feathers, discs, butterflies and fabric, he creates drama and excitement. Crossing boundaries and challenging convention, the work is extravagant and reaches places I could never dream of. If even just once I could make a garden that was the equivalent of a Treacy hat I would be happy; if I could construct something of such exquisite quality and detail, a garden that was a story in itself, that would be plenty for me. It's the continual striving, however, that makes designing such fun.

There are others: Jim Denevan, the 'Sand Man', who walks the California beaches with a rake, brush and stick, creating huge and magnificent geometric patterns that last for just moments before the tide comes in. Or Zaha Hadid, who pushes the boundaries of architecture. Or another Irish fashion person, Orla Kiely, whose assured work with repeated pattern and subtle colour is satisfyingly smart. There are lessons for me in so many places, often outside the garden. Window shopping, flicking through books, visiting exhibitions, hitting on an idea and being inspired by things outside the world of gardens is wonderful.

CHELSEA NO. 4, 2005:
THE HANOVER QUAY LAVENDER GARDEN

Midsummer, anticipating the following year's Chelsea, is a time for pacing the room. For me the questions are generally the same. What would I love to show? Am I obsessed by any particular style? Is there something I would love to exhibit? Are there people I would love to work with? A time of thousands of ideas and a prison of none. Decisions need to be made. Forms need to be filled in. An illustrator needs to be commissioned. So I have to imagine looking at and walking through a garden that doesn't yet exist.

I have books of inspiration – torn newspaper clippings filled with images or phrases, pictures of plants and expanses of water – that spark ideas. I have hundreds of drawings and sketches of gardens that were built and some that never were. Occasionally the solution is quick; sometimes it is agonizingly slow.

In the summer of 2004 I was back in Dublin. From the balcony of our flat in Finglas I gazed at the communal open space four storeys below. On it were a few railway sleeper planters and lots of gravel. In the sales brochures there had been pictures of a lovely garden on the site. The block was in a pleasant location on the banks of the River Tolka. In spring I'd watch as across the water a large horse chestnut tree lifted its lobed leaves, like an umbrella being raised, and soon beautiful cones of creamy flowers appeared. What a shame that the gravel didn't allow any space for recreation. I started to think: what would I like to see there? An idea for Chelsea the following May emerged, an undulating garden for a communal space, one that could suit a block of flats or offices, something that would have intrigue in its topography, individual areas for people to sit alone or in groups, and that could be easily maintained.

I did some sketches: ten metres by twenty-three, a long side wall and another at the back, roughly two metres in height. Could I create a simple garden at Chelsea using only two plant species, spherical clipped box and grasses? From a height of two metres at the back, the garden would dip down like a gentle roller coaster and softly rise, possibly into a hump, before ending at the front, slightly elevated. Four concrete spheres, outdoor rooms, would settle among the planting.

The box, *Buxus sempervirens*, would be set in a diamond pattern, and grasses would inhabit the rest of the space, just one species, probably *Miscanthus sinensis*. I loved the combination of the two textures. Linking the pods and allowing for access through the site I planned a catwalk of pink polished concrete, slightly elevated and interconnected. This would be laid on metal legs. It would appear to hover, creating a shadow line underneath. Crisp. The back mound, with one of the spheres embedded in it, would form the entrance, possibly from an underground car park.

Illustrator David Thomas was a new recruit to the studio. I sat with him and planned the features. He began to draw. Walls would be clad in highly polished black granite. We went outside, into the courtyard. We estimated lengths and heights and proportions. Back upstairs, David sketched. We gathered around. Everybody liked it.

The following morning David shouted across the long desk:

'Do you want me to colour in the lavender?'

'Lavender?' I said, 'It's not lavender, it's miscanthus!'

'Oh,' he said, 'I thought it was lavender and box.'

What a wonderful idea. Two of my favourite plants. What could be wrong with lavender? I could imagine the scent as I walked out on to Portobello Road and around the corner to the bookshop in Blenheim Crescent where I'd seen a picture: a field of lavender with a single olive tree The lavender sloped, planted in rows for ease of harvesting.

I burst back into the office.

'This is brilliant! I love it!'

David reached for colour. We were months late. Where would

we get lavender? It flowers in midsummer, not late spring. I love English lavender for its soft mound-like shape, for its gentle, small silvery-green leaves, for its flower spikes that shoot up in their dozens, for its aroma and for its colour. I didn't mind whether it flowered or not.

Hester spent weeks on the phone, contacting every lavender nursery in Ireland, Britain and the Continent. We needed them to be of a certain size, and we decided to aim for flowers.

The RHS accepted the design, but they wanted more species. They wanted more colour and they wanted vegetables. I should have just stuck to the original plan. The garden was to be simple, somewhat quirky in terms of its land shaping. Anyway, we got on with it.

Months passed. Marshalls had agreed again to provide the pathway: it was beautifully created, a problem taken care of. Finding someone to build the concrete spheres was more difficult. We hit on a company called Shotcrete. The lavender was the problem.

We found two growers, one in France, the other in Spain. They both had English lavender, which they were sure they could encourage into flower. Hester took control and talked to the growers on a weekly basis. Digital images would come in from both countries, and the whole studio willed them on.

In January I was back in Dublin in a radio studio, being interviewed for RTE, the national station, by Marian Finucane, one of Ireland's best broadcasters, a national treasure. Marian has an inquisitive mind and a common-sense approach. I was talking about the previous year's Chelsea and our plans for the next one.

I went for a coffee with the producer, Claire Prior, and told her about an idea I had. I was going back to Chelsea, and every year that I had taken part I had been inundated with requests from people who wanted to come and work for a day or for a few days, people who felt their lives would be enhanced by this experience. We'd had a band of such merry volunteers the previous year, most gardens do. So how about making this a feature of the show, I asked? How about sending out an invitation for people to apply to come and work in the garden that I would be making?

It was an *X Factor* for gardeners. Listeners were asked to write in with their pitch. And they did in their thousands, one using gold ink to pen an ode on the plate of a spade. We arranged a get-together in the Botanic Gardens in Dublin, where various colleagues talked about their love for gardens. We set little tasks. George Dunnington, the cloth-capped gardener whom I had met at Harlow Carr in Yorkshire, flew over for the day, not wearing his blue overalls for a change. Jackie Llewelyn-Bowen, Laurence's missus, came to tell us about her experience of gardening. I gave a lecture, Claire recorded everything and we divided people into small groups and asked them to design their own show garden. Each group had to agree on one design to put forward for presentation. We watched and looked and listened. Lots of smiles, eager faces, men, women, boys and girls, from seventeen to seventy, all with a dream of coming to Chelsea.

At the end of the event we started the selection process. There were definite favourites. We picked a shortlist, a group of volunteers who would help over a few days to create a garden for children with special needs. From this we would make our final selection of volunteers.

I drew up some plans, and Barry Cotter, a classmate of mine, organized equipment, materials, plants and skips. Over the period of a few days, those selected came from all over the island and worked individually or in teams. A garden for little people was created. There were lawns and borders, a pavilion to give shelter and wendy houses, play equipment and lots of different textures. Water spouted and the sun shone.

On the Monday the *Marian Finucane Show* was broadcast live from the garden. It was fantastic introducing children, including Sophie, a special friend of ours, to a safe and delightful outdoor space.

I've no head for names, but soon I had to sit down with Claire again and make a final selection for the fifteen people to travel and work with us. Photographs had been taken. Some volunteers had already found fulfilment in creating this garden. Others had arrived in groups, which made it difficult to take one and leave two. Claire was a skilled editor, and soon began the task of ringing the successful applicants. Many had exchanged email and mobile numbers, so messages were flying across the country and soon people had an idea of who they'd be working with. There would be three groups of five. As one group departed after five days' work, another would arrive. And then, when the garden was built, they would all be reunited to look over the new landscape that we had created.

We had employed a team of contractors to oversee the build. We had a sponsor, a firm called Park Developments. The garden would be known as the Hanover Quay Garden, as after Chelsea it would spring to life in a new development on the quays of the Liffey in Dublin city centre.

I rarely have the freedom to be on site. I try to ensure that we have a good team, a budget and that people know what they are at. And then I'm off away somewhere to record some telly, build another garden, or maybe write a book. I can be missing for a few days. The excitement is all about what is happening on site. I obsess about every detail. I don't sleep. I annoy the project manager by phone, looking for news. At day's end I'll arrive as quietly as possible and amid the chaos try to catch the eye of whoever is in charge of our plot and ask for the lowdown.

Chelsea has to be approached like a military operation. You need the proper equipment for the job, and deliveries have to be scheduled at appropriate intervals so that nobody is standing around. The place is rife with gossip and friendship. People stop by for a chat. It's very noisy, a din of continual traffic, reversing trucks, cranes lifting, cement mixers mixing and angle grinders grinding. The weather can be tricky. From cold and damp to hot and sunny, you can't plan. So your site can be parched or sodden, with puddles of mud.

The first morning is always the same: a stretch of ground cleared of sod running up to the avenue of London plane trees, and behind you the marquees and pavilions, already erected. There's one main entrance for trucks and deliveries, the Bull Ring Gate at the Embankment. And the gate itself is relatively narrow. As drivers arrive they join the queue. With luck they will have a contact number for their project manager. They ring, and someone is sent out to see they are OK. How long it is before we can expect them to be unloading on to the green verge to the front of our plot? Everybody wears high visibility vests and often hard hats. Machines trundle past you, going forward or backwards, and cranes swing huge trees and blocks of marble and sculptures above your head.

A health and safety briefing on each site is mandatory, and inspectors are always on the look-out for anyone deviating from agreed practice. I hate the hi-vis jackets, the fluorescent colour reflecting in your eyes. It doesn't help the planting process.

The first job is the boundary wall. Designers and contractors who share a boundary will have contacted each other. There are rules on how high structures can be within a garden. The aim is to try and cleverly create a plot that's a unit, a garden that doesn't impose on its neighbour. The height of the wall and what pops up above it, either planting or trellis, can be an issue. This year I was lucky: my neighbour was the delightful Sir Terence.

The next stages are levels and foundations. Our garden would undulate. I enjoy playing with levels. Few landscapes are naturally flat, yet we spend so much time with shovels and rakes creating even surfaces. Incidentally, the soil at Chelsea is the worst in London, dug up, built on, compacted and reseeded on an annual basis. At the very back of the garden there was to be a subterranean room. I had the idea of bringing in an old shipping container to create the bulk, and we piled soil against it and on top of it.

Next we created foundations for the raised path and the plinths that our concrete pods would rest on. Our first five volunteers were digging, shovelling and tidying under George's watchful eye.

Later that year, three of them – Nicki Matthews, Jackie Ball and Valerie Duff – would get together with George to write a book about their adventure, *Off to Chelsea with Diarmuid*. It's interesting to see the experience through other's eyes. They tell the story of the whole group, all fifteen of them, of their lives at home, highs and lows, and why as individuals they wanted the adventure of coming to London to help me. Their experience echoes so many days and nights that I've had: arriving in London, nervous but excited, and clean; checking into a hotel; getting to know new colleagues, and on that first morning wandering in with back stage passes to the greatest gardening show on earth; apprehensive about what they may be asked to do; enjoying being an insider, walking around from garden to garden and seeing what others are up to; the excitement of the exhibits being mounted in the pavilions; stopping, talking, chatting, making friends, shovelling and sweeping, shifting plants to one place and then back again; and every evening returning to the hotel wearing heavy boots caked in muck, and a quick drink at the bar because you are too exhausted to go out. When eventually you do there is a little pile of Chelsea soil under the table. You might be too tired to eat. Adrenalin provides your energy. Early the next morning you wait to be told what to do. At eleven you go for coffee. Lunch is from a burger stall.

The three groups would have different jobs. The first would work on the foundations of the garden, maybe seeing some of the big features, the pods, being craned in, contouring the soil, getting that sweep right from high at the back, dipping in the centre and rising slightly at the end. The second would welcome the plants and settle them in. The third would finish the garden. The last week has the longest days, as you try to get everything as good as it can be.

The lavender arrived. I was there for the unloading. The back doors of the delivery truck opened. We had debated where we would order the hundreds of plants from. Spain had won. The grower had insisted they would be ready in time. He was positive. He would deliver them himself. If they weren't in flower he would run around the grounds of the Chelsea Flower Show…naked.

I stepped into the back of the truck and lifted a plant. They were wonderful – big and rotund like everything else in the garden. The foliage was delicious, almost silver and so crisp. The scent from the truck was overpowering. They had brilliant flower spikes shooting out at all angles, erect stems, sturdy with elongated buds. Elongated green buds. No flowers. All eyes were on me as I stepped out of the heaving lorry. I was happy. They would look beautiful with or without flowers.

Soon trolleys and trays of lavender were everywhere. The box balls had gone in. We had laid out lines of string and let them hang gracefully like washing lines over the site. Then we criss-crossed these with other lines, and placed a box ball at each intersection. Our pods were in position, nestled into the soil. The lavender would gently slope from the front, the flower heads rearing like the flower spikes of ornamental grasses as they swept around the entrance to create a soft vista.

The polished black wall to the side reflected everything. The circular pathway had evolved into concentric C shapes, one sliding underneath the other, almost the Coco Chanel logo. It looked beautiful. The extra planting, the colour anemones, achillea, dicentra, delphinium, geranium, digitalis looked fine knitted into the lavender, garlanding one or two pods. And the vegetables, grown by Medwyn Williams of Wales, were superb. Our extended team had worked hard.

I create my comfort zone on site. I'm nervous. I need to work with a few people who I know, maybe so I can ask the same question fifty times: 'What do you think? Will it be all right? Do you like it?'

To others I can appear quite removed. I do take every group who arrive for coffee, I roll out whatever scraps of paper have survived continual inspection at the garden and explain where we are at and what we are trying to achieve. We go to the pub once a week, an hour before closing. Exhausted, hungry, but satisfied. Stories from the site, tired laughter, all of us on the one journey, even if I'm at a slight distance from the rest of the group. I never remember anyone's name, and at times feel a twinge of jealousy for their camaraderie.

By Monday morning the garden was finished. Marian Finucane arrived from Dublin and all the fifteen looked clean in fresh clothes. Some, the last group, the ones who had worked late into the evening before, were proud as punch. Others who had been there the first week wandered through, inspecting the finished product. There was a party atmosphere. There was an outside broadcast van, and Marian went from person to person to hear stories of the week. She talked to George. He was delighted. They'd all worked wonders for him. Alan Titchmarsh came along to add to his comments, and my old sparring partner Laurence Llewelyn-Bowen joined in.

The judges arrived. The moment was captured beautifully on the airwaves. We were asked to leave the plot. Later the pop band British Sea Power came and played a small concert. I sat with Annette Dalton, a friend from County Kerry who works at Kew, on a pink pathway buried in a sea of lavender. Alan came back again, this time with Terry Wogan. The three of us had fun. Another Chelsea garden completed.

During the show I had another agenda. The office was getting busy. Our work was sought after around the world, and I needed more designers. Finding somebody experienced and interesting was proving difficult. I had asked everybody to keep their ears open. Hester reported some interesting news. She had talked to Steve Reilly, who was the right-hand man of Andy Sturgeon, another Chelsea designer.

Originally from County Wicklow, Steve now lived in Brighton. He had indicated that he might like to look at opportunities abroad, maybe Australia. Hester said, 'Would that mean you are looking to move on?' Steve replied that he might be. A meeting was set up and Steve joined our studio at the end of the summer.

People move around in the small circle of garden design all the time. I was told that Andy wasn't happy. I should have informed him that Steve was coming. Word was out that I was poaching people. My priority was my studio and the gardens we were creating, not anybody else's. The design world is full of spats: who's leaving who to go where?

In his first week, Steve caught sight of drawings that David and I were labouring over. I'd been developing a garden for clients in County Kilkenny. The design had its origins in an earlier *Home Front* project. He felt it looked very similar to what his former boss was planning to exhibit at Chelsea.

Andy built the garden at Chelsea. I wasn't happy and I said so. He wasn't happy about what I said, and said so. Solicitors' letters were exchanged. Proceedings were issued. Eventually we both settled and that was that.

After a family Christmas in Dublin, I arrived in London to open the studio. Among the post was an anonymous card. On the front was a photograph of a garden similar to the one Andy created at Chelsea, with Jesus, Mary and Joseph superimposed on top of it, shepherds with sheep in the foreground. It made me feel sick.

CHELSEA NO. 5, 2007:
THE WESTLAND GARDEN:

My next Chelsea presented me with a different kind of problem. My friend Edward Conroy rang. He is the managing director of Westland Horticulture, a successful company in Northern Ireland that he has helped to build from scratch. Everybody likes Edward. He has energy, a curly head and a twinkle in his eye. We'd crossed paths at social events and conferences for years. He wanted me to do a campaign for his compost. I don't add peat to gardens, but most plants I buy are grown in it. I'm very aware of environmental concerns, about the depletion of our boglands, the habitat for so much wildlife. He'd ask me if *I* would do a TV ad.

'You know I can't, Edward. I can't promote the use of peat.'

We'd sip our stout.

'We should be working together,' he'd say.

The following year, another conference, the same thing. And then one day he rings me up.

'Diarmuid, will you do a television commercial for me?'

I said, 'You know I won't.'

'I've come up with a solution. We've developed a compost, Westplus, much reduced in peat. We want to pioneer this for the mass market, it's an exciting innovation for us. You have been part of it. What do you think?'

I laughed. I was pleased that I had played a minor role in the development of this more environmentally aware product.

'OK,' I said, 'You're on.'

As soon as I dozed off that night I woke up again with a start. The reason I didn't do ads for gardening products was that I wasn't permitted to while I worked for the BBC. What had I done? I kept quiet about this for a while. How was I going to get out of this mess?

We shot the ad on a snowy day, in February I think, on the outskirts of Belfast, using someone's suburban back garden as a set. The trickery and drama of these shoots always fascinates me. Huge lights created a summer scene. From the back of a truck big shrubs appeared in full bloom, creating an instant border. In between takes I groaned to myself. How much trouble was I going to be in? I hadn't long to wait to find out.

A gardening magazine got wind of the campaign. They rang the BBC, who rang John, my agent. I was called to his office. Chelsea was a couple of months away. Once again I was due to be in the commentary box with Alan, and yet in March I was to have a series of ads on commercial stations promoting Westplus. John rang Edward. Westland had already spent money on booking TV time.

Eventually Edward rang me. 'Listen it's probably best you don't tell anyone about this conversation. I've been talking to John and he's been talking to the BBC. You're in a bit of bother. I've spent the money, I've booked the slots but I don't want you getting in trouble. If you want to pull this thing, we'll do that. I'll get you back again.'

This was pure decency on his part – typical of Edward. But after creating the mess I knew my answer: 'Edward, let's go ahead. I know what you've put into this.'

I'd been in that elevated position at the Flower Show for years. I would sell my granny for any opportunity to work with Alan. But what we were doing hadn't moved on in years. It wasn't my place to move it on. I was lazily coasting, being more errant than usual, grabbing Charlie Dimmock, running out the front gates down to a nearby pub. The attention at Chelsea was overwhelming. Great for the ego but maybe not so good for the soul. For one week you felt like a rock star.

The ad was broadcast. Edward called me. 'Could I sponsor a garden for you at Chelsea next year?'

Help had never arrived so easily. The Westland Garden, which would focus on promoting Westplus, this new reduced peat compost, just needed to be beautiful. So again the question: what would I do?

I have a good sense of design and of what I would like to achieve. But sometimes I get obsessed by ideas that are just wrong, tacky or plain silly. I'll hit on something, obsess about it, think of little else for days, and then wake up and wonder what I'm at. I love to have fun and create gardens that make people smile. I appreciate many different styles, from Art Deco to Disney, from wildly flamboyant to relatively restrained. Mostly, however, I like to make gardens that are practical and that can be used, dressed up with some pizzazz.

I stared at everything and lost sleep again. Someone new to the office had printed out images of our work that inspired them and stuck them on the walls. I found myself staring at one drawing. Val McDonald of Esher in Surrey had commissioned the design for her home, but it had never been built. She and her husband David wanted a garden with two studios in it – a his and a hers – to tuck into a site under a tree. They were so full of life, every encounter with them was exciting. Val could be tempestuous. One day before I arrived she had thrown an axe at David, which had bounced off his car. I assumed she intended to miss. I enjoyed their company enormously, and the plans that had evolved for their garden were exciting and vibrant. Two studios with billowing wooden roofs criss-crossed each other. The planting was green and textural – with many ornamental grasses and sword-like leaves – and the paving took the form of giant flowers, graphic designs inspired by flower power and the work of Roberto Burle Marx.

'Well, I did ask for something different', exclaimed Val as she leafed through my book of ideas. The garden was never built. David sensibly wanted to make sure the house was restored first. And now, a year later, the drawing stared down at me. I'd always loved the scheme. Wouldn't it be fun to see it emerge, not in Surrey, but at Chelsea?

I began to sketch out plans. The billowing roofs of the structure had to be toned down for the smaller space. Inspired by the ramps of a skate park, they seemed slightly restricted when squashed into a smaller plot. As for the planting, well, I had a good idea about what I wanted – grasses, birch trees, one wonderful specimen tree, and the whole thing to be reflected in a pond. Steve Reilly started to work on this element. We travelled to Belgium in midwinter and I picked out a magnificent Japanese maple, maybe thirty years old, for £25,000 – a huge gamble, especially since we hadn't seen it in leaf. We ordered upright birch trees, which incidentally now form green curtains winding their way across the front of our house in the hills of Wicklow.

I had never been able to figure what the paving should be made of, but a holiday in a Portuguese coastal town gave me the answer. Portuguese limestone cobbles in black and white could create graphic shapes, giant daisies, their centres filled with evergreen shrubs. I loved the notion. We worked hard on producing the drawings. Something wasn't right, though. The curved roofs seemed far too restricted.

In December we brought the office to County Kerry for a few days. We stayed in a wonderful hotel, the Aghadoe Heights, with a remarkable view of the lakes. In the conference room we had a couple of sessions examining work we were doing. We spent late nights in the bar. During the day we went to the beach. It was wild and windy. We mapped out the Chelsea garden in the sand with bamboo canes and string. It was hard battling against the driving elements. And while I was pleased with the different proportions of the area, something still niggled.

I set about the plan again. What if the roofs were to go the opposite way, if I were to curve them downwards, creating an almost train-carriage-like effect – could that work? The new pavilion was much more restrained and maybe more elegant. It had two studios, a wraparound wooden roof and glazed walls, spaces to be alone in or together while painting or writing.

Steve was putting so much into the planting scheme that it was only fair that the entry be submitted to Chelsea under both our names. Edward was delighted with the design, and so early that May I found myself in SW1 again. Shomera, an Irish company who have pioneered the concept of the garden room, became our partners. Back home, they built the magnificent cruciform studio. During construction, and before I had seen it, photographs of it were revealed to me in mid-interview on *The Late Late Show*.

Five men came to London from Portugal to lay the daisy-patterned paving of white and black limestone. They had pre-cast the petals in Lisbon. The rest were laid out according to plans produced by our studio. We chose box specimens to form the centre of the petals, so that our paving would grow from being a two-dimensional ground surface to three-dimensional flowers, half paving, half plants. The magnificent maple we had chosen in midwinter without a leaf arrived lying sideways on the back of a truck. It was beautiful, absolutely perfect for what we required.

The rest of the planting concentrated on texture, with silver astelias, carex and grasses, bursts of allium, lots of echiums, which had inspired me with their profusion of flower on a visit during our winter to New Zealand, and big grey-leaved hostas. A pond that edged right up to the glazed side of the pavilion was planted with lilies and beautiful iris. Its murky disturbed water was soon disguised by a type of black ink that can be introduced to create a dark mirror-finish surface. Behind the pavilion, the ribbon of silver birch created a sylvan feel.

As the date for the opening of the garden was fast approaching, I was asked by Sky News to do an interview in a village near Milton Keynes. The subject was environmental awareness. The channel was dedicating a week to green topics. I discovered on this farm a set of wooden loungers made from recycled pallets. We secured these as a loan for the garden, where they were soon joined by acrylic bubble chairs hanging from an outdoor section of our structure.

The show would open to the press on the Monday as usual. On the Saturday evening Justine insisted I take a night off. We planned to go into Chinatown for a meal, a belated birthday treat. Chris, a young student from Nottingham University who worked and lodged with us, came with us. On the way I drove by Pimlico. I wanted one last look along the row of antique shops, in case there was anything that I could spot through the windows that would add the finishing touch, that last flourish for our garden. Two steel-and-wire chairs in the shape of daisies, beautifully made, were prominently floodlit. They were French 1930s I thought, about £6,000, and I had to have them.

I couldn't get those chairs out of my head. All night they stayed in my mind. I was struck by their delicacy, by the imagination behind them, and by how beautifully they had been made. They appealed to my love of craft-based design. I tried to imagine the garden they had been part of. On Monday I went down early, bringing Steve with me. We peered through the window. 'You're right,' he said, 'we have to get them.' The budget was spent. I sat a few doors away in a cafe as Steve went to enquire. They were French, probably 1940s and certainly £5,800. Steve negotiated a better price and they were ours. I promised to put them on eBay after the show.

We travelled to Val's house and loaded up a van with her art, easels, sculptures and furniture so I that could style the studios.

After we'd unveiled the garden, we had a celebration. My favourite restaurant in London is called the Ark, on Palace Terrace Gardens in Notting Hill. It serves Italian food and has been trading for over forty years. With its one long room, it feels like a very beautiful garden shed, with glamorous pictures from the 1930s and 40s on the walls. It was great fun.

The build that year was uneventful. There was newspaper speculation as to why the shape of the studio had changed. Somebody tried to create a controversy but none existed. In truth

I was a little bored by the seamless nature of this build. There were no problems to report. And this garden was archetypal Chelsea. It was practical, beautiful, I think as good as any other that year, and it was a great delight that it had been inspired by a London family.

The champagne corks popped, and once again in the middle of this extraordinary event we held an Irish party in the middle of the garden. A load of friends arrived to celebrate. Our builders were there and our sponsors. Bob Sweet, one of the major RHS figures behind the Flower Show, toasted me: 'I'm sorry, Diarmuid, sometimes I don't know what gets into the heads of the judges.' From this I took that he believed the garden was of gold standard. We'd been awarded Silver Gilt. I realized that however well I achieved, however well I conformed, it would never be enough. My compensation, however, was huge, in the form of hordes of smiling faces appreciating what we had built and planted.

Later that summer I was at the Electric Picnic, a Glastonbury-like music festival in County Laois, with added magic. The owner of the event, John Reynolds, had purchased the pod from the lollipop garden, and it was set under some stately beech trees, being used as a performance stage for bands. I was enjoying the atmosphere when a guy handed me his card, It read 'Charlie Mallon, blacksmith'. A big fellow with no pretensions. A week later, he travelled from County Tyrone to Wicklow. I showed him the daisy chairs, which I still had, and told him what I would love to do. I wanted them to grow on long stems, to become giant daisy sculptures. He made some prototypes with wonderful billowing petals and yellow centres. I loved them.

Back in London, my book with Sir Terence was about to be published. 'How about doing a garden next year at Chelsea?' I asked him. He liked the sound of this new adventure. And that's how the following year's daisy garden came about.

CHELSEA NO. 6, 2008:
THE OCEANICO CAFÉ GARDEN

Paula Robbins, from our studio in Portobello Road, travelled with me to Germany to visit another nursery which specializes in mature plants. I picked twelve very ordinary shrubs, *Prunus laurocerasus*, big, dark glossy-leaved laurels. Their base had been stripped of leaves, exposing beautiful gnarled stems. On top, the foliage had been clipped into a perfect dome. Sir Terence and I were keen to design a garden that reflected both our tastes. We decided on a café garden.

We sketched and developed plans incorporating giant metal daisies sprouting from an underplanting of box balls and grasses. Discs of reclaimed brick created small patios for two or three people to sit on. These were linked by more reclaimed bricks in straight pathways. A wooden pavilion had walls that could be gently lowered, to transform them into decks. Our sponsors were an Anglo-Irish property firm, Oceanico, who developed golf courses in Portugal. They planned to use this garden as a sales centre when their latest development opened.

The structure was built in Terence's back garden by his furniture and outfitting company, Benchmark. Clad in larch, it was subtle and beautiful. We had worked hard to get the shapes, the span and the colour of the daisies just right. Charlie towed them over from Ireland on a trailer and bolted them into position, allowing us to set our paving on top and place our planting.

I'd come across the work of sculptor Stephen Charlton, who had designed a set of comical mice. His *Mouse Having a Ball* made us smile, and we placed it under the laurels as a final focal point.

It was a simple garden. I spotted a mistake early on. The planting was too low for the daisy parasols. The highest box was about 750mm and then it was about another two metres before the daisy canopy gave coverage. I'd wanted to keep the scheme as uncomplicated as possible, but I ended up almost with a void. The paving was really beautiful, and the back of the garden, underplanted with the laurels, was delightful with shafts of sunlight streaming between the clipped domes. The laurels had not long finished flowering, so the foliage was covered with a profusion of flower spikes. They had to be removed one by one, thousands of them.

On the Tuesday evening we again took over the Ark restaurant and invited our friends to dinner. It was a great celebration, one of those magic nights. Kim Wilde, who had helped me for a week with the planting, sang an acapella version of 'Kids in America'. And then Moya Brennan, the voice of Clannad, who the previous year had played the harp as the Queen passed, joined in with her hits. We had 'Robin, the Hooded Man' and the 'Theme from Harry's Game'. Terence made a speech about our experiences at the showground, concluding that our garden was fun.

I made a speech and told everyone that the garden was dedicated to my mother-in-law – Terry. It was the second year running she hadn't made it to Chelsea. She had a dreadful time in hospital after an emergency operation on holiday. She never complained, just got on with things. She was looking forward to future visits to London. We raised our glasses in unison to Terry.

On behalf of the guests, my father-in-law made a speech. Ronan had been Chief Justice, a distinguished gentleman who was enjoying his first visit to this amazing show. I felt very proud to be the recipient of his public congratulations. At the end of the week, with the garden about to be packed away and sent to Portugal, I headed to Dublin for an appearance on *The Late Late Show*.

The following morning I went directly to the hospital. A week later Terry passed away. She had been my guiding light, the person who, when everyone else advised me to take a cautious road, had looked at me with a twinkle in her eye and said, 'You just go for it!' She'd been delighted by our move back to Ireland and overjoyed to spend time with Eppie, who of course idolized her over-the-top Gran. Terry and my Mum had become great friends, holidaying and shopping together. So often when I have a decision to make or I have scheme to undertake, I imagine knocking on her door, sitting down beside the fire, having a large glass of red wine poured out, watching her widening smile as I tell her of new plans or adventures.

CHELSEA 2011

As I write I am in the middle of the process again, trying to decide will I do a garden, should I do a garden, and if I do what type of garden will I do? The invitation arrived two weeks ago. They'd be delighted to have me. Now, though, they are not taking any chances. A deposit of £1500 is required upon application. If you pull out after a certain stage you won't get your money back.

This is possibly inspired by me and Chelsea in 2009. I hadn't intended to enter, and then months after applications closed I was surveying a site at Dublin airport – an airside garden I was to create for licensed premises. This had moved on to become part of a television series I was working on, where I travel the cities and towns of Ireland creating communal spaces. How about bringing this Irish bar garden to Chelsea? It had never been done. A pint of stout among the verdant greens, a pint that I could slowly pull myself, seemed too good to be true. I sent Alex, manager of the show, a text: 'I have an idea, can I take you to lunch?' Her reply was typically delightful, and a week later over pasta I asked her over pasta what she thought, would I be allowed? She positively beamed with delight and gave me some rough deadlines, I think for after Christmas. That's how late I was. Proposals for plans are usually in by late July or early August.

Within a few days an email arrived from the RHS, from Hayley, who is in charge of press: 'Can I take you to lunch, Diarmuid?' 'Great.' She brought a friend from the office, another delight. Typically, I was nearly an hour late. Hayley laid it on the line: 'To be frank, Diarmuid, you are the one that matters to us. There are other names, but most people have never heard of them. To have you doing a garden at Chelsea is fantastic for us. What can we do to help?' I was shocked. In so many places I go people say to me, 'Oh they hate you don't they? They need you more than you need them,' and I bluster my way through a response. The RHS don't hate me: they have never been anything other than wonderful to me. They let me in as an unknown, and through that they gave me a life. Well, they changed my life. They taught me loads and made me confident. The RHS introduced me to a whole new world of gardening and gardeners, and they have always treated me well. Their staff whether, in head office at Vincent Square, at Wisley or Harlow Carr, the places I have had most contact with, have been welcoming and delightful beyond reason. The volunteers mainly superb, and overall I have immense respect for them.

Sadly, it wasn't to work out. After all the ideas, I was offered a plot that wasn't on the main stretch backing on to the London plane trees. That is the only space I think worth while. I'm not surprised. As usual I was late putting forward my idea. It was no time before the press were on the phone. What had happened to my garden? They had heard I might enter. Why was I in one day and out the next? This can be tiresome. Even if I am not at Chelsea it is a little scandal. I have a responsibility in life to make sure that my dreams and my ego, my desire to show off at Chelsea, are practical. I must be fully sponsored and able to pay my way. At last I am learning that while it was all right to wing it in the early years, the consequences of displaying a garden when I can't afford to are too much. So if I'm not happy with everything – the plot, the budget, and most importantly the design, if I don't feel this overwhelming desire to display – I'll walk away.

THE CHELSEA FORMULA AND SUBURBIA

There is a formulaic style that achieves top awards at Chelsea. A central pond or canal, symmetry, a vista of a beautiful statue, ferns, grasses, purple tulips, alliums, and roses, clipped box and yews, magnificent specimen trees (the older the better) and Portland stone. These features can be used in any number of refined configurations, bordered by walls of hornbeam or lime trees, preferably pleached, or interlaced. The picture is completed by inviting the backdrop of London plane trees into the scene.

For visitors, the gardens with perennial appeal are chocolate-box versions of a British village idyll: the post office, lock keeper's cottage, or abandoned railway sidings. Other ideas continually revisited are the Japanese garden, the Beatrix Potter extravaganza, or the coastal retreat. A recent influx of eastern finance has resulted in a sustained prominence of Islamic courtyards and oases. Laurent Perrier and the *Daily Telegraph* love to sponsor exhibits that appeal to their clients.

The gardens that have stood out for me over the years include a simple water meadow garden by Mark Anthony Walker, Dan Pearson's roof garden, Arabella Lennox-Boyd's romantic woodland, Paul Cooper's Greening of Industry and Julie Toll's Forest – all different and all managing to portray beauty with subtlety or exuberance.

There's no doubt that the Chelsea Flower Show, and gardening television shows, have reflected and inspired an immense growth in popularity of domestic gardening. Sadly we still lack good, sensible design in suburban gardens. Suburbia remains a dirty word, even though it's where most people live. And it's where my love of gardens was nurtured. The new frontier in design should be a refinement of the many lessons learned in the past fifteen years – a resurgence in the craft of growing and composting, propagation and cultivation, and an eagerness to use the simple rules of line and shape, proportion and volume. New practicalities – smaller spaces, the desire to work from home and the requirement for entertainment space – present new challenges.

The recent economic doldrums mean budget limitations, which will ensure that we dig deep and explore different ways of economizing in materials. Which materials surround us? In the days of new austerity, what can we reinvent? How do we re-present simple local resources in a new way? Within an open box, an enclosed space with no lid, we are compelled to create interest. We have the magnificence of the natural world to fulfil the requirements of a client. As gardeners we get so much help. We are surprised by the reaction of plants and delighted by their ever-changing appearance. Ours is a wondrous world.

PART THREE

MOVING ON AND MOVING BACK

RETURNING HOME

Our years living in London had been wonderful. It had been a very privileged life. I had had some money in my pocket, and there were constant invites to events or dinners. On Furness Road our neighbours were great. Our home was surrounded by great parks and a brand new school and leisure centre. Down the end of our road was Harlesden High Street. The area reputedly had the worst murder record in the city but I could safely leave the door unlocked. Apart from the odd incident inspired by my television status, we had created a wonderful haven. The house was always busy with friends coming to stay. In the back garden I'd built a garden room, a cabana complete with shower, mini-kitchen and a bed that folded out from the wall. What had been a rather sweet suburban garden, with its shed and concrete path, lawn and roses, had received a few makeovers during my tenure.

When Eppie was born we'd moved back to Dublin for a year, renting a house in Sandycove, right beside the sea. This allowed Justine and her young baby to make use of the family support system. Over in London, I'd endeavoured to turn the garden into a bachelor pad, lifting a huge sauna and hot tub over the house by crane. To keep out the occasional press snooper on the hunt for comments from me or Justine after I had been deemed too bold at Chelsea, we erected a beautiful wooden wall two metres high, with a pocket across the front planted with lavender. So we were safe inside our courtyard.

After a year by the sea in Dublin, Justine and Eppie moved back to London. This coincided exactly with the time when I began to work in the Irish television industry, so I was always commuting, spending my week filming in Dublin and then back to London at the weekend.

Ireland was in the midst of a huge property boom. There were more construction cranes on the Dublin skyline than in Dubai, and every social conversation over dinner involved prices. Where do you live? How long have you been there? How much is it worth? I'd been careful with property. I had grown up listening to others say that they had regretted selling various homes. If they had only been able to hold on to them what a good investment they'd have made. Not wanting to be that person, and with a good income, I had kept hold of our various addresses through these years.

I began to feel a pull back home. Eppie had loads of cousins who couldn't wait to see her, and Justine and I had our families there. My years on UK television had created a big profile for me back home, and work was pouring in. This varied from property developers wanting me to plan gardens for new schemes to television commercials and television shows.

We settled in County Wicklow. Immediately south of Dublin and known as the 'garden of Ireland', Wicklow boasts beautiful gentle mountains, lakes, a sandy coastline and Peak District-type bogs. I had some talks with the management at RTE to plan a strategy for a return from London. Lots of production companies were proposing programmes, mainly gardening ones, with my name on them. RTE (the national broadcaster) sent me to work with a particular company on a makeover idea.

I WANT A GARDEN

After all those *Home Front* projects, I felt there must be an easier way to create gardens, without the broadcaster or production company taking responsibility for everything that happened. I'd admired the format of *Grand Designs*, where the viewer was absorbed into the projects through the stories of the people who wanted to create their own homes, drawn in by their beautiful designs and limited budgets, and by the challenge, 'Will they be in by Christmas'? So many people wanted gardens, and I was in the wonderful position of knowing that thousands wanted gardens designed by me.

So that was it: a series called *I Want A Garden*, where I would arrive, meet clients in their homes, look over their sites and produce a book of designs based on their requirements. They'd let me know their budget and I'd attempt to stick within it! I worked with a great young team of producers and directors, all very eager to do a good job. Going into a new project I'm always wary. I want it to be the best it can possibly be, and despite our tiny population compared to that of Britain, I never believed that television programmes depended on spending great amounts of money. Creativity was about telling stories, identifying good contributors and developing some empathy. It could also of course be about the exact opposite: creating something or working with people in a situation that was so disastrous that people watched through morbid fascination. Sadly this approach has become more popular in recent years.

We wanted a feel good programme, though. There were worries that people wouldn't want to spend the sums needed, or that renovating a house was one thing, but would their passion transfer into the design and build of a new garden? Straight off, it was a massive success. I discovered in Britain that if you give people things, they'll often want more. When the BBC arrives it is perceived to have a bottomless cheque book, and perhaps understandably some of our clients were never going to be happy: they wanted to grab as much as they could while they could. And what if you gave people the ability to achieve a new garden for themselves? Well, they appreciated everything you did for them. *I Want a Garden* became my most successful series and subsequently sold throughout the world. It is dubbed in many different languages, and has opened surprising doors for me.

At its core is a simple idea. I have to listen to the client. I'm not peddling contemporary designs. I am trying to find out exactly what people are looking for, and how they would like to express themselves through their outdoor space and love of plants. I must listen, absorb the requirements, nod at the budget; then it's my job to bring the garden somewhere else, to tick all the boxes but to take the gardens further. And we'd feature a whole range of projects, from tiny courtyards to really rather massive affairs.

Our first programme was at the smaller end of the scale. Karen was a single mum who had lived in flats all her life, with no access to her own garden. She had two lovely little girls and had moved to a groundfloor apartment in a high density scheme. At last she had her own small outdoor space, measuring some six metres square. What could I do? The budget, although small, was still a Celtic Tiger one – I think she spent €4,000 and she wanted high design. She loved colour and flowers, she wanted vegetables and she'd like a place for herself and a friend to go and have a glass of wine when the children were in bed. She was prepared to do the work. Access to the garden was very difficult, involving a trail through the kitchen, down a corridor, past a bathroom and in through the children's bedroom. The plans envisaged a garden pavilion made from a new shed, a small rectangular lawn with curved ends, two reclaimed brick terraces in the same shape, and loads of planting. I was keen for Karen and the girls to learn about planting and soil, and to understand that the first investment in

220

a new garden should be generous quantities of well-rotted farmyard manure.

So as I sat on a horse having jumping lessons, Karen and her family filled bags full of their waste in the lashing rain. Karen is a very funny girl and for a week we laughed our way through this build. Much of the promised help never materialized. So a lot of the donkey work was done by yours truly, but I enjoyed it. When this small new garden was revealed to friends and family, Karen gave free rein to her emotions. So the first *I Want a Garden* story wasn't about the garden so much as the client: a bundle of humour who wanted the best for her kids, a girl with a wicked turn of phrase, who in that week achieved one of her dreams.

At the other end of the scale altogether, Jimmy and Charlotte lived in County Meath, virtually on the beach. Their elegant Georgian home had been in Jimmy's family for generations, and despite enjoying magnificent views of sea and ships, their garden suffered through wind and gales. Salt-laden gusts would rip through any flimsy foliage. Charlotte would give Martha Stewart a run for her money: tables groaned with food every time you called. Pavlova for breakfast was a favourite of mine! And Charlotte and Jimmy wanted a garden for their young family. They socialized a lot, a wide circle of friends came to visit, and pristine and comfortable as the house was, a trick was being lost outside.

We wandered the bare green lawns and climbed down some rickety steps to the beach. Heaven. But how could I create a garden that was useable here? An off-the-cuff remark by Charlotte gave me the clue: 'The only thing I can imagine,' she said, not seriously, 'is digging down.' I knew she was right, and a week or two later came back to show them plans a series of sunken garden rooms, open to the sky but dug into their green lawn. It was to be a huge operation, and pretty and exciting as the illustrations I brought with me were, the requirement to get the job finished within six weeks was daunting.

As with most of our clients, though, this was embraced as a challenge. 'We'll build it, and we'll build it exactly as you've drawn it,' said Charlotte, "I suppose you won't be back until the last day?' It never works like that. If people are adventurous enough to join me on the extraordinary journey of creating a garden, whether gentle or dramatic, I need to see it at every stage. If my flight from London arrived at eleven o'clock in the evening, many a time I would creep up to a house and peer over the fence, or if I saw a light on knock on a window to see what had been happening.

I get transported to another world and am in awe of the physical act of garden-making. To see space turn into ideas and then to have those ideas work is hugely rewarding, and for a garden designer the rewards work on many different levels at different times. Finding a solution when I'm at the drawing board, imagining combinations of plants, making decisions about materials or lighting; nervously awaiting a reaction when you present your book of ideas to your clients; and finally going on that journey with them as their gardens spring to life: every stage carries with it a constant excitement. I try always to be around for the planting. This is when a space becomes a garden. And then over the season, or over the years, to see these places develop and to receive the occasional letter or text, sometimes years later, to hear how people love their gardens and to go back, to give advice and to eat or drink in those gardens: there can be no better job.

Fourteen stone masons toiled for weeks to create the sunken courtyards. A golf course designer oversaw the building of a series of mounds to separate front from back, and at four o'clock on the morning of the final day, Jimmy was despatched to Wales to buy two bubble chairs that would hang from an open pavilion that looked past our constructions and straight out to sea. As we planted furiously in the last few hours, Charlotte was in tears by her kitchen sink: 'I can't believe all these people are working to give me a beautiful garden.'

Pat and Mary were something else altogether. Their house in County Carlow was an island within a large garden, itself set in a rural location with 360-degree views of wonderful hills on the horizon. In the distance, just visible from the house, trucks trundled along a motorway. Their brief was interesting: they wanted *Lord of the Rings* hills and hummocks, places to disappear into. I enjoyed the company of these free-spirited people enormously.

I went away scratching my head. An idea had come to me of a reclining figure, a woman lying down in the landscape. Certainly this has been done before, perhaps most recently in a small garden at Chelsea. But I had something different in mind, using grass mounds to create a sculpture, one that would be huge. It might be possible to sculpt a female form that would block out the motorway and create a physical end for their garden. I put it out of my mind. But it wasn't to go away. The project had been scheduled for fairly early in the series. I wasn't ready. My series producer, the wonderfully pragmatic and inventive Alex Hatton, talked to me. Why was it such a problem? What was I planning? 'Brilliant', she said when she heard my ramblings, 'Let's do it.' Well, we could only do it if it was appropriate, and of course if Pat and Mary liked it.

My idea was that we would take a studio photograph of a woman reclining on the floor or a bed. David from our office would draw her, I would develop a presentation based on this fantasy figure, and I'd bring it down to Carlow to reveal my design. Who would the female figure be? We'd talk about this for months. I had a friend Ellis who lived in north London. Years before, I had done her garden. Ellis was an agent for models, and on her books was Jerry Hall. The idea of a reclining Jerry, her long beautiful hair falling over shoulder sculptured into furrows, reclining at large, creating a landscape, stuck.

It took a long time to arrange the practicalities. Jerry was in London, so off we went. My cousin Niall is a fashion photographer.

We booked him, his assistant and all his equipment. Louis Walsh
lent us his flat. It was packed with Warhols, some of them of Mick
Jagger. Discreetly, I turned them to the wall. Jerry arrived dressed
in a summery floral outfit, and I gave her a brief. We would try a
number of different poses; I would need her to lie down for three
of four hours, occasionally shifting position; she would be
photographed and drawn, and from this I hoped would emerge
a concept for a figure resting in a garden, 150 feet long, 25 feet
high, and with no guarantee that the clients would commission
the design and build her. It was a risk. Jerry was perfect, wonderful,
beautiful, shapely and professional. She made her own suggestions,
and I joked that it was in my power to make her bum as big or as
small as I wished. David walked around her, leaning down, peering,
getting different perspectives as he sketched furiously with a
pencil. I pinched myself. Full of the joys, we had made this happen,
we had hired a model, she was wonderful and I was about to
present the clients with an idea that was completely off the wall.
But I was sure it was right.

Furiously we worked up a book of concepts, and off I headed
to County Carlow. Sitting on a patio in the garden on a sunny
summer's day, I handed over the book of plans. There was a sharp
intake of breath. A black-and-white drawing of bumps and hollows,
hills and valleys in the shape of a very leggy Jerry Hall. Gasps. 'I
don't know what to say,' said Mary. She was excited and nervous.
Pat was unsure. The cameras were turned off and we paced for
a while. They wouldn't be left on their own, I would help. It was
all possible if they liked the idea, but it came down to trust. They
decided to go for it. And so within a week David from the office
had based himself at their home. Graham Knuttel, a very popular
artist from Dublin, took the train down every day and made a
three-dimensional clay sculpture of the shape we were trying to
achieve, and truck after truck arrived with loads of top soil.

It was a crazy few weeks, but soon Jerry appeared from the

ground, and finally she was covered in a coat of grass. Pat and Mary put their heart and soul into sculpting her, and our little group was tremendously excited as Jerry came to life. They loved her. We finished building her on a Sunday, and the programme was broadcast exactly a week later. The radio buzzed from the Monday morning with pro- and anti-Jerry comments. 'How was she going to be mown?' was the most asked question. The only person who wasn't worried about this was Mary, who has happily trimmed the lady with a hover mower ever since. Soon helicopters were hovering overhead to get a glimpse, and locals getting married stopped at the house to have their pictures taken with this reclining form.

Near where Mum and Dad live in Rathfarnham, I was asked to design a garden for Anne-Marie and Eamonn and their three sons, Oisin, Diarmuid and Gavin (I'm not kidding!). They had a suburban lawn running away from the back of the house, and then suddenly a precipice – a dangerous slope leading down to marshland beside the river. A budget had been set, and Eamonn had spent months installing foundations for a series of decks that would step down the back. It was all too difficult and had been abandoned.

What could I do? The house rang with energy and laughter. But the danger lurking at the end of the garden concealed a great opportunity. A picket fence across the end of the lawn was a real shame. Wonderful trees had sprung up everywhere. If you looked past the danger and across the river there was a sylvan feel, as if you were in a forest. Sketching on my notepad, I developed an idea for a bog garden down below, making use of the ever-present moisture. I drew ligularias and hostas, massive tree ferns, skunk cabbage and gunneras, even bamboo; all plants that would love this environment, plants that had different shapes and different coloured foliage, plants that would create an adventure play area for the children. Up the top, looking out from the house, would be different. I wanted to build on the idea that Eamonn had started with, a series of terraces. These would be different, however: a series of rectangular wooden terraces that would launch out into the abyss, striding over the damp land below. One would step into another, and they would have billowing roofs, arcs of wood in the form of skateboard park ramps. I wanted the roofs to launch out into the crowns of the trees and claim visual ownership of the environment beyond. I have always liked the rope bridge from *I'm a Celebrity, Get Me Out of Here!* That was the shape that would reach into the trees.

Before my first visit was over I knew what the plan would be. It completely broke the budget. Without the billowing roofs I might have been able to stick to the allocated funds, but I told the clients that I was going to produce drawings showing the ultimate, and they could pare them back if they wished. They had about a month to construct the garden, and I wondered if they would be daunted.

Anne-Marie and Eamonn sat at the kitchen table. I handed over the book, they leafed slowly through it, said 'Wow.'

'It looks very difficult,' said Anne-Marie.

'Ah no,' I said, 'it's not really.'

She looked at me: 'It is.' Nothing would stop them, however. Eamonn set to work, and telegraph poles were delivered. These would be set into the ground at angles and all the structures hung from them. Eamonn devised a little trolley – one end of the long pole set on two wheels – and dragged eight of them through the narrow passageway from the front to the back garden. He developed a concept to build the structure, and soon he had a team working all hours.

For me, this job was the perfect mix of structure and planting. I was away in London a lot, and our director Bonnie Dempsey, a superb filmmaker, kept me in touch with all developments. At times it was knife-edge stuff. At one stage halfway through, the whole thing began to sway. Structural engineers were called, and

226

Anne-Marie and Eamonn patiently debated the consequences of abandoning the build. They kept faith. A few adjustments and work started again. It became a brilliant programme, in fact two. The episode was judged so nail-biting that it was divided into two parts. The first ended at a point when gardening armageddon seemed inevitable and everything was left hanging in mid-air. But just two weeks later, friends and family gathered to watch me swing a bottle of champagne against the superstructures to officially launch them. And as was so often case with this series, the family became great friends, holidaying with us in California. Anne-Marie became my business partner.

The future of television, I think, lies less in handing over big budgets for projects and more in people doing things for themselves, which is much more fascinating. The viewer can identify with a personal quest. And a lot of the issues that develop when a television company is paying the bills don't arise when it is just documenting a story. *I Want A Garden* was a difficult programme to make. I had come from working with the BBC, the best broadcaster in the world, and I brought with me the scale of ambition and ideas that I had learned. Creating an aspirational garden design programme for a smaller audience with a tiny budget was challenging. In the end, however, the commitment of the participants and production team made this the television I have most enjoyed making.

THAT'S ENTERTAINMENT!

One of the peculiarities of plying your trade through the medium of television is that it opens doors on to other disciplines. When the audience is interested enough in you and what you are doing, you become a face. And you are often encouraged to step outside your own area of expertise. What's known as reality television has always been around, but an explosion of interest about ten years ago led to whole genres being mixed up. If an audience was interested in you as a gardener, they might also be curious to know what you are like and how you react to situations outside your role.

I'd been through obvious dramatic life changes. My new career in the media had shot off like a steel bearing in a pinball machine. I was launched at dizzying speed into this new world in a different country, and for years it felt as though I was bouncing off walls and obstacles, being sent in ever more eclectic directions, occasionally hitting the jackpot. I was lucky in that all the projects I was involved in were good. The jackpot was to be the programmes that were right down my alley, and that would eventually become my own: *Home Front* and *Home Front in the Garden*. With these I worked very hard and was in heaven.

Once you were noticed as a new face, other people took an interest. I became a reporter for the Channel 4 series *Collectors' Lot*, travelling Britain, examining people's collections of milk bottles and tarot cards, every day a different town or city, a different story. I was an occasional panellist on *Through the Keyhole*, giddy with excitement at meeting the iconic David Frost, playing guessing games in his studio in Leeds. Dictionary corner on *Countdown* was fun for the week I was there. And incredibly I got to co-present *Top of the Pops* with Fearne Cotton. The announcement that it was to be axed came a mere two weeks later – just a coincidence!

I was never any good at quiz shows that required general knowledge. I should have been, because I know a lot about a broad range of subjects, but concentrating on facts or detail isn't my thing. Laurence and I did *TheWeakest Link*. We signed up because we had heard Sharon Osbourne was to be one of the other contestants on that particular celebrity edition, and a duel between her and Anne Robinson wasn't to be missed. In the end she wasn't there. The final nail in my coffin was driven in by some grumpy fruit and veg man. Laurence lasted a couple of rounds longer.

I was fascinated by many of these programmes and wanted to see how they work. My usual television set-up doesn't involve studios, make-up or a control box with directors and editors barking out split-second instructions. Like anybody else, I am intrigued by the mechanics of the magic, and especially so with Anne Robinson. I had met her a few years earlier doing an item for *Watchdog*. But now I was faced with an inquisition by the Queen of Mean. I discovered that she stays in character for the recording, and at the end disappears without even giving the final two contestants the benefit of her nod, wink and smile. In that last moment of the show she simply turns her back on them.

I feel I got the best of our encounter. She quizzed me about a gardener being let in the building. Would I not normally arrive via the back door? Knowing that at her country mansion her gardener was the immensely grand Penelope Hobhouse, I shot back, asking if she let her help in through the front door? Anne turned just a little red and bowed her head.

On *Mastermind* my fellow competitors were Paul Ross, Lembit Opik and a *Coronation Street* actress. My specialist subject was the life and times of the Irish rock band U2. I did as much as I could to memorize release dates for albums and years of tours. The fear of the chair is ridiculous. I came fourth out of four, but with a respectable 21 points. Like all his family, Paul Ross is an intelligent, articulate and knowledgeable man. He ran away with the programme with his answers on the writings of Ezra Pound.

All these programmes were great fun to do, and I was learning a lot along the way, but the big departure came for me in 2004 with *Strictly Come Dancing*. It was the second series, a relatively new show presented that year by Bruce Forsyth and the previous year's winner, Natasha Kaplinsky, while Tess Daly was on pregnancy leave. It was a startling change for me. I have two left feet. This show attracts the full gamut of ability: some contestants they know will be hopeless, others are athletes and former stage kids assured of good progress.

My partner was a lovely South African girl, a champion dancer called Nicole Cutler. I immediately felt sorry for her. It was too big a challenge to turn this oaf into anything. My class of 2004 included Carole Vorderman, Esther Rantzen, Denise Lewis, Jill Halfpenny and Julian Clary. But thankfully I wasn't to be the worst. I already had a good rapport with car enthusiast Quentin Wilson. We'd met down through the years. He is a man with a good sense of humour. Finding ourselves in the same rehearsal hall, we giggled and continually asked each other were we mad, what were we at?

'But I can't do it, I can't dance,' he'd say.

'I know', I'd say, 'I can't do it, I can't dance.'

We'd collapse with laughter again. But then I caught sight of him through a glass panel in a door. Well, I couldn't dance, but he couldn't move. I liked him even more. There were fittings for costumes and argy bargy about sequins. I didn't want any, wearing the strange shoes was bad enough. I had the body of a gardener, not of a mover. I practised initially a couple of times a week and then almost every day with Nicole. She had the patience of a saint. I had the footwork of a sinner.

It's clear these days there's not a problem attracting familiar faces to strut. Back then, though, it was another revelation to the family in Rathfarnham. They were sniffy, until I mentioned Bruce

Forsyth's name. Wow! This must be big. So I had support of sorts. Saturday evening television had lost its lustre, I think, and these were pre *X Factor* days – event television hadn't yet been reinvented. Try explaining it to friends. Oh yeah, well, I'm going to be dancing. I'm learning to tango, to foxtrot with a fixed smile and an arched back. What was I at?

Justine was pregnant. We lived about seven minutes by car from Television Centre, straight up the road. The baby was the important thing in our lives. It had been a busy and difficult year, so maybe a month or two of dancing was OK. It's all a hazy memory: training, meeting Nicole, interviews, dancing, costumes and laughs. I had no natural rhythm and found it very difficult to conquer the steps. There was camaraderie among the contestants. We eyed each other up, but not really. Straight away it was obvious that some knew what they were doing. A few were desperate for success and others, well, the rest of us, hung on from session to session.

The professionals were wonderful – Erin and Camilla, Ian, Anton, Darren and Lilia, and of course the boisterous Brendan. It's brilliant working with experts, people on top of their game, not searching for fame for its own sake. Each had a special bond with their celeb partner. They desperately wanted us to perform to our best potential, to share with us the magic of good steps and rhythm, of a successful interpretation of the chosen music.

For some of us, being prepared in any way for that first night was a minor miracle. As with all the other challenges in life, you step up to the game, a little anyway. I think it was the first night we met the judges. I don't watch myself on television, so you hear about your performance through others. Maybe I escaped strong sarcasm initially because of Quentin's presence. He was endearingly hilarious, but pretty soon Arlene was looking at me po-faced, Craig was being demeaning, Len was gazing at me with a sorry smile, and Bruno was telling me that I wasn't in a potting shed, that Nicole wasn't a plant. I survived a number of public votes – two, three, four weeks went by. I spent daily sessions in dance studios or gymnasiums, Saturdays always at Television Centre.

I would be nervous dancing at a family party, so dancing in front of millions was something else. I think the key to it is not to take yourself too seriously. Do what you can, do your best, and take plenty of instruction. Waiting to go down the steps as your name is announced is very strange. But this type of programme is part of your job. You are paid to train and paid to entertain.

In my last few weeks training got intense, but work commitments had to be squeezed in. I was involved in a project for Save the Children, designing a Christmas tree that was due to be auctioned off weeks later in front of Princess Anne at the Natural History Museum. The Waterford Crystal craftsmen wanted me to inspect progress, but Nicole needed me to dance. The Beeb arranged for her to accompany me on the short flight from Luton to Waterford. There was a small camera crew with us on the plane. As we landed, I peered out of the window and groaned. The airport and the good people of the crystal works had arranged a welcoming committee – good luck banners for Diarmuid and a full troupe of Irish dancers; a silver bucket, champagne and two crystal flutes. On the factory floor, after seeing the amazing creation, Nicole and I went through our paces. There was applause from the machinists, and that night my friends, the craftsmen, took me out in the city as they had done on every visit. Late in the evening in a nightclub, Nicole and I joyously took to the floor. She demonstrated a particularly vigorous step needed for the following Saturday's routine. I embraced it enthusiastically. Drink is a great anaesthetic. The following morning I woke in pain. The crystal works doctor was summoned. I had a groin strain from dancing. Idiotic.

In the evening Justine would make the short trip in her sporty little Mazda and sit in the front row, her bump burgeoning. And the following morning the two of us would walk in Roundwood Park with the dogs and giggle at the ridiculousness of life. Monday would see me back training again.

Those weeks were rich with incident. I travelled to the ITV studios where Claudia Winkleman's *It Takes Two* was recorded. She was wonderful to me. Radio shows from Ireland would ring up. The public support was huge, but didn't I know I couldn't dance? My final challenge was a Paso Doble, with me as the angry bull. I think I was legendary for all the wrong reasons. I do remember a complicated manoeuvre that I conquered flamboyantly – a series of dangerous steps over Nicole's twisted torso, complete (on my part) with snarly face. I'd made some progress, but dramatically – in week four – I was out.

It's horrible to subject yourself to any of these shows where you line up like rabbits in headlights, in front of an audience and with millions watching at home. Everything is an effort: for me nothing but gardens comes easily. I never took it for granted that I would go through to the next round. The drum roll beats as the guillotine blade is raised. That's what it's like – a pounding heart, public humiliation, the relief if your name is called, and the dread if you find yourself in the last two. And then when you're out, pretending you don't mind and trying to convey a state of grace and happiness, while everyone gawps at your rejection. When the roller coaster ride was over I didn't feel like walking in the park. I was bruised for a day, embarrassed by my peers and by public rebuff. The drama is in your presence, it's in your embrace, it's written all over your face. At the Chelsea Flower Show it's different. Your award or lack of it is delivered quietly: it may be broadcast nationally that evening but you don't have to be there, you never have to react. For *Strictly* to work, the pleasure and the pain need to be on full show – that's entertainment!

On Monday I was back in the studio on *It Takes Two*. Claudia had donned a bald wig and wailed along to Sinead O'Connor's

'Nothing Compares To U'. Her favourite was gone. I felt bad for Nicole; she didn't get exactly the pick of the crop. And then Justine and I concentrated on waiting for Eppie.

A few weeks later, the day before she arrived, we were in the Portland Hospital watching Donny Osmond being interviewed. The person he had fallen in love with during this weird series was Diarmuid. Donny Osmond. Knew. Who. I. Was.

AGENTS AND ADVERTISING

Just as I was developing skills on the job as a broadcaster, I was also finding out about television production, the roles of producers, directors, researchers and assistant producers. I arrived at a time when cameras and equipment were changing. The move to the digital age had begun, and cameramen were full of questions about what size the picture was to be broadcast at. I had to get used to terms such as 'ptc' (piece to camera), 'vo' (voiceover) and 'strawberry filter' (when you are filming a contributor just to keep them happy, knowing that the piece will never be used, the cameraman says he will insert a strawberry filter), which were bandied about freely. On one of my first shoots I was informed by a cocky soundman that the presenter always carries the camera legs. They never do. Presenters are treated with kid gloves and after a while begin to act accordingly. From that first day on I have always carried the legs.

If you are a presenter you are not meant to negotiate your terms and conditions, your contract, directly. You need somebody in between, an agent, who looks after your interests. I seemed to explode onto the scene, with loads of broadcasters wanting to work with me. I didn't understand the concept of an agent. After I'd worked on one early production where the backroom people weren't so pleasant, however, somebody whispered to me that I needed to get one. Back home in Dublin I looked in the Golden Pages (the Irish equivalent of the Yellow Pages). Agents. I rang a couple of numbers. They dealt in show bands, booking light entertainment acts into venues in the rural hinterland. They were thrilled to hear from someone working in television in England. I thought better of it. What would I do?

I rang Rachel at Pebble Mill.

'I've been told I need an agent. Who do you think I should talk to?'

She'd had a guy ring her up about a gardening client and travel to Pebble Mill from London to meet her. She had been impressed. His name was John Noel. I rang, and eventually a meeting was arranged at a mews office in Primrose Hill. It was for a Friday afternoon. There was a leaving do and most people were out at the pub. I talked to a lad there called Brendan, and then John returned to see me. He was quietly intrigued. John is from Manchester. He's a sharp operator who loves fun. On his books were Denise van Outen, Davina McCall, Russell Brand, Dermot O'Leary, Katie Thornton as well as prominent figures from Radio 1 and Radio 2. I told my story. He listened intently. But he didn't give anything away. John likes mavericks because he is one. He has a love-hate relationship with the business. If he's bored, he'll create some trouble. And as an agent who believes in you, he is fantastic. John looks for something in people. He is not inspired by anyone bland or pretty. He likes a challenge. He tends to see something, stick with people, and develop talent.

I haven't read Russell Brand's *My Booky Wook*, but people tell me that John is a significant character in his life. He sticks with people and sees them through troubled patches. He sees beyond addictions to drink and drugs, and sticks with any spark of originality, humour and danger. He's tough on broadcasters and can be tough on clients. I walked into the office not needing work. I'd loads of offers but I have always needing producing and management. I am tricky. I need somebody to talk me away from an emotionally charged precipice. John likes fun, parties and danger, but he also demands that you do your job, that you turn up on time and that you don't act the diva. He enjoyed the fact that I was Irish, and in particular loved working with Sean, who also in time signed with his agency. He likes people who can do stuff, make stuff, create. In the early days of *Home Front* he would travel to site. I loved when he came to see what we had made. He'd stand there, arms folded, and smile. My Dad was back in Dublin and had a good twenty years on John. John was my English dad.

I'd be frustrated by other designers who I felt didn't really 'get' gardens. John's point was that this series was going in my direction. I had a gift and the series would be mine. He was right. 'There's only one Diarmuid Gavin,' he would say, 'Don't worry.' There isn't, of course. Everybody is disposable, and over the years I was good at creating problems that John would need to sort. I would take against people who I didn't want to work with for whatever reason. John would receive another call from the Beeb. There was nothing better than driving around London in John's Range Rover, him bursting into Irish folk tunes.

On occasion, when schedules were getting too harsh, I would lose the run of myself and disappear for a few days. Nik, John's son, worked with me on a daily basis, making sure all my arrangements and deals were in place. If Sean and I escaped to Ireland, to enjoy the entertainment in local hostelries, Nik would arrive, enjoy our facilities and then lead us back to England for more gardens. Nik left me for Russell Brand. I think I prepared him for what was to come.

Every so often he would have a look at his books, see who his clients were and get rid of half of them. When John felt he could no more for me, if I was creating more trouble than I was worth, I would be culled. It happened three times. He never really meant it though. When Nik moved on, Polly, John's right-hand woman, took over looking after me. She always has my best interests at heart, always strives for the best deal and comes with an innate understanding of how I work. It's a very happy arrangement. They don't go in for masses of publicity, and they have a good sense of what is right for me. I'd never be encouraged to go on the likes of *Big Brother* or into the jungle. If there was a programme with an interesting, stimulating challenge, it could be right up my street. Every Christmas, John hosted a big party.

Dermot O'Leary would be behind the bar pulling pints, with producers, directors and talent crammed together to celebrate another busy year. Burlesque dancers or strippers would perform. Mum came over from Dublin, pretending to be outraged by the mad decadence but secretly loving it. So many phone calls from John started with, 'I've just had a phone call from so and so, what have you been up to?'

With Russell going to America, we have a whole new set of contacts. Last year myself, Justine and Eppie spent a summer living in a house at Venice Beach, California. I met agents and publicists and had loads of production meetings. We had the time of our lives. Disney asked me to prepare an installation for the launch of *Alice in Wonderland*. I worked on the development of an *X Factor* type gardening series with Fremantle. They said every series needs an angry Brit. That was to be my new classification. An old friend from London, who I'd worked with on *Strictly Come Dancing*, was now in charge of *Dancing with the Stars*. We'd meet and swap stories of the differences between British and American television. Not only talent had agents, but also producers and agents. You can't talk to anyone without going through a chain of representatives. We had fun in the sun.

When I started working in Ireland, Dave Fanning, the iconic DJ, introduced me to Noel Kelly. The Irish television industry had developed, and now there was a super-agent. I had been away for such a long time that the landscape had changed. I didn't know Dublin any more: there had been a building boom. New roads and railways abounded, and I had few connections in the media business. I had struck gold with John in London, but if I wanted to work at home, I would need somebody with a similar capacity for understanding my foibles, who would develop and work with ideas that suited my skills and temperament.

Noel comes from a sales background. He has a direct marketing company which works countrywide on promotions. Through this he had begun to hire individual personalities to front campaigns, and he subsequently developed a business to look after them. Like John in London, Noel prefers to stay in the background. He gets frustrated dealing with the politics of large organizations, and strives for clearcut results. In a relatively short space of time he signed up radio and television broadcasters, writers, sports people and artists. And at home, along with Niamh Kirwan, a young lady full of good sense and humour, we are guided through the rigours of life in the media. Noel became a very good friend. He won't accept you hiding behind a personality, he wants to know you, the good and the bad. He likes things to be straightforward. Both our families connected. The social aspect of careers in Ireland is as important as the work. I'm not an easy character to deal with and sometimes I can be elusive. But loyalty and consistency are traits that I possess and that I admire in others. So through good times and difficult ones this is how life is managed.

If the television audience believes and trusts in you, you become a valuable commodity for advertisers. Before I became known to the Irish population at large for gardens, I was hired to appear on a series of comical ads sponsored by both the northern and southern environmental agencies. We filmed about seven different scenarios over seven days, with a massive crew, north and south. The set-up involved a renowned Ulster actress, Olivia Nash, playing the role of a desperate housewife. I was the gardener with a cheeky grin. Olivia had twinkling eyes. Recycling was the last thing on her mind. Acting yourself is an odd experience. When you are filming, whether it is bit parts in dramas or for advertisements, you are expected to know what to do. Home for a few hours or days is a Winnebago, complete with bed, shower, kitchen and flat-screen television. Every five minutes somebody will check that you are OK – do you want another tea or coffee? There is a catering truck and all sorts of special effects machines.

The ads were a huge success. The agencies were able to chart a direct correlation with environmental awareness and waste being recycled.

In Britain I was soon also in demand. Lots of suggestions come in from agencies and judgement on these situations is important. They can pay a lot of money, but you must look after your credibility. I would never promote something that I didn't use or believe in. I've done ads for Hellmann's, Stena Line and Oceanico, who develop golf and holiday resorts in Portugal where I build gardens, as well as for the Swedish outdoor maintenance equipment company Husqvarna. And I have been to Costa Rica with Kenco coffee and the Rainforest Alliance to see how the benefits of fairtrade prices to farmers can affect a whole community.

Strangely enough, the most important work I've done in gardening has been with Morrisons, the supermarket chain. Five years ago, I filmed an advertisement for bread for their Market Street. A series of celebrities were used to press home the idea of the freshness of their produce. In Tunbridge Wells I filmed their Christmas ad with Lulu, walking down a street, wrapped up in a scarf, fake snow swirling all around, winking at Lulu.

The relationship developed into a stimulating campaign called Let's Grow. Morrisons came up with the idea of encouraging children to appreciate where fruit and vegetables come from by launching a voucher scheme. Schools throughout the country are encouraged to sign up. They are sent information packs and starter kits. Shoppers are given vouchers with every £10 or so. The vouchers are collected by children, who bring them to school. The school can then exchange them for gardening equipment, packets of seed, compost, pots and containers, wheelbarrows, greenhouses, raised beds, wellington boots, aprons and gloves. Hundreds of items can be ordered to encourage children to grow plants from seed, to understand where food comes from, to show

The biggest pair of bitching queens since Elizabeth I and Mary Queen of Scots, visit Marrakesh

Strictly Come Laughing end of series party, 2004

Myself and Nicole Cutler in an awkward publicity still,
Strictly Come Dancing, *2004*

Putting on the boots, Chelsea Flower Show 2004

Our pod covered in 5,000 enamelled balls travels down the Chelsea Embankment

Paul Cunningham and I discuss our next garden plans, Lollipops Garden, 2004

*Lollipops Garden at Chelsea Flower Show 2004, with blue geraniums in the foreground
and the giant pod in the background*

Bunny Guinness in her boat race themed garden, next door to us at Chelsea Flower Show 2004

Charlie Dimmock and I having a swinging time

Presentation from Sophie, Countess of Wessex, London, 2003

Bouncing water baby Eppie and her Dad in Spain, 2005

Lavender and box ball garden, Chelsea Flower Show 2005

Laying out our box balls before the invasion of lavender at Chelsea Flower Show 2005

Poseur!

Hester Leneghan running operations
from Portobello Road, 2005

Myself and Rhys Ifans at Jools Holland's Hootenany at the BBC

With Cherie at Downing Street

Suburban woodland garden, Rathfarnham, Dublin

Steel pavilion in the leafy suburb of Foxrock

Steel meteor lands from outer space in Stoke Newington, Home Front in the Garden

Jimmy and Charlotte's garden in Laytown, County Meath

Our cruciform pavilion at the Westland Garden, Chelsea Flower Show 2007

With my favourite Irish Chelsea pensioner

Eppie photographed by her fashion photographer godfather Neil, 2006

The team at our Portobello Road studio, 2007

Receiving the IFTA Best Documentary Series Award from Mel Gibson for Blood of the Irish, *the first series I wrote*

The pony kids with Jane and Louise at Brennanstown Stables, Wicklow

Alan Titchmarsh and Terry Wogan with me
at Chelsea Flower Show

Myself with Justine and Eppie receiving an honorary
degree from Nottingham Trent University, 2007

Meeting the Queen with Sir Terence Conran at Chelsea Flower Show 2008

Our illuminated giant daisies, Oceanico Café Garden, Chelsea Flower Show 2008

With the Zulu planting crew at Pat's garden in Durban, South Africa, 2009

Me, Hannah Waterman, David Gest and Sherrie Hewson, Come Dine With Me, *Christmas 2009*

Getting ready to saddle up in Iceland for
No Frontiers *travel programme, 2009*

With Cristina, Eddie and family in
Rich, Famous and Jobless, *December 2009*

that gardening is fun from the earliest age. Teachers and community workers come in, areas of the school ground are given over to gardening, soil is tilled and potatoes, lettuce, corn, cabbage, tomatoes and peppers are sown. From 2010, thousands of fruit trees will be sent to schools by post.

My role is to be the Morrisons ambassador, to front the campaign and film ads, and take part in photo shoots. The fun part, however, is visiting the schools. I travel the country as the growing kits are being received or as the crops are nearing readiness for harvest. I arrive for morning assembly, where hundreds of little ones sit on the floor, sing me songs and ask questions. It is wonderful – they are adorable. The enthusiasm of a child learning about worms and soil, understanding plants, and letting you know that they bring these ideas home to mum and dad, and that they encourage their parents to start their own gardens – be it in a trough or window box where open space isn't available, or growing in the allotment with granddad – is entrancing.

The support the campaign receives from teaching staff and gardeners in the community is great. And maybe it is my age, or maybe it is Eppie at home, watching us create our own vegetable garden, that makes me realize that catching children at a young age and instilling in them the basic values of gardening is so important. We rounded up all Eppie's friends on the street one day and each of them got to plant a fruit tree. Eppie's was a cherry, variety 'Stella'. Her best friend Hannah from next door has an apple. There are also pears and figs and plums. After all my time spent championing the contemporary, building flashy water features, creating lighting effects and escaping into dens, what matters most to me is relaxing and encouraging the next generation of gardeners to take over.

ONLY FOOLS ON HORSES

In 2006, Sport Relief approached me about a television show-jumping series they were planning to raise much-needed funds. I had a meeting in Shepherd's Bush at the offices of Endemol, who made *Changing Rooms* and *Ground Force*, but also ominously *Big Brother*. Could I ride a horse? No, never been on one in my life. (Once or twice as a kid didn't count.) They wanted to take ten of us, of varying ability in horsemanship, and turn us into show-jumpers after a couple of months' training. There was then to be a ten-evening event to be shown live on the BBC, in which we'd be in open competition. We'd live in a converted stable block with twenty-four-hour camera surveillance. We'd receive the best training and any equipment required. Being Irish, it was expected that I had some kind of horsey pedigree. I didn't.

The nuts and bolts of it were that the BBC was going to provide me with lessons, equipment and a showcase to learn a new discipline. The pay off, once again, was that I would be subjected to humiliating public scrutiny. Without a doubt, it was worth it. I mentioned it at home. In my life you never know what the next conversation is going to be about. Justine's reaction was to worry about injury. Justine worries. About everything.

I understood. I work for myself, always on the go, travelling somewhere, generally abroad every other day. Anything that precluded me from doing so might jeopardize the mortgage. I was single-minded, utterly dismissive of any danger. Having just embarked on the *I Want a Garden* television series for RTE, I was spending a lot of time at home. Training was arranged at Brennanstown, Kilmacanogue, County Wicklow. The odd afternoon and Sunday mornings seemed to be the only time I was free. Clothing and equipment arrived. They seemed strange: tight jodhpurs, black boots, hard helmet. I dressed up and felt foolish. But at the riding school I fitted in. I was heaved onto a horse, called

Bailey I think, and all but sat facing the wrong end. Predictably, I was a disaster. Never brilliant for following instructions, I bounced on and off that horse, spending most of my time on the ground laughing. Jane, my tutor, was desolate. 'How is this ever going to happen?' she'd mutter. Oddly, I was enjoying myself. It was usually just the two of us, maybe with a little Jack Russell nipping at Bailey's heels, in a big steel shed. I don't think I was that concerned: seemingly, despite all my faults, I had a good 'seat', whatever that meant. I didn't feel in danger, and any bit of speed that Bailey could gather I found exhilarating. And then there was the jumping. Again, I had no aptitude but I loved it. I was bruised and battered. Eventually, after a month of these sessions, there was a vague sign of improvement. The dates of the summer competition were drawing ominously close.

Back in London, I started my training at stables in Ealing. A gaggle of pony kids, teenagers and younger girls, would sit on a paddock fence and giggle at me. I was to be assessed by our main trainer, Tim Stockdale. Tim had pedigree, as one of Britain's foremost jumpers. He is a Yorkshire man, plain-speaking and rugged. In the television industry he was already famous for the time when he had trained a participant on the Channel 4 programme *Faking It*. Back at Brennanstown, when I told them who was in charge, there was a sharp intake of breath. Wow, he's one of the best. I took to Tim immediately. And he laughed his way through my first demonstration; he thought I was hilarious on a horse. My arms flapped up and down like a chicken trying to take flight. I had complete disregard for protocol, and a care-free attitude. At the end of the session Tim had tears in his eyes and a red face. He had enjoyed the session, but was worried about me. Did I think I would be OK? Did I think I would make it? He would have to report back to the bosses, it wasn't too late to have me replaced. I was enjoying myself and wanted to do this. Training continued. One Sunday morning back at Brennanstown, Jane said to me, 'You know there's something really odd about you, you're a disaster on a horse, you won't take instruction, you completely forget the course, and yet sometimes, just sometimes, I wonder are we the butt of a joke? Are you sure you haven't done this before? Are you sure you haven't been in competition?' I laughed and rode away. How mad is that? I'm doing it all wrong and yet they are saying this is something I can do.

For two weeks immediately before the live event we were invited to participate in intense training every day. The location was a beautiful farm in rolling countryside, an hour from London. The owners were members of the Dutch national equestrian team. It wasn't so much a farm as a ranch. An outhouse near the stable block was luxurious, with a sort of living room that we changed in upstairs, a kitchen area, and oddly a bedroom. Looking back, it must have been somebody's flat, taken over by this motley crew of amateur jockeys. I met my fellow contestants: Ruby Wax; the Olympian Sally Gunnell; Duncan Bannatyne from *Dragons' Den*; Matt Baker from *Blue Peter*; Anna Ryder-Richardson, late of *Changing Rooms*; veteran actor Paul Nicholas; actress Josie D'Arby; Matt Littler from *Hollyoaks*; Jenni Falconer from GMTV; Suzi Perry, Nicki Chapman and Radio 1's Sarah Cox.

That was our side. And on the other side were Tim, and a brilliant collection of show jumpers and trainers who daily put us through our paces. We were photographed together, standing in front of and sitting on the trunk of a fallen tree, and our colours were handed out – my blazer was wine-coloured. We got snowy white jodhpurs for the live events, neat short-sleeved shirts and ties. Gloves were mandatory; much store was placed on how you were presented. Show jumping was an elegant and courteous sport. We were introduced to our horses. Mine, Isa, was OK. Bailey back in Wicklow had given me a run for my money: I think Tim maybe felt this new one was a safer bet. Having ongoing gardening commitments, I wasn't able to stay locally like some of the participants, but maybe that was lucky. Seemingly the accommodation was over an hour away. I'd arrive, and get dressed with everybody else – another disparate set of characters that I would never normally meet in my life. The joy of this collection of people was that everybody excelled at something in their own right, some, like Sally, exceptionally so. And here we were, all of us in the same boat, nervous about what was to come. Tim barked at us. We loved it. He was strangely reassuring, even when screaming blue murder. In his hands, we thought, we'll be OK. Ruby, of course, was a character, and looked amusing on her horse. Sarah, Nicki and Sally had done a bit of riding before. Duncan had an accident, fell off and broke his arm, so never made it to the event. That was a sharp warning for us. And Matt Baker turned out to be an accomplished all-rounder – a British judo champion and world record holder for something or other. As well as presenting *Blue Peter*, which he had recently left, he had over the years become a director on it. Here was a man who knew how to achieve, a winner.

I arrived early one morning, stumbled up the narrow stairs, battered and bruised but ready for another day in a dusty paddock. It was always wonderful sunny. I burst into the sitting room, dropped my bags and waded in through the bedroom in search of my uniform for the day. To my surprise there was someone in the bed. For a moment I felt like an intruder, then I got over it and retrieved my stuff. Fully kitted out, downstairs on a grassy bank I drank black coffee and exchanged greetings with the others as they arrived. Soon there was a huddle of us comparing bruises, talking about yesterday, gossiping about the property owners – then suddenly someone burst down the stairs and straight over to us, with a face of manic excitement. 'Do you realize who that is in the bed?' No. 'It's only Carrie Fisher – you know from Hollywood – upstairs in a bed in our stables.' Oh yeah, someone piped up; I'd heard that she's a friend of Ruby's. They went out last night and had a good time. So Princess Lea from *Star Wars* joined our little party, standing by the wooden fences to watch a strange group of people jump over some circular poles. The camera rounded in on her, she pledged support to her friend, said she'd be great at the event, the rest of us better watch out. Over our picnic lunch I got talking to her. And as she left she wrote her name and address on the back of a business card – Coldwater Canyon, Beverly Hills California 90210. If ever I was in town I was to get in touch.

We carried on with the training, and all of a sudden the big day was upon us. En masse, we decamped to a riding school at Braintree in Essex, not far from Stansted Airport. Horror was etched on our faces as we walked the first course with Tim. It seemed huge, and thousands of show-jumping enthusiasts would fill the stands that night. We were introduced to the panel of judges: Jodie Kidd, whom I'd met when we were discussing options for her garden; Robert Smith, an old-style show jumper, reminiscent to me of Harvey Smith, with a slightly comical face and no-nonsense attitude; and finally the chairwoman, Jessica Kuerten. I knew of Jessica, a blonde-bombshell Irish show jumper who didn't suffer fools gladly. A cross between Marilyn Monroe and Roy Keane: a woman of high principals who railed against unfairness in her sport, and who was currently number two in the world. Her role was to be critical – often. That first evening we paraded into the ring, terrified. The presenter Angus Deayton brought his scathing *Have I Got News For You* wit to our large barn, aided by the sweet and sporty Kirsty Gallacher. They made a good team. The applause from the floor was thunderous: show jumpers love any attention being given to their sport, and they especially liked our pony girls. Matt Baker, thanks to his get-up-and-go attitude on *Blue Peter*, also went down a treat. We jumped. My main ambition was to remember the course: jump 1, jump 2, then it's a double, then turn left…I think I had a few down. For the moment of judgement, you dismounted and stood in front of your jury. Jessica called me a 'big eejit'. This wasn't going well.

Inevitably someone was for the chop. Your hope in these situations is only really to get past programmes one and two, then anything else is a bonus. I survived. Exhausted, the remaining riders were rounded up and led to our new home: a built-for-television stable block focused on an open courtyard, with three sides containing stalls for the horses. There was a tack room that served as a diary booth, with an antiquated phone that would occasionally ring with instructions. And at the top of the yard was a living block. I was fascinated. There were cameras everywhere, and those large one-way mirrors inserted into most walls. Once again, I was bewitched by the mysteries of television. I cased the joint. The boys were in one bedroom, the girls down a small corridor. Automatic sputnik-type cameras were positioned in the corners of each room. Loos were clear of cameras. Our main living room was a long country-style farmhouse room with dressers and locked bookcases. The fridge was amply stocked, and fresh meals were prepared for us every evening. Games would be provided and encouraged. With Nicki, I went on the prowl. We discovered camera runs – little corridors built immediately behind the living room and the bedroom. In the dark, we stumbled across cameramen huddled behind black drapes. Like a naughty pair of St Trinian's schoolgirls, we ventured on till we'd found everything and everybody. Back with the group, food had been delivered – delicious meals every evening after the competition, ice-cold champagne and bottles of beer. A ritual ensued: we'd grab a bucketload of beer, find our way to the forbidden door and silently drop a couple of bottles at the feet of the shrouded cameramen. A whispered thank you and back out to join the fun.

And it continued, day after day. We were isolated from our families, but every night our nearest and dearest would arrive in the audience. Justine would have our next-door neighbour Ann for company, and little Eppie, only one and a half, would instantly spot me and scream out for her Daddy. It was an odd situation again – isolation and a common cause together breed instant and deep connections, or so it seems. But it's often superficial, lasting only until the final whistle. And while you may make countless cups of tea and endear yourself to your fellow travellers, you are continually sizing them up while calculating the length of your own stay. But you do cling to each other for the short period. In your stable block you would hug everyone in the morning, during lunch and in the evening. Snatched conversations can be gossipy: who you are feeling sorry for, who is a little bit weak. The joy and relief of returning to the stable block having lost one of your party are very real. And the production team always made sure to have fresh cold alcohol available, so that tongues might be loosened.

My riding improved dramatically. Uncannily, again one of the trainers sidled up to me during the week and – while telling me how terrible my technique was and what a great laugh it provided for all back stage – asked was I sure I had never been in competition before? To reach the age of eighteen and not be any good at anything but dreaming, to find a true passion for making gardens, then to find a voice and some energy to carry me through to some achievements, to be picked up for television and develop a career in broadcasting and writing, and now at forty- odd to find a sport that I had a natural ability and aptitude for: this wasn't what life had planned for me.

Soon it was just me and Matt in the boys' room, with about four girls left. Our horses were getting tired, as became clear when they were changed for fresh ones during a relay. Never had I felt so comfortable – racing round, jumping poles, turning tight corners, feeling wonderfully in control. Jessica began to say lovely things. One evening we did a pre-record. Now that the field was narrowing, they'd insert a second event in the live programme through VT. The race involved us jumping on and off horses, passing batons against the clock. We were divided into two teams. It was a mess. The instructions over the tannoy didn't add up, the judges were shouting one thing at us – to jump fences, get on horses, get off again– the trainers another. I felt safety was compromised. Some in our group were quite shaky, so there was a revolt. There was no way we were doing this again to make it appear perfect for the live show. Like a militant trade unionist, I summed their feelings up angrily. This was the evening that John, the agent I shared with Nicki and Josie, appeared. From across the stands he could see an argy-bargy, and he smiled to himself that the old passionate Diarmuid creating trouble hadn't gone away. Tim was called for, and in an instant – because we trusted him – poured oil on troubled waters. We jumped on our horses and completed the course without incident.

I made it to the last four, and then my time was up. In these situations, when you are out, you are *so* out. There was no going back to the stable house: a group of my own peers, with whom I had shared so much over the past month, had voted against me. I waited around, did the secondary television programme, the after-hours edition, was patted on the back, told what a good sport I was and sent in a taxi to the hotel. I wandered in to the Radisson at Stansted Airport and walked through the heaving bar feeling like a conquering hero. No-one blinked.

The following evening, on television for Sport Relief, a true hero appeared. We had been a bunch of performing monkeys jumping on gentle horses over a few sticks. David Walliams had swum the Channel – a cold, lonely and isolating feat, achieved by few – in a brilliant time.

DIARMUID'S PONY KIDS

Despite finishing my *I Want a Garden* series straight after Sport Relief, my head remained a bit in horsey land. A few years after our wedding, Justine and I had bought our first home, a flat in Finglas, on the banks of the River Tolka, very near the Botanic Gardens. It was what we could afford two bedrooms that within hours of the builders leaving I had started to destroy. I pulled down walls and made one big studio apartment with massive folding wooden doors, and decorated it as an elaborate and luxurious hotel room. It suited us perfectly as my work in England took off, being near the airport, stylish, and a perfect studio-type place for television programmes. Its location, however, raised some eyebrows in Dublin society. It occupied a strip of land at the end of the genteel suburb of Glasnevin, but ran up to an area that was notorious for its poverty, drug-related gangs and unemployment. But as with any community, it was also a place of great pride and strong values. There were regular stories, especially on the radio, of a disturbing rate of young suicides, particularly among teenage boys. Finglas and its neighbouring Ballymun got a very bad press and had suffered decades of neglect, with burnt-out cars, bonfires and loose horses on the roads as regular features of life. For many comfortably off Dubliners, these areas were no-go.

I was well aware of this other Dublin culture from the time when I was a student at the nearby Botanic Gardens, and now even more so, having bought a home in the area. When I was a child, my Dad had on occasion brought us to the Smithfield market in central Dublin, where horse and ponies were traded on the first Sunday of every month. It was unique and rough, combining the essence of rural horse fairs with the hoodie-wearing youth culture of the day. And where I lived was where many of these horses ended up, children and teenagers riding them through open fields, bareback, using ropes as reins. These kids were well beyond any social boundaries. You'd hear about the horses when AA Roadwatch reported the animals loose on the motorways as commuters tried to get to work. Driving in her relocated sporty Mazda into the underground parking base beneath our flat, Justine was startled by a number of horses nonchalantly wandering out. Alan Parker's film of Roddy Doyle's *The Commitments* has a wonderful scene where a freckled young lad is about to take his young horse up in the lift of the Ballymun tower block, where they both live.

What had amazed me in England was that if you were prepared to have a go with horses, the equine fraternity took you to their hearts. They really appreciated you having a go. And Sport Relief had put showjumping back on the map for the first time since Harvey Smith's infamous V-sign to the panel of judges. I had felt welcomed into that world, and I had got to know some of its senior figures, including the great Irish show jumper Jessica Kuerten. When she invited me to come her castle in the centre of Ireland, I decided to discuss this other side of Dublin with her. Did she know of these kids and their horses? No, she was from Northern Ireland and based in Germany, she had never heard of them. She was fascinated, though.

I set about writing a television series, with the idea of taking a number of these children and to see if they would be embraced by the show jumping community with the same enthusiasm as I had been. It was a love of horses that united these different parts of society.

The Dublin Horse Show is a grand event on the international show jumping calendar, taking place in August every year. Its highlight is the Aga Khan Trophy, the Nations' Cup, in which national teams from around the world compete against each other for a magnificent award. It attracts national and international interest. What if these kids could be trained to ride with saddles?

What if they could learn the proper way to treat an animal, with mutual respect? And what if some could be saved from difficult life situations? I brought the idea to the production company who made my garden shows. Together we took it to the broadcaster, and almost instantly it was commissioned.

And so the summer was planned out: we would recruit some of these young horse-lovers, create a daily equestrian camp, enter them in local competitions, give them a bit of international travelling, build them up so they would be fit to ride out directly after the Aga Khan Trophy on the final day of the Dublin Horse Show. For successive months we paid visits to Smithfield to let people know what we were up to. The first Sunday of every month it always seemed to rain. The place was fascinating. I felt an oppressive atmosphere, though I may have arrived early before the camera crew and felt a bit intimidated. Smithfield is an ancient part of the city that still has its cobbled streets. The square itself is now bordered by luxury apartments and hotels.

On the mornings of the horse fair, security guards stand at the hotels' entrances, refusing the casual visitor even a cup of coffee. But spending some time there, beginning to relax, allows you to observe the sometimes silent, always fascinating business of horse dealing. Ponies and stallions, some of them wild horses recently removed illegally from British moors, are scared and untamed. Rough-looking characters abound, and open trucks sell all sorts of tack, saddles and bridles. The odd tourist wanders through, mystified but intrigued. And policemen keep well to the side of the action, watching; obviously the place has been trouble in the past.

Dublin Corporation would love to see this ancient market moved out of the centre of population. No water troughs are provided for the often thirsty animals, and specialist officers in the prevention of cruelty occasionally appear. Children as young as six and seven man two-wheeled horse-racing carts. Slightly older youths jump on top of fierce beasts and physically wrestle them to submission. Palms are spat on, firm handshakes indicate a sale, cash changes hands. For as little as €80 you can buy a small pony. You feel sorry for these animals.

It's a knotty problem: do you bring your education, your knowledge of animal welfare and your liberal views into a traditional cultural situation like this? How can you affect it, make it better for everyone?

We gave out leaflets and talked to as many youngsters as possible. They had gathered in the centre of Dublin not only from Finglas and Ballymun but also from other places such as Firhouse and Tallaght, mostly areas that were socially and economically disadvantaged, and that form almost a complete ring around the outer limits of the city. There weren't many smiles, but furrowed brows and earnest conversation revealed the depth of their passion. The camera crew proved a mild attraction.

'Do you like horses?'

'Yeah, mister.'

'Where do you ride them?'

'In the fields behind the houses.'

'Do you ever use a saddle?'

'Naw.'

'What do your parents think of you owning horses?'

'Ah, they used to own them too.'

'Do you look after them?'

'Yeah. Mister, what are you at? Am I going to be on television? Am I going to be on the news?'

We told as many as possible and set up an audition of sorts – youngsters with their guardians were invited to a council-run stables at Fethercairn in Tallaght. Jessica flew in from Germany, and our little team was complete when trainer and jumper Ronan Corrigan joined the fray. Kids sat up on their horses and tried to jump some low fences. They found the saddles awkward. Often it was hilarious. One lad completed a little trot around but wouldn't approach the jumps. Jessica asked

'Do you like riding?'

'Naw, I hate horses.'

'Why are you here?'

'It's a day off school.'

We had one day to find five individuals, boys and girls. Thomas had a go. A big strapping good-looking lad of about sixteen, he was from the traveller community. He was disastrous on a horse. He hadn't much experience, he told me, but he really wanted to do this.

'But Thomas you're not much good.'

'I know, I just need a chance. Can I have another go?'

'No, sorry Thomas.'

He waited all day and got his second go at the end. He was no better.

At the end of the trials, Jessica, Ronan and I sat in a room. All of the participants had been photographed, and a little polaroid was paper-clipped to a printed sheet with their written details. We went through the selection process. That Dean guy was brilliant, cocky but with real potential, Ronan said. There were two brothers, Darryl and John from Finglas, both smilers. Darryl got the nod. And Darryl's friend from just down the road, another Dean, showed real promise. His nickname, used by everyone, was Squeaky. Only two girls had applied: Amy, diligent and quite assured, and Jade, with blonde ringlets, who was tenacious but had fallen at her first jump. She cried but got back on the horse and tried again. That won her a place. And finally we were down to one. I couldn't put Thomas out of my mind. There was something about him, the begging for a chance, needing a second go – how many of those was he going to get in life? We agreed. What a day.

It wasn't over. We had had a great success, achieving a lot before Jessica had to depart for the airport again. We had five youngsters, all enthusiastic, who we hoped would carry the same passion they had shown that day right through the summer. The next job was to tell them that they had been selected. We knew they loved horses, well most of them anyway, and that, combined with the attention that television brings, made an intoxicating mix. I was about to go to all their homes to talk with them and their parents, to let them know they had been successful. The nearest was Dean in Tallaght. He was embarrassed to see me again so soon, and tried to run away with a big smile on his face. I managed to pin him down and told him the good news: the smile got bigger and quick as a flash he was gone to his mates. In the house, I sat down with his mum and sister. They hoped this would mean something, they hoped one of the family would be able to achieve something. There were other sons, difficulties were suggested, and notes of regret hung in the air.

Then it was on to Jade, obviously beloved and full of excitement, a little princess. It was my turn to turn red when she told me her aunty fancied me. The next port of call was Thomas. Our procession of crew cars went to the given address. The director rang our car. Thomas didn't live at the address he had given. We waited in a laneway. Twenty minutes later he appeared. He didn't want us to film where he did live, and so, with him surrounded by a group of his cousins, I gave him the news at the side of a country lane.

'Are you serious?' he asked me, 'are you serious?' He looked away. 'Jesus', he said, a smile breaking out. 'You're not joking me?'

On then to Squeaky, a little thin lad whose whole face lit up on hearing the news. His mother hugged him. And finally to his friend just around the corner, the difficult one. We had to choose between two brothers, and Daryl had been successful. Life was an obvious struggle at home, with parents who were lovely but battling their own demons. This would be a great hope, and John was genuine in his happiness for his brother.

The relentless training started. Four days a week, they'd be picked up at any time from seven in the morning in the one minibus, and at nine they'd arrive at their new base, an equestrian centre in Mullingar. They'd always fight on the bus. They were from different tribes and anything could set them off. The fights would be vicious but generally verbal. It was hard on Jade being the only girl, but when it came down to it, she gave as good she got. Every day, Ronan put them through their paces. They were ill-disciplined, and some had a bad attitude towards the animals. They felt more important than the horses. The beasts were there to serve them. There was one member of the production team for every child. Despite their only being youngsters, these minders were needed: things could get unruly. In a way it was all to be expected.

The quality of their riding differed greatly. Some were naturals; others, like Thomas, were woeful. Discipline was important. The head of the Irish Show Jumping Association came down to present them with their membership. They'd need this if they were to compete in Dublin at the end of the summer. They were almost polite.

My role, in between digging my gardens and drawing lines on paper for others, was to appear occasionally, to troubleshoot. And every week Jessica would jet in and keep them in check – she could scream louder than them. We had a wonderful producer, Clare Kavanagh, a real Irish beauty with inbuilt tolerance and strong affection for the children, and Conor O'Mahoney, a solid director. He'd need to be. But fair play to the kids, they attended every day without exception. They also fought every day without exception. But they were on those horses in the ring, learning how to jump with saddles.

Strict procedure about qualifying for any appearance in the Royal Dublin Society's show grounds was to be relaxed to allow them to participate. It was still felt that they should appear in some local shows throughout the country to gain a little experience, however. I witnessed one or two. Generally it was the same. Squeaky had a natural ability, with a twang of arrogance. Thomas was always pulled at the last minute. The set-ups were often the same, not a hundred miles removed from *Father Ted*: a little cubicle or caravan with a tannoy, generally some lady announcing 'and Squeaky is riding such and such.' Onlookers were bewildered. Who were this bunch? A million miles from the equestrian world.

The group was brought to Homestead Saddleries, where they were fully equipped. The street clothes were replaced by riding boots, shirts, ties, jodhpurs and blazers. It wasn't long since I had undergone a similar transformation. This felt more dramatic, though. In the shop they fought like cats and dogs, resorting to horsewhips to attack. Jessica yanked them out of trouble by their earlobes. Lined up, they looked cute.

As time went on, we arranged a surprise day trip to Jessica's state-of-the-art base in Germany. They loved Jessica's place, and her husband Eckhart treated them to a barbecue. They were fascinated by a sauna for horses. Jessica had succeeded in connecting with them all, so for most of the day their behaviour was good. A few days later in Mullingar, their tales of wonderment poured out. More local shows followed, Squeaky jumping better than ever, the others bringing up the rear in a progression of downward steps, Thomas always left out. He was scared of horses and they knew it. Dean was joining Squeaky in the arrogance stakes. They knew they had ability. Darryl had great ability, but would get frustrated. With Jade there were lots of tears. She remained plucky. I witnessed one incident where a horse was belted. The offender was hauled along with a few colleagues to the Dublin Society for the Protection of Cruelty to Animals. They were astonished at some of the images they were shown there, and resolved to behave better.

When I set out on this project I had had the idea of taking the kids away on a trek, somewhere like the wilds of Canada. I had imagined sitting around campfires eating baked beans, having to rely on each other, and the children coming out of themselves and maybe understanding responsibility. Nowhere to go for a smoke, no smokes to be had. There was a budget, of course, and I was told that Connemara on the rugged west coast of Ireland was where our teens would be let loose for a few days.

I set out for the west of Ireland, not quite sure about what was planned, on my way to meet Willie Leahy, who did some horse-trekking. He wasn't hugely happy when I arrived. All he knew was that some inner-city kids were coming and the television crew had negotiated a cut-price rate. We also wanted him as our companion, which would mean he'd have to leave his group of high-paying Americans to an assistant. When the kids arrived, they weren't the most polite bunch in the world. They were tired and angry after their long coach trip, and not at all impressed when informed they would have to catch their own horses in a field and saddle them up themselves. Their language was intemperate. Willie wasn't pleased at all. Our escapade looked doomed.

I said to Clare, 'I hope we're not going as part of a larger group. These kids needs to be together, no one will understand them.'

Further negotiations. Willie's mood worsened. After an hour he led our little bunch, including me, down a country road. The kids wanted to gallop. He screamed, 'slow down! I have to see ye first, see what ye are like. It's not safe!'

He led us on to a beach. The kids took off. He scratched his head under his leather stetson.

'By God,' he said. A smile crossed his face. These were cowboys, they could hold their own. The kids raced backwards and forwards. Whenever he cried slow, they speeded up. He gathered us all together. The mood had softened. We followed in a line as we were told. The children appreciated the new twinkle in Willie's eye. He was an old boy but a bit wild like themselves, they sensed. And then we arrived at a beautiful small bay, with gentle rolling waves and a headland across the water. The kids – dressed, riding on saddles with reins and long leather boots – went straight for the water. Willie screamed at them to come back, but there was no stopping them. One after another they rode their horses into the drink.

'Mine's swimming!' a shout went up.

'So's mine. This is a gas. Hey, Diarmuid come on in!'

I sat there with Willie.

'In fifty years,' he said to me, 'I have never seen anything like that.' He smiled. 'They're in there with their bloody saddles, fully dressed. They don't care, do they?'

I joined the kids, I had to. If I didn't I wouldn't survive the slagging. It was magic. Out of Dublin, away from competition and stress, on the backs of swimming horses, the kids were having a ball. An hour later we sat by the side of a hedgerow to have lunch. Willie pointed to a pan of sliced bread, a few pounds of ham and butter. There were flasks of tea and cold water. No protest. The kids munched away happy, happy to be kids. They joked. That evening they played football and ping-pong in their bed and breakfast. On another little beach they borrowed buckets and spades and made sandcastles. Innocence.

I was worried about our next trip. I knew Zara Philips socially, and she had been kind enough to welcome our motley crew to her mother's stately pile, Gatcombe Park, during its three-day eventing course. Zara, a wonderful girl who was fun, was competing. Our plane landed at Bristol Airport, and as we drove we revealed our destination to the kids. Jade's eyes lit up.

'Is she a real-life princess?'

'No, not exactly, but her mum is.'

'Wow!'

There was huge excitement. I got the kids out of the minivan, leaving just a couple of the them unsupervised. Minutes later we heard screams – we rushed in, and Jade and Dean had to be separated. In the pristine, turfed car park of Princess Anne's home, Jade screamed at Dean and Dean screamed back, their faces red, hotheads, name-calling.

We were brought to meet the non-princess at her stable block. She was dressed in top hat and tails and about to compete in dressage. Her horse, Toytown, was beautiful. Zara was worried though. 'He's often a bit naughty at home, he can play up.' The kids gathered round and fired questions. Zara didn't know what to think, but she could give as good as she got. Amused by this bunch of urchins, she smiled sweetly, found their innocence endearing. They liked her. Today would be OK. 'Right', she said, 'I have to get this competition out of the way, and then the rest of the day I'm with you lot.' We followed as Zara took centre stage. Dressage has never been my thing. It's interesting to watch but there's too much control of the animal for me. Out of nowhere a bank of photographers appeared, about twenty of them. As if by magic, with long lenses all hoping for Zara to fall for that one shot, Toytown played up. Despite being in her mum's back garden there was no home advantage, and Zara, disappointed but stoic, retreated to the stables to change. The kids continued to fire questions. Lunch first, she announced, and then we're going to walk round the course. She drove us up and down the mounds, explaining all the jumps, the water, the tunnels. The kids were in the palm of her hand. This was the essence of the programme that I had written: a common interest such as horses, or indeed gardening, breaking down barriers. Passions shining through and perceived roles forgotten. Programmes were signed and we waved our goodbyes. 'Will you come to Dublin to watch us jump, Zara?' 'If I can, I'd love to.'

The day in August was nearing. We were nervous and the show

grounds themselves were getting twitchy about these kids. Who exactly were they? Would they behave all right? Could they jump? All of them had done OK, Squeaky and maybe Darryl excelling, though Thomas still was a major problem. The morning arrived. Jessica and I joined the kids in a minibus, driving through their estates, right through Dublin: everyone was very quiet, the nerves were real. We disembarked on the site, the main gates on the leafy southside road. Little was said. We were given our own little room, gathered together for a pep talk on behaviour and nerves by Ronan and Jessica. I'm sure we hugged. It was a beautiful day.

We did press interviews to promote the programme. The kids weren't interested, gave one-syllable answers. A succession of journalists asked pointed questions, nothing to do with the programme. Jessica kept her cool. Family and friends arrived, but before they were let loose the kids changed into their green blazers and white jodhpurs. Names were drawn from a hat to establish the order of jumping. I wandered around with Jessica as she pointed out all the characters. It s another world: men in bowler hats and ladies in tweed skirts looking on as characters on horses perform and rosettes are awarded. There were gaggles of girls, pony kids, thrilled to see their heroine Jessica in the flesh.

We went out and sat on the wooden benches in an old-fashioned concrete stand to watch others in the arena. There was tension in our group, nerves were beginning to show. Darryl decided he didn't want to take part. A message came through from Buckingham Palace – Zara, who couldn't be there on the day, wished our little group well. Memories of our day at Gatcombe Park buoyed the atmosphere, and then Willie Leahy arrived with his family from Connemara. This was something he wasn't going to miss. The kids were thrilled. We went down to the practice ring. Ponies trotted round, and one by one Jessica cajoled them over jumps. Nothing had changed. Squeaky was speedy, Thomas reticent. Moments before the bell rang in the main arena he still wasn't performing. It was time.

The rest was a blur. I remember most of the group going out, Squeaky achieving his clear round, thousands of people in the stand. Glancing for a moment at the VIP gallery, there was Dad in prime position beside the President of the Royal Dublin Society. How did he get in? How did he know? These kids were unknowns, but their family and friends managed to create an infectious enthusiasm that was picked up by the rest of the spectators.

Jessica and I watched as Thomas emerged to cheers. He didn't have his leg on. There was no power being transmitted to the horse. A trot up to the first jump and a refusal. After all the cheers, the crowd went quiet. The jumps weren't high. Thomas trotted around again. A second time. Same thing. Jessica and I shouted, 'keep it going, don't worry, try again!' Seven times. The look on Thomas's face said everything, embarrassed but determined. And on the seventh attempt, over the horse went. And over all the jumps. The crowd erupted in a frenzy. The nerves of the big occasion were set aside. Our five little kids had stood up to the big occasion, and in front of thousands of people. Immediately after the Nations' Cup, they had jumped in the main arena on the final day of the Dublin Horse Show.

There was a formal presentation of rosettes and mementoes, and then they took off like mad things on a lap of honour. We had tears running down our faces. And then some commotion in the distance. Squeaky's saddle fell off. How, we don't know. Bareback, he cantered round the ground one more time. The cameraman ran up to him.

'Are you missing anything, Squeaky?'

Squeaky looked back with that impish grin and an emphatic 'No!'

Our bareback riders were bareback once more.

A few months later we gathered together in a hotel in Finglas to watch the first programme go out. Jessica was in Germany. We all had a chat with her by phone. We made an unusual group –

the television production team, family and friends. It was very happy. Despite all the problems, these kids had kept their side of the bargain. They'd taken on board any discipline doled out, and all of them had managed to jump in Dublin.

The first programme showed the selection process and gave a hint of the turmoil ahead. Everyone loved it. I'm used to lots of attention, but if by an accident of birth you are from an area hit by deprivation, often very few people care. You miss out on being singled out for encouragement or praise. For our group and their families this was what was happening. People would see them, appreciate them, and the opportunity could be a springboard for something positive.

As he was leaving, Squeaky's dad Tom came over to me. 'We're having some trouble with the council. A whole group of us got together and created some temporary stables with containers in the fields that kids have used to keep their horses for fifty years. We've been trying to make this better for them and their horses. Since we've organized ourselves people have stopped burning cars there. Something really good is happening. We have a tack room, stables and dry food for the horses, all under cover. Some lads doing building across the way have laid a pipe so we have water there now. But the council put a note on it saying we have no permission.'

I was concerned. A group of parents and friends from the community helping themselves, trying to keep kids away from danger, creating an environment where a vet visited every few days, and the council was threatening it all. Nobody does anything for these kids.

'Tom, anything I can do?'

'Don't worry, Diarmuid. We've arranged a meeting at eleven o' clock on Friday with the council. I'm sure it will be OK."

'Just give us a ring if you need anything.'

I thought nothing more of it. The first episode of the programme did really well in the ratings. The whole country seemed to be watching it. They weren't sure about these kids. On Saturday evening, Clare the producer rang me.

'Did you hear anything, Diarmuid?'

'No,' I said.

'There's been trouble with some of the kids' horses. The council destroyed their stables.'

I rang Tom. He was in shock. 'We are sitting around a little bonfire here. The kids are in tears. Everybody else is scratching their heads. You wouldn't believe what went on.'

'But you were having a meeting. Everything was going to be OK.

'The man from the council rang me at twenty to eleven on Friday. His mother was ill. He asked could he rearrange. I told him I was very sorry his mother was ill and we could certainly rearrange but I was worried they would do something. He told me not to worry. On Saturday morning at five I got a call from a neighbour who lives next to the fields. It seems hundreds of police arrived in riot gear with council workers and trucks. What they couldn't lift, they mangled. They rounded up horses and ponies. One neighbour ran out and managed to get a load into his yard before the police could get them. I raced up there and saw one policeman taking off his gear and throwing it on the ground when he saw what he was being asked to do. I saw a council worker in tears.'

On Sunday morning I visited the site to see for myself. It was a crushing picture. Mangled bits of containers with sharp edges that horses had run into, cutting themselves, discarded bits of temporary stable, and a devastated group of people who had only tried to make their children's lives better, to keep them off the streets in an area with the highest rate of young suicides in the country. It was mystifying. I took notes and photographs, and interviewed as many people as I could, including the community who lived next to these fields. What they had seen was brutal. I went home and rang the newsroom at RTE radio. Then I rang Clare the producer. I was asked to come in and do a live interview soon after eight o'clock on the Monday morning. Clare came with me. I described what I had seen and what I had heard. The official bodies would give no information other than denying that animals were injured. I'd seen the gashes on the legs, not caused by the children. A foal just weeks old had been left while its mother was taken to a pound. I went for breakfast with Clare. The production company rang her: 'Tell Diarmuid not to do any more interviews.'

Claire protested. 'He's only doing what's right. This is nothing to do with our programme. We didn't film there. Most of the kids affected weren't on the documentary.'

The reply came: 'Tell him to stop talking to the press.'

I don't believe in the idea of television using contributors as material and then dropping them. These people who had given us a programme were from one of the most vulnerable parts of society. I'd been welcomed into their lives and houses. They'd given us the material for programmes which at that year's national awards won best documentary series. I couldn't be blind to what was happening in their lives. The council huffed and puffed in the media, issued denials. Embarrassed by the overwhelming reaction from the press and public, they began to work with the community. I got a letter from the production company thanking me for my work, but they wouldn't be pursuing another series of my garden series that they had also produced. They told the press they had no plans to work with me in the future. I was dropped like a hot potato.

Some time later, when the broadcaster RTE wanted them to produce another gardening series with me, I was offered the role by that same production company. I turned it down. I took it on myself to look after these children, to manage their expectations and to encourage a possible future in the equine industry. I brought them over to jump at the Christmas show at Earls Court in London, where Jessica teamed them with five of the best show jumpers in the world. Squeaky has recently returned from Tim Stockdale's stables in Nottingham. Tim reckons he should be a jockey. It's a delicate time in these young people's lives. There are two roads they could take. Keeping them on the right one is important.

COME DINE WITH ME

Like many others, I have retreated to cooking as a form of television entertainment, watching Nigella and Jamie strut their stuff rather than me having to. At home, when cooking comes around, well, I dress the table, I clean up, grab a beer and retreat to the sofa as the sweet and savoury smells waft through the house. My guilty secret was *Come Dine With Me*, a bitchy cookery dinner party show that since its beginnings in 2005 has become something of an international phenomenon. Made by Granada for Channel 4, it started off as a cheap daytime idea: invite five strangers who live in the same area to get together and on successive nights cook dinner in their own homes for each other. Each morning the four that weren't cooking would receive the menu, and they'd give their first impressions, commenting on their likes and dislikes and how they expected that evening's chef to do. There's no presenter to get in the way, just a catty voiceover written by a team of comedy writers and delivered by David Lamb. The fascination is on so many different levels: getting to look inside people's houses, to see how they cook, how they prepare, how the guests react and how they nose around each other's properties. It's fantastic television: voyeuristic, fun, sometimes poignant thanks to the personal stories that emerge across the dinner parties. As the guests leave each evening in a black taxi, slightly the worse for wear after too many tipples, they score each other out of ten.

Now I'd never dream of going on a cookery show – a proper one, a competitive one. The call came – would I be interested in doing a Christmas *Come Dine With Me* special? The programme had jumped from daytime to prime time, and in these episodes there were just four participants. The concept was exactly the same. Well, I was intrigued. Because I watch it so often, I was dying to know how the programme gets made, all the little secrets. Who are the team behind it? Was it done four nights in a row? How much do you get to spend on your menu? But also, who would possibly be my fellow dinner guests? My kitchen as such is in County Wicklow. In London I eat out for every meal. I don't even make coffee. What would I do? Where would I do it? The guests weren't going to travel for one night to Wicklow from central London, so it seemed impossible. But I was hooked. I said yes, and I'd figure out the practicalities later.

There followed a nervous month trying to see if a suitable mix of people and places could be arranged for this very special Christmas celebration. I assumed it had all gone away. But all of a sudden everything was confirmed. The team came around to my little place on the Portobello Road and loved it. They asked for my ideas on what my menu might be. They had to know by the following day. I hadn't a clue. Christmas dinner. Well, Christmas to me is about tradition – food, drink, music, certainly the turkey and the ham. I'm not particularly fond of either, but I'd hate for them not be there for Christmas. I had watched my mother and my wife successively battle in the kitchen every Christmas morning and debate the preparation for a month beforehand. Was this what I was getting myself into? What would I do? It was Thursday afternoon. I rang Bord Bia (the Irish food board) in Dublin and asked for help. I went to their offices, went through heaps of menus and started to harness my ideas. Only a week to go…

There was a dress code for the week. This was revealed at the last minute. The first night was to be glam; the second, mine, well I just wanted an elegant Christmas look; the third somebody had decided to have a fancy dress and they would supply the costumes. And the fourth was rock and roll. How do you plan for a week like that? I went in to Alias Tom on Duke Lane, and from the bowels of his emporium Tom set me up for the entire week.

Everyone's involvement was a secret: we weren't told who the other guests were. The first night I was driven mysteriously to a

Georgian townhouse in Islington. There were three other Mercedes all pulled up outside with blacked-out windows. I was self-consciously glam in a golden jacket – Alias Tom had pulled out all the stops. My attention was diverted as the first guest was led in. Soon it was my turn. I rang the doorbell and Hannah Waterman, daughter of Dennis and herself an *Eastenders* actress, let me in. Upstairs in her flat was David Gest, ex of Liza Minnelli. And I was thrilled to see an old friend, Sherrie Hewson, latterly of *Coronation Street* and more recently a panellist on *Loose Women*. The stress on Hannah's face was clear to see. We had champagne and quails' eggs, all very polite. It turned out she wasn't at home. This was an apartment she had seen for the first time that day, arranged by the production company: she had never cooked in that kitchen. Dinner was served. I'm not a fan of fish, and never have been. In my office earlier that morning there had been real glee among the camera crew when the menu was revealed – trouble straight away. But I vowed to be fair: if someone wanted to serve fish, well I'd have a go. I didn't feel it was very Christmassy, fish pie for mains and scallops for starters, but hey. The scallops were delicious. The fish pie, well, I'm sure it was lovely. I tried. But David and Sherrie gave Hannah such a hard time that I went the other way and was over-the-top effusive. I was excited to see how things happened, especially the marking. We were all put separately in the same taxi, which had been rigged up with cameras. I gave my mark, an eight. As things would work out it was a silly mark, far too high – but what a great girl and a fun night. Everyone had relaxed in each other's company. David turned out to be a hoot.

And then the day I dreaded. When I say I don't cook I really mean it. The weekend before, I had taken the precaution of being taught to cook a meal by a wonderful chef, Monique McQuaid, who runs the cookery school at Donnybrook Fair in Dublin. She'd been brilliant, but the menu we had both come up, with help from Bord Bia was Christmas with a twist, lots of it and slightly complex.

The trial run at home had gone well. Our Sunday guests, my gardening television director Bonnie Dempsey and her film producer partner Dave, lived to tell the tale. But Monique had been watching over my shoulder.

Alone in Notting Hill, my weekday base, I could feel my confidence evaporating. I'd brought over the little Golf from Dublin port, stuffed with everything I'd need. I wanted the menu to have an Irish flavour. We had goodies from Avoca, a local food emporium, cheese from County Wicklow and wonderful turkey fillets and bacon from Irish producers. I had Irish whiskey sauce and every herb and spice imaginable. And seeing as I don't cook in London, the car was weighed down with every plate, kitchen implement, chopping board and Christmas tree decoration from our house in Kilmacanogue. When I had got the car to London, I had flown home to Dublin again to give my meal a trial run, and on the flight back to London I sat beside Craig Doyle, a super chef. He made me go through every course in detail. Sitting a few rows behind was Sammy Leslie, from Castle Leslie in County Monaghan. I asked her what she was at, and it turned out that she was over to launch her new range of smoked salmon at Harrods. So that was the salmon sorted. The budget for the meal was £125, and as it was Christmas there was an additional £100 for decorations. The vegetables were to be from Portobello Road: the markets are directly outside my front door, and I have known Tony, the nearest stallholder, for years. Whenever we have a garden at Chelsea, he brings his mum down in her wheelchair and we have fun. Tuesday is generally his day off, but he set up stall especially for me and made sure it was packed with everything I needed. So I bought my potatoes, my sprouts, my baby carrots, beetroot, clementines, passion fruit and fresh thyme a couple of yards from home!

So, on to the cooking. Desserts were first, as they had to set: twenty clementines squeezed, strained juice of passion fruit, caster sugar added, and gelatine dissolved. A refreshing clementine and Muscat jelly to cleanse the palate. I worried about them all day, would they set in time in the fridge?

Next, a potato cake mix for the canapés: blinis topped with either smoked salmon or black pudding. Potatoes boiled, added to eggs, milk and spring onion and seasoned; a camera over my shoulder that I wanted to scream at. Oysters arrived from my favourite London pub, the Cow on Westbourne Park Road. Then the gammon had to be boiled and the butter clarified. I had to make a sauce to go over the ham, which involved making caramel and adding whiskey. Secretly I had stashed a way a little from the Dublin trial in case it didn't work out. I slaved over a tiny cooker all day – it was a nightmare. Between that, running and dressing trees, choreographing two live reindeer and a 'Victorian' choir to sing carols, and then arranging for a keg of Porterhouse stout to be sent from Dublin by my friend Oliver Hughes, there weren't enough hours in the day.

Soon I heard rumours of the guest arriving. The crew could see I was in a mess. The sound man on side winked at me and told me that he would mike them all extremely slowly, giving me another precious twenty minutes. And so they trundled up the spiral staircase, one by one, all relaxed and happy. Not me, though. I was in bits. I hardly had time to change my shirt – elegant I was not. I served them poinsettias – a drink suggested by Monique, consisting of Prosecco, Cointreau and cranberry – as a welcome. Then it was back to the blinis and straight into the office room across the rooftop (my London home is strange) for a pint-pulling competition with a barman from the Porterhouse in Covent Garden. The blinis were a little cold. The oysters, for those who could take shellfish, were delicious. As soon as everyone was set up, I dashed in to the kitchen and starting roasting my beetroots – the salad was mainly rocket with orange segments, melted goats' cheese and whole walnuts. At the last minute the beetroot went

on, and we were ready to sit down. I had begged my favourite Jasper Conran dinner service from Wedgwood, and the table looked great.

The night went by in a dream, or was it a nightmare? But the guests were pleasant and they seemed to like the food. The carrots were not a success, but that was all. The main course had been turkey escalopes and well-seasoned gammon in breadcrumbs with the whiskey sauce – a triumph, thought everybody, which surprised me – with potatoes in roasted in duck fat and pan-fried brussels sprouts. The plates were cleaned. Afterwards the jelly had set and it was delicious. The night became a blur of champagne. When they all left I collapsed. It was very late. I scrubbed until the early hours and went to bed still not believing it was over.

By the following evening I was giddy. I was ready to party; it was Sherrie's turn to cook. We never knew where we were going, so the car picked me up from a book signing with Terence Conran at the Conran Shop in Marylebone High Street. As a committed chef, he couldn't get his head around the show's concept. I left with him with his Christmas gift of Wicklow cheese. The car brought me just three streets away. And when we got there I was given my costume, a horrible polyester Christmas pudding. I waddled in, and there was Sherrie dressed up to the nines as Mrs Santa Claus, in a beautiful red dress with a white fur stole and carefully arranged snowsdrops in her hair. David arrived as an elf and Hannah as a Christmas tree. We weren't happy. Sherrie looked brilliant, but we looked ridiculous – and things were only going to get worse. Sherrie seemed happy enough, though. She had hit the bottle early and had obviously thoroughly enjoyed the preparations. Champagne was found and we sat in our costumes watching her do, well, do things. An hour passed. No food. Not a crisp. David was itching in his elf gear. He's allergic to polyester.

Another twenty minutes passed. Sherrie had forgotten we were there. I was in playful form. I whispered to Hannah. And together we legged it, down the stairs and out the front door. Swiftly followed by camera crew, producer and director, who knew we were up to no good: me playing the part of a plum pudding and Hannah looking marvellous as a tree, we wobbled through the streets of London.

Regulars in a lonely nearby pub were startled to see us fall through the door. After a lovely pint we were enticed back. Food was ready. Yippee! Sherrie wasn't happy, and David was, well, a very annoyed polyester elf. The starter was unusual: Yorkshire pudding and strawberry compote. We stared at each other, then at the food. Sherrie left the table, and quick as a flash we bounded down the stairs again, this time with David in tow. And back to the pub, where no one even blinked this time. David ordered a pizza. And after half an hour someone told us that main course was ready. Back to the house. There was a frosty reception. Dinner was served, the full Christmas works. I complimented Sherrie on the stuffing, delicious with apricots. The others looked at me. I was the only one with it on my plate. And then, with much aplomb, the pudding arrived. Home-made, looking gorgeous, it was soon smothered in cream and decorated with chocolate buttons. As she delivered it to the table, Sherrie slipped and dropped the whole thing on the floor. And then she fell in its wake. What a memorable night.

Thursday morning I was exhausted and just a little hungover. Going to dinner three times in a week and having guests round is tiring. I tried to do some work in the office, without much success. At noon I had an appointment with the crew on the South Bank. This was the daily routine. On the morning of the dinner, the menu would be revealed and you would be asked a few questions about the previous evening. Because Sherrie was recording two episodes of *Loose Women* back to back, the crew had picked a location near the London studios where it was filmed, so she could hop out in her lunch break and have her say. The location for me was the upstairs room in a nearby pub. I set off on my bike and had a glorious cycle on a beautiful autumnal day through Hyde Park, down to Chelsea, across the river and down the embankment on the other side. In the pub the shot had been set up, and at the bar waiting for me was a pint of stout. I removed it. If I never saw a drink again I'd be happy. David's menu was revealed: lobster salad in a Russian sauce; veal in a sauce with capers, with roast potatoes and puréed nutmeged veg; and some Christmas surprise pudding. Wow! And he said he couldn't cook. This was a beautiful menu. And who knew what other surprises the bold David would have lined up for the evening?

His dress code was rock and roll, so it was on with the leather jeans and frilly back shirt, find a guitar, and at seven o'clock I was collected, bound for an address in St John's Wood. The evening was to kick off at seven fifteen. There was mayhem in the foyer, with people coming and going. The doormen gave me hints of what was happening upstairs. Life, they said, was always interesting with David living there. It was about twenty past eight before I was told to go in the lift as the first guest to arrive. I was exhausted, nervous and intrigued. As soon as the lift door opened, there was Santa Claus, Mrs Claus and their two kiddie Clauses.

Refusing to sit on Santa's lap, I instead opted for Mrs Claus. She gave me my Christmas stocking, which I would later discover was stuffed with Tiffany boxes full of gifts that he and Liza had been given for their wedding. And so, inside. I was met by two little people (don't ask) and two Chinese girls, then Mickey Rooney and family, and to round off events a full gospel choir.

David lives in a posh flat in St John's Wood. All the walls were covered with gold discs, the furniture was beautiful Art Deco, and on display everywhere were the results of a life spent collecting rock and roll and Hollywood memorabilia. Michael Jackson stuff was everywhere. David was his best friend. The place was fun. In the kitchen a celebrity chef oversaw David's cooking. The lead gospel singer transformed into our waitress, and the food, course by course, was very good. We had to praise the Lord a lot and the cabaret was the best I'd been to.

David was a great host, he could definitely cook and his stories of a life in show business were enthralling. It was especially poignant when he talked of his friendship with Jackson.

The eventful week ended with David and I being crowed joint winners at three in the morning. Hours later I packed my car up with gifts, left-overs and pots and pans, and drove out of Notting Hill, through London and towards Wales, where I got the ferry to Dublin. Home sweet home for Christmas!

71 DEGREES NORTH

In late 2009 and early 2010 I took part in two television series which presented two very different kinds of challenge.

For *71 Degrees North*, as part of a group of ten celebrities, I travelled to the Arctic Circle on a survival mission. We were all apprehensive when we met at Gatwick Airport for the flight to Oslo. The names of the rest of the team hadn't been confirmed to us. One or two I had met before – Andrew Castle from GMTV, and Shane Richie from *Eastenders*. There was also the Welsh rugby player Gavin Henson, Suzi Amy, Chardonnay from *Footballers' Wives*, and the Glasgow entrepreneur Michelle Mone. The format had been running in many other countries for up to eleven years, and ITV had commissioned it for a British run. I had to undergo full medical and psychological tests to see if I was sane and fit enough to spend time isolated in white-out conditions, in freezing temperatures and performing competitive tasks. We were to live in tents, and to be divided into teams that would be pitted against each other to win privileges such as hot meals and nights in luxury hotels.

Suddenly I was one of the older people. There were a couple of athletes and very fit young body-conscious actors. I was in my mid-forties, with a middle-aged belly, no sporting skills to speak of and a fear of heights, but I did possess some stamina. The conditions were quite unbelievable. We were given very basic training and health and safety information. There was a crew of about sixty, each and every one of us wrapped for the Arctic conditions. Our kit was extensive, and if we neglected to pack a single item – gloves, mittens, goggles, long johns – this could result in our team losing the task. You watched out for everybody and they watched out for you. You were always just minutes from mild hypothermia, which can lead to hypothermia and frostbite, disorientation and loss of consciousness. There was a heightened

276

sense of awareness and of fear. This went beyond a television programme and became a personal challenge.

Just as in the school yard forty years before, team captains were appointed and I was picked last. Our tasks ranged from riding sleighs, carrying passengers and driving huskies in a thirty-kilometre race, to climbing ice waterfalls with picks, swimming in fjords and building snow caves. It was difficult, claustrophobic and challenging. I loved every second of it.

I was out way too early. I would have enjoyed a few more programmes. The experience left me with a continuing sense of wonder about the places I get to – remote towns and villages, snow-covered landscapes – working with people from so many backgrounds.

Rich, Famous and Jobless was a totally different kind of challenge.

An invitation to appear on a reality show came through from the BBC. No information other than the fact that I would be removed from my normal environment was forthcoming. I was told to dress well, as if I was going out to a do or to meet a client. I would be collected by car. The Mercedes brought me to a cavernous disused warehouse south of the Thames. I was told to pack for ten days, and at an allotted time to walk into the warehouse pulling my suitcase.

This was the start of the programme *Rich, Famous and Jobless*, a contemporary television take on the issue of people who survive on benefits. The production company, Love Productions, had already made a similar series about homelessness, using celebrities as a device to garner interest. I hadn't seen it, but I knew that the concept involved embedding participants in different situations and communities.

Back at the warehouse, I met my fellow participants, Larry Lamb, of *Eastenders* and *Gavin and Stacey*, Meg Mathews, a designer formerly married to Noel from Oasis, and Emma Parker-Bowles, car mechanic and niece of you-know-who. We lined up with our belongings in front of us. Two experts from the world of unemployment came to brief us. The atmosphere was spartan. We were given statistics and a challenge. Our possessions, mobile phones and money were to be removed. We'd be stripped, given street clothes and limited provisions. We were handed envelopes – £39 in each – and told we'd live in four separate locations around the country.

We broke for lunch and the four of us huddled together. What were we going to do? How would we survive? This might be the last proper food we would have for some time. Where would we be going? How would we cope? And before we could blink we were back again in our line-up under the spotlight, being told that we had to go out there, survive and understand how people lived. We should try and make money, we should look for work, and we should form opinions. In five days we would be brought back to the warehouse with our spoils – money and experiences – before being sent away again, this time for something completely different.

And then we were bundled into people carriers. I, it seemed, got lucky – for me there would be no four- or five-hour journey to Hartlepool or Wales as there was for the others. I was going to Hackney in east London, a journey of half an hour. But it was one of the most crime-ridden parts of Britain. The stats read out to me were frightening, and the unemployment rate very high.

Personal security was a huge issue. I was introduced to my two 24-hour-minders: for the duration of the programme, wherever I was, they would lurk in the shadows. One was ex-SAS, the other ex-French Foreign Legion. They didn't smile when I said hello.

I was handed an envelope with an address on it and a set of keys. With cameras rolling, I walked up the street of small council flats. I stopped somebody in the street for directions and started chatting – what did they work at? They were coy initially but after a couple of minutes they told me they were on benefits, that everybody was on benefits. Everybody I was to meet would be on benefits.

Was there any hope of finding work? I asked. They were young, well-dressed, healthy, funky looking. They shook their heads: 'There's nothing going on around here, anybody who works around here leaves in the morning and travels way out. There are no jobs.' They had been looking for jobs for years. With a wave they wished me luck.

Up a narrow stairway I put the key in the door. I was home. There was a very narrow hallway, one door locked, then a dishevelled bedroom and living room where everything appeared to have been upside down, and a kitchen which had an amazing smell. There was a small, grubby Ikea sofa and then a letter on top of some bits and pieces. I'd never seen such a filthy place in my life. Well maybe I had, but not one that would be my home. It was quite astonishing that people lived here.

The note said: 'Welcome to your new home. The flat is partly furnished so you will need to get your own mattress and essential house furniture.' I felt the £39 in my pocket. 'You will need to pay rent for your stay tomorrow – this costs £6 which you pay at the Post Office. I've left you the light and gas key which will need paying for as well. This can be done at the local supermarket. You can buy all the supplies you need at the local stores. I don't really have any friends in the neighbourhood but just watch out for the gang of youths that hang out on the Southwold Road. I hope you enjoy your time here.'

I was dumbfounded. I had moved into somebody's life. I couldn't believe they lived here, I didn't know who they were. The note was sweet and elegant, but I was shaken by it. It was half past six. It had been a long day standing in the warehouse, and I was tired. Suddenly the lights went out. No more electricity. I stood and I looked out through the dirty panes of glass. The flat was on the first floor, and there was a street lamp outside. It glowed a warm orange. I stared at it. Oddly, it made me think of the sun setting at Venice Beach, California. Right, get your act together.

The camera crew were there all the time. I told them I was going out looking for work. They said, what about dinner? I said I'm not eating, I'm not buying food. I had £39 in my pocket. The following day I had to pay £6 for rent. I had been given a mobile phone, a pay-as-you-go with £5 on it. That was my life, my worth, my credit. Every penny was precious. If I was to eat, I had to earn the food. I wasn't going to endanger this person's flat. I set off and walked. I'd walk a lot that week. There was no money for bus fares or the London Underground. I was dreading this. I saw my first shop, a fried chicken takeaway. I'd have to start somewhere. I went in and asked – 'any work?' A quick shake of the head. I went on my way again into the next shop, a convenience store. 'Do you have any jobs?' No. Out the door and to an off-licence. 'Do you have any work?' No. 'Where would I get work?' 'Not round here, mate.'

Another five shops in a row. The pattern of trading places repeated. It was chicken takeaways, betting shops, off-licences, barbers, hairdressers, some sewing places. I didn't discriminate. I went into every one. Asian people seemed to run the convenience stores. I asked them, any jobs? 'No, nothing. Listen mate, I can't pay my own tax, no jobs, no work. You'll get nothing around here, nothing.' The man in the off-licence pointed out a supermarket down the road. In the wholesaler's he paid £12 for a bottle for gin. They were retailing it for £10. He owed money. A restaurant with no one in it. I wanted to work for my dinner that night – 'Sorry, nothing.' The bank wouldn't give them an overdraft of £20,000 – this was a medium-sized restaurant in London. They were waiting for the Olympics in 2012, they thought there might be an upturn then.

Across the road I walked and walked and walked. Occasionally in the shadows I saw the security. One was on foot the other was in a car. When I went down the street a car would hop from behind in front of me, wait till I passed and then hop past me again. Across the road I spied a shop that said organic something or other. I crossed over and went in, trailed by the crew. In the organic shop the shelves were almost empty. There was a guy in a Rastafarian hat behind the counter, chatting to a friend. He looked up at me. 'Do you have any work?' Behind me he saw the crew. Quick as a flash he grabbed a machete, screamed, jumped over the counter and ran at us. He chased them out of the shop and down the street. It was wild. When he came back in the shop I was still there, frozen to the spot. Then security stepped in. This was some introduction to my new world.

I carried on: eight o'clock, nine o'clock, walking, talking, asking. A cold, rainy night in Hackney, the neon lights of cab companies and chicken houses reflected in wet pavements. I found a pub and went in. I asked the guy for a job. 'Have you had any bar experience?', he said. This was the first opening, the first hint of something. I thought back to my days as a lounge boy in the Yellow House in Rathfarnham when I was sixteen. 'Not behind the bar', I said. 'Oh, well then no, sorry mate.'
'I'll do anything.'
He looked at me. 'I might have some cleaning in a day or two.'
I couldn't believe it. 'Are you serious about this?' I looked at him. I said, 'I'm a worker.' He nodded and wrote down his number, Sal was his name. I was elated. The tiniest chink of light, a possibility of some hope. I was shocked by this turn of events. Smiling away to myself, I ambled down the road, more shops, no luck. There was another pub, an Irish-looking pub but the owner was Turkish. I asked for work. No, nothing going on. I said, 'I'll do some work, whatever you want me to do, just for some food.' He shook his head. 'I'll tell you what', I said, 'I'll do some work for free, just give me a couple of hours' bar experience, I need to get experience.' 'No.'

It was pushing eleven o'clock. I wandered into a chip shop, bought a single and ate silently, crouched in the doorway. It was a long walk back home. I'd been given a new quilt. I wrapped myself in it and slept on the floor. In the morning I was determined to be up and ready before the crew arrived. I didn't want them to see me going to bed or getting up. That made me feel vulnerable for some reason. So I got to the bathroom early and made some decisions. I scrubbed a tile clean so I could lay down my toothbrush. I went into the smelly kitchen, gathered anything I could to scrub the wash handbasin, and in the cold water I washed my hair. I resolved to do this every day, and then I left. A routine was what I needed. Up and out early. My first full day looking for a job. I walked back towards the main street. £3 in my pocket. If I didn't bring money I couldn't spend it. The rest was under a cushion. Into the first shop. No jobs. If I wanted to apply to head office, send a CV. I trailed out and the sun came to greet me. Passing by a warehouse-type building I peered through iron gates and saw a skip. There was a guy filling it with something, and then another lad, two lads working. 'Is there any work?' I asked? They mumbled to each other. The boss was upstairs. He came down. I said, 'I'm looking for work.' He said, 'what sort of work?' I said anything. 'Hold on a sec', he said, and disappeared. Within a minute he was back. 'I'll try you out for a half an hour'.

A crew had been working on a loft-type flat for months. Someone hadn't turned up. It might be useful to have an extra pair of hands to do some priming. It was amazing. I was in. My job was to clear cobwebs and to paint over faint cracks to get it ready for its final coat. I couldn't believe it, I was pinching myself. The half hour went by, then it was an hour, then coffee break. I sat round with three lads, belonging, even temporarily; I was part of the gang. And someone made me coffee. I couldn't believe it. The crew couldn't believe it. I had found a job on the road that I lived on. Everyone expected to be pounding the street for a day, and I had lucked out in an extraordinary way. After a few hours it was like I had always worked with these people. At lunch the boss came.

It was Friday. Every Friday he bought them lunch – a delicious Thai takeaway. My £3 was safely in my pocket. I was munching away, talking football (of which I know nothing). And then there was a mattress there, about to be dumped in a skip. I said, could I have that? No problem. At half past four I left the flat and walked home, the mattress on my head and a fresh £45 cash in my pocket.

And one day fed into the next. I'd stay out till ten or eleven at night. I'd walk the streets, I'd go to libraries, to a Baptist church, and during the day I'd go and look for work. And I got it every day. Sal had me back to the pub. I cleaned an upstairs room – he had family coming from Turkey to stay. I did a good job, so he let me do another room. I worked into the night. He paid me well, again in cash, and gave me a shirt and a pair of trainers and a can of beer. And I went home and opened the beer and stared at the lamp on the street and imagined it was the sun setting in Malibu.

The next day I tried a hardware store, and the man behind the desk rang his wife who needed some garden clearing done. I arrived the following morning as arranged at half eight, a Sunday, It was lashing down with rain. I stood on her porch, a drowned rat, and I looked at her and said, I really need to work, let me do the job. She did. My jeans were caked to me, mud ran down my face. The weather changed and I dried out. Using my pay-as-you-go mobile I sent a text home: 'Please ring me but I'm not allowed to talk to you'. In Wicklow, my little girl was celebrating her fifth birthday. I sang 'Happy Birthday' down the phone and worked till seven in that garden in the pitch black. There was another job in the house that needed doing, and until half past eleven that night I was on my hands and knees sanding floorboards. All sorts of memories came back to –me – as an eighteen-year-old no one wanted to do anything, looking for work, never being good with money, getting into difficulties.

It was a week of single-minded determination. While the whole community around me was full of no hope, I had a background, an education and experience that have led me to believe that if you look hard enough there are answers. I am also white and middle class, and learned early on how to approach people in a way that's appealing to them – to be clean, polite, good-natured, to look somebody in the eye in a way that lets them know you mean business, and maybe, just maybe, that you are desperate. I had to separate myself from the idea of a television show. My quest for me that week couldn't have been more real. I'll never forget those days, even though I've blanked out much of what's happened in the past fifteen years, and what I learned was that I am able to provide and I don't need the things associated with perceived success. Comforts actually mean very little to me.

This was only the first part of the experience. I was shell-shocked. As a group we gathered together back in the warehouse to relive our experiences in front of the cameras. Again we were to line up. I walked in. Larry and Meg were already standing in a line. It was great to see them, as they had been through something similar to me elsewhere. How did you get on? I was greeted by full smiles. Fantastic! We had a great time, it was brilliant, met loads of people. Did you get work?

'Yes I got work,' said Meg. 'I worked on a tiny market stall selling chocolates for Christmas – I lucked out!'

Larry: 'I met amazing people!'

I looked at them. Tears started to well up I didn't want the cameras to capture it, so I ran behind the pillar. What the hell was going on? Everyone ran after me: it was all to close to the bone, my week hadn't been easy.

Emma came in. She'd had a hard time but she had done OK. I'd earned the most money by quite a lot, and I'd probably had the most vivid experience. Larry hadn't tried – he'd stuffed fifty quid down his sock and survived on his rations. Within an hour he was celebrity in Hartlepool. Emma got mad at him: she screamed across the line-up that she was effing pissed off. And bloody hell she was freezing as well. There's a tough nut inside that vulnerable-looking exterior.

The experts appeared again and set us up for the next part of the challenge. We'd again be going to different parts of the country. One of us would go to a single mum living on benefits; somebody else to a family where the dad has always worked and was a new middle-class recipient of the dole; there was to be an ex-convict not long out from prison; and then someone was to get a young couple with five kids and another on the way who were on long-term benefits. That was the only one I didn't want. One by one we sat in our people carriers, and then I was given an envelope. I said, it's not the family of five? The producer nodded with a smile. Off on another adventure.

It was a long drive. I was getting twitchy. They kept us in the warehouse till seven, and now I was being sent to an underprivileged family in Manchester and wouldn't arrive until eleven. Would you do that to a middle-class family? Would you arrive on their doorstep at eleven o'clock at night? I was agitated. But I was told they were excited. What celebrity would they like to have arriving? Orlando Bloom! That's who they were hoping would walk in the door. Instead this middle-aged, slightly rotund gardener from Dublin stands in the doorway. They'd never heard of me but were wonderfully polite.

It was a madhouse. If you have ever seen *Shameless* you'll have an idea: kids everywhere, mum and dad, his dad and friends in a rented red-brick house. There was a dog, the family pet, and nine of her puppies upstairs in the mother's bedroom. And then a Rottweiler strolled out of the room I was to sleep in, having left a puddle in the middle of my bed. And by two o'clock in the morning nothing had changed. The one-and-half-year-old was beating up the six-year-old, to the merriment of everyone. There were no drugs, no drinks. What I encountered was a loving family, but one without rules. I think they were confused by my presence, but not as confused as I was. At three I went to bed. The crew were about to depart for a nearby hotel: they put their cameras on me for the last time and there were tears again. This time I laughed until they dripped down my face. What was going on? Why was I here, I choked? Next door the video games and the movies were running till late in the night.

Eddie the dad knocked on my door. He was going to the shops – could he get me anything? I was fine. I made a bed by putting a quilt on the floor and pulled another over me. My head raced. The previous week hadn't been a walk in the park. I had spent a lot of time alone with my thoughts. Now I was in an altogether different situation. Why was I here? What could I say? And who was I to say anything? I'm not a fount of wisdom. It was coming up to Christmas, and ironically I was being well paid for this experience. This family hadn't a clue who I was. What would they expect of me? I didn't know what to expect of myself. I looked for sleep. It wouldn't come. Too many images. I was drunk on thoughts. Eventually I settled. I would stay. I'd see what tomorrow brought. I would calm down and relax.

And then it was obvious. I couldn't. Of course I couldn't. What was I thinking of? An hour earlier I had gone into my room and a Rottweiler passed me in the corridor. They had a small child. The Rottweiler was visiting, staying for a few weeks, and I was aware of what could happen in these circumstances. Just a month before, a dog, again a stranger to the household, had killed a child in Liverpool. Calmly I got up, sent a text message to my minder who was parked in a car a bit up the road, told me him to meet in ten minutes at the corner, and began to figure a way out.

It was half past three. There was noise coming from the living room. They were still watching movies. Right, just tell them you can't sleep and you're going for a little walk. I folded the bedclothes, packed my stuff into a polythene bag and left it all behind me neatly. In the living room, three bodies were sprawled on the sofa, dead to the world. I opened the front door and walked down the road. I was picked up.

'What do we do now?' the guy asked.

'Just drive, drive down the road, drive around the corner. I need to get away.'

The crew had been alerted. There was trouble. At a quarter past four, bleary-eyed, they had set up their cameras by the side of a motorway. What are you doing, what are you thinking of? Calmly I explained that the situation I was in was wrong. I knew about dangerous dogs. I could appreciate my hosts might not, but if anything happened while I was sleeping at that house I would have condoned it by my presence. I was direct, clear, not relaxed but strong with conviction.

'What are you going to do now?' they asked.

I looked at them. 'Excuse me?'

'What are you going to do? Where are you going to go?'

'I think that you probably have a duty of care to me, you got me into this mess.'

There was another question, a bit bolshy. I got very angry.

'Right,' I said, 'That's it.'

I walked away.

There was no one I could ring; I hadn't a clue where I was. It had been a long day for all of the team, and this experience was getting to me. I don't mind tough conditions, but when I felt something was inherently wrong, flawed, I'd made a call. And now was I being abandoned? The director saw that I might have been pushed a little too far. I walked off. I don't know where. Down the central reservation, across the road, the odd car whizzing by. I saw another road, I walked into the shadows. It was a cul-de-sac. Back up to the main road. I was being trailed by the security car.

They pulled down a window. 'Hop in.' I did. We drove to a car park. The crew followed in another car.

'Tell them where to go,' I said.

Eventually, after an hour of continually saying I didn't know what I wanted to do, I was booked into their motel. I was shattered, sleep came fast. At ten I rang home. Justine reassured me.

'You do make the right decisions, Diarmuid. Just don't worry about it. Let them sort it. Just do what you feel is right.'

I rang Polly. Ever practical, she asked, 'What are you going to do now?'

'I'm not sure... they were lovely people. I am quite embarrassed now but I can't stay there.'

The producer of the series rang me: 'Are you OK, are you sure you're OK?'

I said yes.

Cars were racing up to London. The production team told me to rest for a few hours, have breakfast, relax. The experts arrived, the producer arrived. I had quiet chats and then was interviewed. I had no problem going back to the house, but I felt the situation was wrong. While there was a dangerous dog there I couldn't sleep there. Simple as that. I believe the production team hadn't known about this dog. They hadn't realized Eddie's dad would be staying for a few weeks and this was his pet. It had been a shock to me and a surprise to them. However the dog issue would never be broadcast. I would be shown departing without explanation, walking out. I understand this. Television is full of compromises.

Noises were made about me having the courage of my convictions, of taking a brave step. I was crushed. I hadn't wanted problems on this programme, I had wanted it to go well, I had wanted to learn and I had walked away from a situation. I felt I was right to, but I had still left. Word came back from my hosts, Cristina and Eddie. They were chilled, fine, relaxed. They had heard I didn't want to stay. That was OK: 'Whatever makes Diarmuid comfortable.' We arranged to meet for a coffee at a shopping centre that afternoon. They had no issues. Their generosity in the face of a guest upping and leaving in the middle of the night was startling.

Over the next four days I was to learn a lot about this family. They were in a difficult situation, receiving a lot of money from the state on benefits. Eddie wanted more children. Cristina didn't. They had lost a son and Eddie hadn't dealt with the emotions of the tragedy. I hung around in the house and began to understand how they lived. I talked about my experience in life, the fact that I was briefly homeless, albeit in very different circumstances. I saw the food the family ate, frozen food from the supermarket chain Iceland. In my mind I compared the children's upbringing and Cristina and Eddie's to my own. Mum and Dad had struggled to start me off with the best in life. Down the road from Cristina and Eddie's house was a different world, a middle-class housing estate. I walked with Eddie as he looked for a job. We bought him long trousers, shoes and a shirt. He took out his earring and he knocked on doors. He was intimidated, but took one step at a time. Back at the house, we talked about growing vegetables. They had ample space but they hadn't even considered the notion that they could produce some fresh food for the family.

In long conversations cradling cups of tea, I confronted them about the amount they were receiving from taxpayers to support their growing family. Cristina got upset. I was bewildered. And then it was time to go. We shed tears and waved goodbye and promised to keep in touch. I'm now a very proud godfather to their new baby son.

Wherever I go, people know who I am. In London, every black cab driver has something to say to me. It's a funny way to live your life, especially being so reticent myself. I just wouldn't know what to say to anyone to strike up a conversation. And yet wherever I go, whatever street I walk down in whatever town, people will greet me with nice words and a smile. 'Great to see you, love your gardens, will you come and do my garden?' In hotels and restaurants they all know who you are. Managers come out to you, always with kind words, always so pleased that you are there. You go into a shop, and the people looking after you mightn't want to say, but they just look at you, their heads slightly bowed: 'It is you, isn't it? Oh, you look better in real life. When are we going to see you on the telly next?' 'I used to love you and that Laurence fellow.' There are very few places where this doesn't happen. Because I made so many series for the BBC, most of which are shown on BBC World or BBC America, I get post from the oddest places. My own Irish television series are broadcast in all sorts of places. I regularly do gardens in France, where people expect me to converse in French because I appear to do so on their screens. But it is a pleasant form of recognition. Unless you are at a gardening show, it is never heavy. People are a bit intrigued as to why you are where you are. Why are you visiting here? What are you at? And always there are smiles. This is celebrity at the level that I have it, and it's a privilege. I think back just fifteen years to walking down the street. If anyone glanced at me I would go bright red. I think of all the parties I went to as a young lad where I'd leave after five minutes because I didn't know how to talk to people. I would make deals with people not to leave my side, even to go to the loo. If I did get involved in a conversation I would bore people to death and hope they wouldn't leave. So once again I would be a lone island in the middle of a room of chatter. All that's gone. The really funny thing is that it's now my job to go and strike up conversations, to chat, to be the first to speak, to initiate conversation and to make people feel comfortable. And you do find yourself in funny situations. Not long ago I was on a couch in a hotel in Dublin talking to Rene Russo on one side about gardening (she loves roses) and Bo Derek on the other about horseriding (she loves horses). And then just a week ago I was the pre-dinner entertainment for twenty-five captains of industry, leaders of FTSE 100 companies. I have been able to bring my mum to visit Tony Blair in Downing Street. I've been at quite a few parties in Buckingham Palace and have assisted the Duke of Edinburgh in giving out awards at St James's Palace loads of times. I have introduced acts on stage in Trafalgar Square and had drinks with Pamela Anderson. Because you assume a role, simple as that. Every situation requires a certain type of behaviour. Wherever you are you are there to act the part.

My family keeps me grounded. I owe everything to them. My life completely changed when I got married, and it changed again when Eppie arrived.

As I write, Eppie is five and a half. She has blonde curly hair and large blue eyes. She has just completed her first year of proper school. The report card said that she lit up the classroom every day. She lights up our lives every day. She's packed with smiles, good humour and optimism, and hugs like a boa constrictor. Her name is unusual. When Justine was just a couple of months pregnant I was digging in Chelsea. It was the third day, and the row with Bunny was just over. My phone rang. We'd been discussing potential names and we knew we were expecting a girl. We weren't striving for anything unusual, but we did want something that reflected how precious this child would be to us. Justine was reading *Silas Marner* by George Eliot, and in the book there was a little girl, no more than a baby, whose mother perished in wretched conditions while on a journey. The baby Eppie crawls to a cottage, the only place she can see a light. She curls up by the dying embers of the fire. The owner of the cottage wakes up, and in the half-light thinks that the child's hair is a pile of gold coins that had been stolen. Eppie becomes his redemption. He manages, against all the odds, to adopt her, and he brings up this beautiful child as his daughter. What did I think of Eppie as a name for our little one?

I knew this girl. I had studied *Silas Marner* – it had been on the curriculum in school, and what had struck me was that as a child she asks Silas to build her a garden, to enclose an area with stone walls around the cottage to grow flowers. And eventually she marries a gardener. I was delighted. We decided we would wait to meet Eppie, to see if she and her name were a fit.

She arrived at the Portland Hospital in London. We were full of the worries of expectant parents, which she instantly dismissed. I took one look at her long yelling form and felt I knew her personality immediately. I laughed. Eppie wasn't going to cause any problems, then or ever. I rang our parents, who were variously in London and Dublin, waiting for news. 'What's her name? What? Eppie?' There was a strong sense of disapproval. Where does that come from? It is derived from Hephzibah, a name for Israel which also translates as 'all my delight is in thee'. She would always be Eppie though. She couldn't be imagined as anything else.

She has a warm and loving personality that people are drawn to. She makes friends instantly. Bringing her home from hospital was the first adventure. I settled her mum in bed, with Eppie in a Moses basket on a stand beside her. Monkey, a black-and-tan King Charles Cavalier spaniel, had been around for a few years, and he wasn't best pleased. He leapt up onto the bed, sniffed the air and peered towards the basket, then leapt in on top of the new arrival, meaning no harm, just curious.

We remember every day: the big occasions, her first solid food, and her first steps in the early evening in a pub in Norfolk. People tell us, watch out they grow up so fast, you won't see them change. We watch and remember and love every day. The best parts with Eppie are watching her wake up, lying in the bed, seeing her eyes open, the wonder of the new day. She gazes around, looks at you and straight away a smile crosses her face. She is a perfect mix of Justine and me. She'll take after her granddad Ronan, she's going to be tall. And I'm lucky to have a very close relationship with her. Because I travel a lot I make sure that when I am home we spend a lot of time together. We breakfast together on a Saturday morning in a café in town or climb the Sugarloaf Mountain with the two dogs. She will have lots of benefits in life, but it's important that she is prepared for and knows about her world. To everyone's surprise I am quite strict. I value the manners that I was brought up with and respect for people and property.

Life with Eppie is giggles, tickles, smiles and answering a million questions. She travels with us everywhere, right the way around the world. She's a plucky little thing. Our job is to create a well-rounded individual, to provide a secure home life and a good education. I doubt she will be a gardener. She has seen us build the vegetable beds, she's eaten the new strawberries, the freshly dug potatoes and the broad beans. But her exuberant singing and dancing and her talent for people will allow her to enjoy a different direction.

HOW THE BOY NEXT DOOR TURNED OUT

In 2006 I was spending most of my time in Ireland. Between television series and the booming property market, with its attendant requirements for ever newer and ever more dramatic gardens, I'd spend my days driving the length and breadth of the country. Back home in London, Justine would strap Eppie, aged two, into a little buggy and walk her down the busy Harrow Road, turn right onto Ladbroke Grove and eventually, as they reached the Westway, turn left for the babyminders'. Eppie was developing a strong character and loved to be among her bunch of mates at play school. Justine would then go and run the Portobello office for the day.

Life was comfortable in London, Eppie an utter delight. But we were missing our families, missing them seeing Eppie's first steps, hearing first words, sharing how adorable she was. I found myself by chance in a show house in a new development in County Wicklow. It was at the foot of a beautiful landmark, the Sugarloaf Mountain. The house was a big block, architecturally not particularly distinguished, and inside it was draped with gold curtains, black carpets had invaded the space like an oil slick, and feathers hung out of every chandelier and lampshade. A friend was showing me around, and although not looking to buy a house I got an incredible feeling of being at home. Upstairs was a wraparound landing, and as I stood there an image of Eppie running out of a bedroom and down the stairs on Christmas morning rose before my eyes.

But I had a home, I wasn't in a position to buy a house, the family was in England and so was the business. What was I thinking? Within a week I had done the deal. The following year we moved. Justine, Eppie, me and two dogs, Monkey and Coco, moved to the hills. It's funny living in a show house. You act somebody else's life for a while. After a month or so we got rid of the rococo trimmings, slapped some paint on, put pictures up and began to make it our own. We were among the first here, and we've watched as other small and large families have moved in up and down the road. I brought the sales brochure to the boys in the office in Portobello. To a person they fell around laughing. 'That's not you! That house couldn't be further from the type of place you'd live in!'

I started out my life as just another boy in just another house on just another suburban road. And now, as my parents did before me, I have moved back from London and become another boy next door. I don't see myself as a man, because I haven't really grown up. The ideas and the thoughts in my mind are still playful. I'm still excited by childish possibilities. Maybe seeing the world through the eyes of a little one makes me aware of my responsibilities – of protection, guardianship and education. I don't need to run around the world. I love being at home, and we will make it a home by making it our own. Where do I start with the garden?

When there are a few quiet moments, I look back on life and the adventures that have made the last fifteen years – the places I have been to and the people that I have met. After a few years of being on television I would occasionally be referred to as a celebrity gardener. It's a label I dislike. After a while I accepted it. Celebrity meant to be celebrated for something, but often I meet others who aren't celebrated but maybe really should be. My mind goes back to a trip that I made to Kenya early in 2006 with the charity Christian Aid. My job was to act as a witness for the effect that climate change is having on communities far from home. I met a Kenyan farmer, Damaris Ndunda, in the hills of Kilone, east of Nairobi in rural Kenya. She is somebody far removed from my life, but who like me grows plants for a living. Ten years ago she was told she couldn't grow crops on her land. She farms on a slope in a four-acre smallholding, baked tawny by the sun. She had been told that all she could grow was maize and beans. What she achieved is a little miracle. The land suffers from droughts and floods. Damaris, whose husband works in the city, was desperate to send her children to school, but she had no money. She wanted education for her kids and a varied diet. She needed extra income to educate the children. Single-handedly, she built five water tanks and created a series of gutters, sloping pavements and channels that catch every drop of water. She has her own irrigation system and has dug a well. And now she has citrus trees, beans, maize, pumpkins, kale, onions, cabbages, pau paus, mangoes, bananas and more. She has developed a small nursery and carefully tends 140 citrus trees, growing produce not just for herself but for the village and to take to market. Through her willpower she has transformed her life, that of her family and those of her neighbours, against all the odds. She has a stoical pride, and her simple architecture, her devices for collecting water and how she manages the moderate wealth were inspiring. At quiet times I wonder what has happened, how she is doing. Has the small community been lifted off its knees by the resilience of an individual?

Part of my role in Kenya was to officiate at the opening of fresh water wells. In a number of locations the villagers, the women and children, had previously to walk up to ten miles a day, carrying the weight of water in containers on their heads. The water in these wells originated from the snows of Kilimanjaro. On the plane out from London, I had read how owing to climate change the snows of Kilimanjaro were melting. It was bittersweet, as I enjoyed the singing, the dancing, whooping and smiles, to know that the celebrations were coming too soon. The west was having such an effect on climate, and the people who were going to pay the price, directly and immediately, were those who could least afford it. Looking to the future, our concerns – both politically and personally – must centre on the environment. We are handing our children a time bomb. For the future, starting at home, conservation of water, home composting and reducing the amount of natural resources I consume will be a priority. Moving to Wicklow and settling in to the house and garden where I will live for many years have hardened a resolve to develop a garden, grow as much food as I can and enjoy the little things. The journey to work used to be down busy London streets; now it's through hills of deciduous woodland and valleys bright with yellow furze. Design hasn't preoccupied me in the garden yet. Plants have. Our little orchard is now reaching the end of its first summer; the cherries were taken by the birds, but the apples and pears look fine. We have allowed a small meadow of very ordinary wildflowers to develop beneath the trees. It wouldn't achieve any golds, but we love it. The raised beds at the back of the kitchen have produced endless quantities of potatoes and purple-sprouting broccoli; the cabbages are ready to eat and I am d ying to explore the onion crop. The strawberries were like I have never tasted before, the corn is thrusting upwards, the broad beans have been heavy croppers; my next step will be planting piles of soft fruits.

I plan to build a pavilion, a small round tower with a tiled conical roof. I will have two terraces of lawns. The site has awkward side boundaries with angled fences. I will straighten these out by creating a series of garden rooms, one with a shed, one for composting, one with a trampoline. I'll have an office in the garden, I'll have a wooden cabin, and I'll adapt the architecture of the house by creating wraparound verandas crossing the back of the house on two levels, topped with gracefully curved New Zealand-style corrugated iron. In the front, Charlie, our blacksmith daisy man who creates wonderful metal flowers, has planted three huge metal daffodils which bow down with drooping heads. They are settled underneath our Chelsea birch trees and are surrounded by a sea of grasses.

We are moving the studio from the Portobello Road to Dublin's Merrion Street. I travel all the time, so I want to make the most of my hours spent in Ireland by sketching in Dublin rather than London. I want to teach – it's the one thing that I am sure I do well. My dream has always been to open a school of gardening and design. I've had fun exploring and learning about so many different traditions that I would like to inspire others with the possibilities, make them question, help them grow plants and explore with them their dreams of a gardening future.

We walk a lot in the hills and on the beaches surrounding the little group of houses that is home: Justine, Eppie, and the two dogs, Monkey and Coco, beating a trail through the bracken up to the top of the Sugar Loaf or down the pier in Dun Laoghaire.

I have all I could ever have hoped for in life. For so long I had a constant desire to achieve, to move on, and to change things. That's disappeared. Happiness is arriving home from the airport having delivered another book of plans for somebody's garden in Geneva, Monaco or Surrey, sitting down in front of a home-grown dinner and maybe a glass of wine, and anticipating the luxury of a weekend, perhaps digging the garden and waving as the neighbours go by, or bringing Eppie to see her grandparents.

I have great fun with ITV doing makeovers for old age pensioners beside parish halls, nothing too challenging and generally not contemporary: a few days on the road creating nice gardens, not feeling the need to change anybody's world. We are about to change some towns that have felt long since abandoned in a new television series motivating inhabitants to take pride in their communities. And we are working on an increasing number of public spaces. We have three projects that revolve around gardens in hospitals. At Frimley Park in Surrey we are creating an enclosed courtyard in a hospital which is used by the public and the military. The design includes a dedicated garden room to allow the terminally ill to be wheeled outside, so that their last moments aren't spent in antiseptic wards, but rather surrounded by an open sky, an avenue of pleached trees and dancing fountains. In Cork, at the amazing state-of-the-art maternity hospital, the dancer Michael Flatley has donated funds so that one of our giant daisy gardens can be enjoyed by visitors, staff and patients. At Temple Street Children's Hospital in Dublin, a tiny space needs to be converted so that children who may be receiving treatment for a day or a year can have some access to outdoor space. Of course they want fun – toys, castles, fish, and cuckoo clocks. Overlooking Monaco, meanwhile, we are hard at work on the gardens of a romantic villa, with views both towards the Mediterranean and inland towards the Alps. We have contemporary town gardens to create in cities, and in front of the Bishops' Palace in Waterford, which dates from 1746, we have to create an eighteenth-century garden based on the terraces of an Italian palazzo. To one side we are allowed go wild, with a new green public space replacing a sloping tarmacadam car park. And on the other will be a memorial gardens for locals who went to Spain to fight the fascists.

Later in the year I will travel to South Africa, so see how our gardens in townships arc developing and to examine the growth, eighteen months after planting, of a special garden next to a marine forest in Durban. At Grahamstown I'll give a talk on my experiences of six Chelsea flower shows.

We are talking to Chelsea about a garden for next year. Our plans are out of this world, quite literally, a garden that hangs in the sky, a garden suspended over one of the world's greatest cities. If I can make this happen I'll be delighted. It will reflect so much of what gardens can have – beauty, excitement, technology and humour, a traditional recipe for garden builders everywhere, brought up to date.

It's been a wonderful journey, one not without heartache and difficulties. I've been very fortunate in the people I have met and the lessons I have learned. It's good to have dreams, but you must believe you can fulfil them. There will be people along your journey who'll want to keep you in your place. But there are even more who will want to help you. Passion is great, but keeping things in perspective is even more important. I've learned to work hard, to make the most of opportunities and to enjoy life. The great gift for me is to have come out of my shell, to be able to converse and relax with people. It's time to look forward now. The world was never against me. It was cheering me on. And now, it's time to go out and do some more digging.

PICTURE CREDITS

We are grateful to the following people for their kind permission to reproduce photographs in this book: Marc Duffy, Helen Fickling, Alan Pollock Morris, Robin Matthews.

Every effort has been made to trace the copyright holders. We apologise in advance for any unintentional omissions and would be pleased to insert the appropriate acknowledgment in any subsequent publication.

ACKNOWLEDGEMENTS

Thank you to all those who have played a part in the adventure of writing this book. To Justine who doesn't feature hugely because that's the way she likes it – there would be no happy ending without you. To Eppie, the brightest little star. To Helen Jones who keeps the train on its track brilliantly. To Lorraine Dickey whose belief in my story never tired. To Jonathan Christie, once again a great job. To Sybella Marlow and Martin and Simon Toseland for crafting some sense from thousands of pages. To Anne-Marie Dermody for guidance, business and fun. To John Noel, Polly Hill, Luigi Bonomi, Noel Kelly and Niamh Kirwan for making so many adventures possible. To Madeleine Keane for sage advice. To all my family and Justine's for never ending support.

This book is full of adventures which many people have had a hand in. Creating gardens isn't a solitary endeavour. I achieve nothing alone so a big thank you to all I have met and all who helped me a long the way. So a special thanks to Jason Stubbs, Sean and Paul Cunningham, David Thomas, Steve Reilly, Ron Wilson, Paula Robbins, Vincent Barnes, Richard Hill, Leigh Scotford and all at Peter Dowles, Brian Cullen, Gerry Conneely, Dermot Kerins, Charlie Mallon; Mavis Sweetingham, Alex Baulkwill, Bob Sweet, Hayley Monckton and Stephen Bennett at the RHS; *Home Front*'s parents Rachel and Dan Adamson; Alan Titchmarsh, Sir Terence and Lady Conran, Laurence and Jackie Llewelyn-Bowen, Maureen Spain, Warren Lange, Jeff Morey, Steve Poole, Alex Hatton, Bonnie Dempsey, Barbara Mantan, Neil Gavin.

I hope to continue creating gardens for many years. If you'd like to contact Diarmuid Gavin Designs please visit our website www.diarmuidgavindesigns.co.uk or telephone +44 (0)207 727 2002 and +353 1 6765794.